HERO, ARTIST, SAGE, OR SAINT?

RICHARD W. COAN

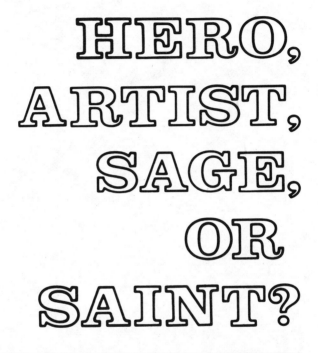

HERO, ARTIST, SAGE, OR SAINT?

A SURVEY OF VIEWS
ON WHAT IS VARIOUSLY CALLED
MENTAL HEALTH, NORMALITY,
MATURITY, SELF-ACTUALIZATION,
AND HUMAN FULFILLMENT

NEW YORK COLUMBIA UNIVERSITY PRESS

Library of Congress Cataloging in Publication Data

Coan, Richard W
  Hero, artist, sage, or saint?

  Includes bibliographical references.
  1. Mental hygiene. I. Title.
RA790.C663   150'.19   76-57751
ISBN 0-231-03806-2
ISBN 0-231-08355-6 pbk.

Columbia University Press
New York—Guildford, Surrey

PREFACE

Throughout life, we are confronted with an assortment of views regarding the modes of living that our contemporaries consider good or bad. Whether the good style is stated in terms of mental health, Christian virtue, manhood, or proper taste, we are subjected to many pressures to conform to it and frequently are apprised of our failures to do so.

As a child I was shy and awkward. Though I did have a few friends, I spent much more time than most of my agemates playing with abstract ideas, studying and composing music, and exploring the inner side of human experience. During my school years, I learned that people like me were sometimes valued for things they produced, but I also perceived that my life-style was not generally considered the best. I envied my more popular classmates who appeared to lead a much more social and carefree existence. As an adolescent, however, I managed to hold this envy in check; I discovered that great geniuses often lead very miserable lives, and I succeeded for a time in convincing myself that I was a genius and that it was far more important to be a genius than to experience the contentment of ordinary folk.

During my college years, I became progressively more involved in the study of psychology and encountered additional perspectives. An introductory psychology course taught the importance of being well adjusted: I was informed that one could adjust in a variety of ways— emotionally, socially, in school, in one's home life, and so forth. Whatever the setting, it was apparently very important to be well adjusted. Having realized in earlier periods that I was a social misfit and then concluding that there was some virtue in being that way, I naturally had a little difficulty in assimilating the adjustment concept. I still have difficulty with it, because I have witnessed too many conditions and developments in this society to which no alive and aware being can reasonably adjust with equanimity. I have also discovered that I am not alone in being a social misfit. Most of us recognize but conceal from others the fact that we have square feet, pointed heads, or double-handed psyches and that we cannot quite mesh with the social world in which we find ourselves. Perhaps in a sense being a social misfit is the "normal" condition.

Obviously the teachers and the textbook writers I encountered as an undergraduate student of psychology did not see things this way. To them, it was important to be well adjusted. As I progressed in my studies, I was informed that it was even more important to be mature. This idea posed a somewhat more difficult problem, because the concept of maturity was not so well defined as adjustment, and it was more difficult to assess one's maturity. Nonetheless, it was obviously necessary to do so, especially if one hoped to become a clinical psychologist—one of those wise people who could help others become more mature. Some of my classmates seemed to have some of the vital ingredients of maturity and were deemed promising candidates for the graduate program in clinical psychology. I had some doubts as to whether I had personally reached this ideal state, but along with my classmates I realized it was imperative somehow to acquire maturity, or at least to act as if I had.

At some point early in my career, however, it became still clearer to me that I really had not reached this lofty goal of full psychological development and that I probably never would. Indeed, if maturity meant some sort of final state beyond which no further development was needed, I was not at all sure I wanted it. Life seemed to me most worth living at those times when I was changing in ways that seemed meaningful. Since then, I have wended my way to the middle years of my life. Along the way I have gone through periods of stagnation and I have gone through periods of changing, and on the whole I certainly prefer the latter. I am still changing, and I hope I never stop.

If there is one ideal mode of living, or one ideal mode of being, for which everyone should strive, it is no clearer to me now what this mode is than it was when I first began to study psychology. But I have learned a few things in the course of many years of study of human personality. For one thing, I have learned the importance of distinguishing between the outward form of behavior and the style of experience and existence that underlies this. The "maturity" of the eager and aspiring young clinicians I knew in my student days served to highlight the difference. I remember that to me and my classmates it was apparent that being mature had something to do with maintaining an air of equanimity and smoking a pipe. These were among the more conspicuous characteristics of our elder role models whom we considered most mature, those professors who had somehow "arrived" in life and in the world of psychology. Needless to say, many of us took up pipes. I recall observing one evening in a seminar with an enrollment of about forty students that every male student present, like the professor, was smoking a pipe.

Of course, I do not really mean to imply that any psychologist would seriously equate maturity with smoking a pipe. But my observation does demonstrate a few obvious facts that the layman often overlooks. It is far easier to notice and record superficial bits of behavior than it is to grasp the basic character of the individual who displays the behavior, and some psychologists at least prefer to confine their attention to the superficially observable realm. All psychologists, however—behavioristic or otherwise—are first of all people, and they make many of the same errors that everyone else makes. We all tend to judge people primarily by the most outwardly evident features of the roles they assume, and we tend to assume that in adopting a new life role we are automatically effecting a total transformation, acquiring all the good features that we associate with the role.

Unfortunately, in the course of my career I have had a number of occasions to note the difference between roles and underlying personalities. In the professional world one often encounters individuals who have carefully cultivated a pattern of behavior that they regard as mature and psychologically healthy, while denying large parts of their own experience and many of their basic needs and impulses. The consequences of assuming a facade that so thoroughly disguises the individual from himself and others can be disastrous. Sometimes the result is merely a very sterile existence, but often enough it is an eventual upheaval that surprises his most intimate associates. There is an obvious lesson in this: we must be very skeptical of the value of glibly prescribing "good" modes of behavior for other people.

I have also learned that psychologists and psychiatrists have a multiplicity of ideas as to what constitutes the ideal condition of the human being. Their ideas are expressed not only by such terms as *normality, maturity, adjustment,* and *mental health,* but also by a host of terms like *genital character* and *productive character,* which express the ideas of particular theorists. Altogether, however, there are many more ideas than there are terms. It seems especially fashionable these days to lump many of these ideas under the heading "mental health." I find this a bit distasteful for two reasons. For one thing, it is implied that there is something analogous between the various conditions of the personality and the conditions of sickness and health in the body. This analogy has certainly outlived any usefulness it may once have had. For another thing, the use of such terminology implies that our concepts are the products of scientific effort and understanding and thus have some unique, established claim to truth.

The more I have studied contemporary concepts of ideal adjustment or optimal personality (or "mental health"), the more I have become aware that they are just as value-laden as any comparable concepts proposed by theologians and philosophers of the past. It does not follow that we should stop using these concepts, but we ought to be more honest about them. It is also evident that our concepts are not simply products of recent endeavors; they have roots that link them to older traditions within our culture. The roots and the traditions are varied, of course, and consequently our concepts do not just represent a variety of desirable conditions—they represent conditions that are to some extent incompatible. We cannot simultaneously be all the good things that contemporary theorists say we should be. Therefore, if we construe all these concepts as prescriptions for the one mode of living that is best for everyone, they cannot all be right.

These are some of the considerations that have made me increasingly leery of any attempt to define and prescribe a universally optimal mode of living. Over the years I have become more insistent on pursuing my own idiosyncratic path and more accepting of the diverse ways of others, whether or not their life-styles and mine conform to any set of standard precepts. At the same time, I have sought to make orderly sense of the prescriptions that have been written for the human condition, and this book is one of the results.

Tucson, Arizona   RICHARD W. COAN
1976

CONTENTS

ONE

BASIC PERSPECTIVES ON THE OPTIMAL PERSONALITY

THE NATURE OF THE ISSUE

In the last few decades, the mental health professions have undergone very rapid growth. As a consequence, there has been not only a marked increase in professional and research activity in the realm they represent, but a burgeoning literature dealing with all aspects of mental health as well. Much of this literature serves, in one way or another, to define *mental health* and various forms of departure from this ideal condition.

Mental health is only one term employed to represent the desired condition. There is a host of other terms whose meanings overlap extensively with this—*normality, adjustment, maturity, personality integration, stability, ego strength, self-actualization,* and many more. Together these terms denote a condition that is currently regarded as optimal or ideal. They imply an absence of disturbing conditions that are deemed undesirable or a low susceptibility to the occurrence of such conditions. They may also imply a positive developmental attainment, a condition that everyone ought to reach in the course of personal growth but which not everyone does reach.

Obviously there is nothing new about concepts of an ideal mode of being or living. What is novel is the amount of writing devoted to

1

the matter in recent years. Also novel is the fact that much of what is said in these articles and books is a product of systematic empirical research or of observations made in the course of the professional activities of psychologists and psychiatrists. The authors of this literature tend to regard their work as having a special scientific status. They are inclined to feel that what they say is less speculative in nature than the things that have been said in the past about the optimal condition. Since it issues from scientific investigation, it presumably has a greater claim to being true.

If we take this literature seriously as a source of insight about the human condition, an underlying question crops up: is the nature of the optimal condition or the ideal personality really a scientific issue? If we pose the question in such terms, it is obvious that we are dealing with a matter that is not subject to total resolution by the methods of science. To regard any condition as ideal or optimal is to make a value judgment. At some point in our inquiry we must make a decision about what to value and what not to value, and that choice cannot be furnished for us by experimental manipulation, by an automatic recording device, or by computer calculation. It is not a matter of truth in the scientific sense.

I would not contend that science is or can be value-free in the sense that the scientist can somehow rise above all questions of value and not concern himself with them. A scientist inevitably makes many value judgments in the course of deciding what to study, how to study it, what use to make of his findings, and how to conceptualize them. The criteria that scientists invoke to evaluate theory are much like those employed to evaluate works of art, and their application is a frequent source of contention; in fact, the most basic controversies regarding scientific methodology and theoretical formulation entail issues of value. Scientific thought in the main is not so different from philosophical or artistic thought as many people think.

Empirical science can best be distinguished from other disciplines by its use of certain procedures for gathering information and testing hypotheses. Nothing in the arsenal of observational and inferential techniques and strategies that we call scientific method, however, provides the scientist with a means for a complete resolution of a question

2

of values. To achieve a resolution we must introduce at least one premise that is not subject to empirical validation. To achieve a definition of the ideal person, personality, or life-style, we must decide what constitutes the highest good of living. This desideratum has been conceived in many ways—as pleasure or happiness, as the maximization of human intelligence or rationality, as oneness with God, or as some balanced combination of qualities. In making this choice, we may focus on the individual, the social group, or mankind, and our definition of the ideal person will vary accordingly. Thus, if we conceive of the highest good as rationality, then we will incorporate this into our definition of the ideal person. If we conceive of the highest good as the happiness of all people, we are likely to regard the ideal person as an altruist who promotes this end.

A few psychological theorists, notably Abraham Maslow, might argue with this position. Maslow felt that a scientific approach to values was possible.[1] He believed that we could identify the truly healthy or self-actualized people by scientific means and that such people would prove to have essentially the same characteristics regardless of the cultural setting in which we found them. He felt that the qualities these people possessed and the things they valued could furnish the basis for a scientific value system, for these qualities and things represented something that could be regarded as inherently good from the standpoint of the human species. Unfortunately, Maslow's reasoning is a bit circular. If we define *good* in terms of the qualities and choices of good people, we still have to make a value judgment when we proceed to identify the good people; to investigate self-actualizers Maslow had to rely on his own preliminary identification of self-actualized subjects. The initial premise in Maslow's argument is obscure, for it is embedded in the implicit criteria that underlay his construction of a list of admirable people. His procedures culminated in a list of traits of self-actualizing people and a list of virtues favored by such people, but these lists serve to articulate the ingredients of the initial premise. I offer this criticism despite the fact that I share most of Maslow's values and I believe his work constitutes a major contribution to our understanding.

To aver that science can fully solve basic ethical problems is to make a needlessly exaggerated claim for the powers of science. It can

3

make important contributions to such problems, however, and it can throw valuable light on the specific issues of the optimal personality. Having adopted an initial position on the highest good, we can invoke both logical analysis and empirical investigation to augment our conception and to identify prerequisite and corollary conditions. Scientific study can thus provide a more detailed picture of the individual who embodies such a basic virtue as rationality or spirituality. Through scientific investigation we can learn more about the total organization of personalities, about the interrelationships of their components, about the social effects of various personal qualities, and about the nature of change in personality—either under conditions of natural growth, in various environments, or in the course of psychotherapy. Such work can throw a great deal of light on the conditions that people have regarded as optimal, and it is also bound to lead to revisions in our concepts of the optimal personality. Thus, science has an important contribution to make here, but to look to it for a total solution is futile.

There is a current widespread tendency in the Western world to invest far too much faith in science as a means for achieving understanding and solving problems. I fear this tendency is particularly strong among some of my colleagues in psychology who believe that by simple innovations in procedures they can solve philosophical issues that have tried the best minds through the ages. To advance our understanding of the optimal personality, let us see what science can offer, but let us not confine our sights to studies published in recent issues of psychological journals with the expectation of finding a novel profound truth. The recent concepts of the optimal personality—whether or not they are cast in such contemporary terms as "mental health"—are products of our culture, and they have histories that we can trace back to much earlier times.

Some of us raise questions about the ideal human condition in the first place because we are dissatisfied with our present lot. We hope to find guideposts that will facilitate our personal growth toward a preferable state. Perhaps we sense a more general tide in human affairs that is sweeping mankind in the wrong direction and think there may be some useful guideposts for people in general. If so, it behooves us to search widely. In this book, we shall consider the varied perspectives of a number of contemporary theorists and consider some of the historical antecedents of their views, and we shall consider views of the optimal condition that come from a variety of disciplines and cultural settings. Then, we shall consider what recent research can add to the total picture. This panorama will not lead us unerringly to the one ultimate truth, but perhaps it can give us a better understanding of the nature of the choices we are making, both in our own lives and in our efforts to define an ideal condition.

PERSPECTIVES FOR VIEWING MAN

Before considering the basic models of the optimal person that have been proposed, we should notice that there are several distinct aspects of human nature and a number of ways of viewing them. It is difficult to deal with them all simultaneously, and we are likely, in our efforts to make sense of people, to attend primarily (if not exclusively) to one of these aspects, such as the biological, the social, the psychological, or the spiritual. These four are neither exhaustive nor mutually exclusive, but they encompass most of the perspectives we are likely to employ. Each provides a somewhat different way of looking at human nature.

With the biological perspective, we view people in terms of anatomical, physiological, and biochemical properties. On the whole, we share these properties with other animals, and our differences from other species can be largely expressed in quantitative terms. Our behavior is to be understood in terms of such things as reflexes, physiological needs, and instincts.

With a social perspective, we attend instead to the individual's relationships to others. Two main levels are possible here: we may focus primarily on the individual's interactions with other individual beings (the interpersonal level), or we may focus on the individual's relationship to the larger society or institutions within it.

The psychological perspective takes us back to processes within the individual, but not ones viewed in terms of biological substance. Two main possibilities here are the cognitive and the phenomenological approaches. In the former, we consider the human being as

5

cognitive

phenomenological

a creature who can know, understand, and perhaps consequently control either himself or things in the world around him. In the latter, we are more concerned with the qualities of experience as such and with people as experiencers of ideas, feelings, emotions, sensations, and the like.

The spiritual perspective clearly overlaps with the social and psychological perspectives, for it may be conceived in terms of certain kinds of relationships or certain forms of experience. Spiritual aspects of personality, however, concern the individual's relationship with God, with nature, or with the universe as a whole or the special experiences that this kind of relationship may involve.

Each of these perspectives is useful and necessary for certain purposes. Each provides a legitimate avenue for certain kinds of understanding and provides the basis for disciplines in which this understanding is sought. Yet there have been major historical shifts in the relative emphasis given to these differing perspectives. According to Peter Drucker, our ideas about people have been dominated by four or five principal myths since the beginning of the Christian era.[2] Christianity itself ushered in the myth of Spiritual Man. According to this myth, people are destined to be free and equal in a world beyond this one, and the present life of which we are aware is understood as a preparation for an afterlife—the true life—in the other world.

Drucker says that this myth ultimately lost its potency and was superseded in the Renaissance and Reformation by the myth of Intellectual Man, which held that our salvation is to be found in this world and achieved through the free exercise of the human intellect. This myth in turn was replaced by the myth of Political Man, which became salient in the latter half of the eighteenth century, a period in which freedom and equality were seen as dependent on changes in the social system and were sought through revolutions. The myth of Political Man subsequently gave way to the myth of Economic Man, which was expressed in slightly different forms in the writings of Adam Smith and Karl Marx.

In Drucker's view, the myth of Economic Man is basic to both capitalistic ideology and Marxism. Both ideologies attach primary importance to economic needs and see the goals of human happiness and fulfillment as inevitable products of a social system that best meets these needs; they differ principally in their ideas about the essential nature of that system. Writing in the 1930s, Drucker believed that the people of Western society had finally lost their faith in both the capitalist and socialist systems as ways of meeting their basic needs. Both ideologies had lost their potency, and the myth of Economic Man had collapsed. It is in this light that Drucker saw the emergence of fascist regimes in Europe. Disenchanted with the ideologies that had sustained their hopes for the future, the people of Italy and Germany turned to leaders who had no fundamental ideologies to offer, or at least none that these leaders themselves or their most active subordinates really believed in. Mussolini and Hitler were essentially the embodiments of power. They appeared to have the will and strength to do dramatic things, and despite the vagueness of their societal aims, they were accepted by the masses. This acceptance could be regarded as a kind of desperate grasping for a new myth—a myth of Heroic Man—to replace the one that had been lost. In 1939, however, Drucker felt that Western society had reached a critical point at which an old myth had been abandoned but no really viable myth had emerged to take its place.

Reviewing Drucker's analysis, Edward Tolman suggested that there was a new myth in the making, the myth of Psychological Man.[3] He felt we were moving into an era in which we would achieve a clearer understanding of all the needs of people and could attempt to meet them in a balanced way. He saw each of the older myths as containing a more limited perspective, each one focusing more narrowly on limited sets of needs. Philip Rieff also spoke of Psychological Man, but as a character type or image of man that had definitely established itself in our culture.[4] Both Tolman and Rieff saw Sigmund Freud as the individual most responsible for the emergence of this new myth. Whether we can best regard Freud as the initiator of the myth or as the most conspicuous representative of a new zeitgeist, it is quite likely that no other single individual has had a greater impact on Western thought in this century. Whether Freud is cited as an authority or

= the general intellectual, moral + cultural state of an era.

7

treated as an object of attack, it is clear that the basic method of understanding human affairs that is developed in Freudian theory has become a dominant mode in our time.

Undoubtedly the Drucker analysis does much violence to the specifics of history. It ignores the nuances and varieties of viewpoint of the past, but it may be as accurate a picture as we can attain by very gross classification, and it does capture the most dominant motifs of the major eras in our history. To get a more adequate picture, we might pay closer attention to subtle transitions in the development of a particular image of man and to various interactions among competing images.

Perhaps the myth of Spiritual Man provided the most durable image between the onset of the Christian era and the beginning of the Renaissance, but other images competed with this one. A history written in terms of political events would reveal their operation. In introducing a myth of Intellectual Man, the Renaissance recaptured an outlook that had been prevalent in classical Greece, involving what we have called a psychological perspective in its emphasis on the cognitive functions and potential of the individual person. In many respects, the myths that have superseded this one can be viewed as transformations of it. It is true that the myths of Political Man and Economic Man shift the emphasis from the inner resources of the individual to the nature of his society. Yet intellectual freedom—the freedom of the individual to think and express his own thoughts—was an important part of the movements toward political freedom and democracy that began in the eighteenth century. The myth of Economic Man is an outgrowth of the industrial revolution, but this revolution in turn is an outgrowth of a spirit that emerged in the Renaissance. As people explored and attempted to understand and control the world around them, their efforts ultimately produced fundamental changes in the means of economic production.

Another effect of the Renaissance, of course, was to spur the growth of the sciences. This growth has been taking place at an accelerating rate over the past four centuries, and we must recognize that at some point during this time span—perhaps during the nineteenth century—an image of Scientific Man began to operate as an important

8

way of understanding what people are and what they should be. During the twentieth century science has become a major factor governing changes in our society and our life-styles, and much of our faith in the ability of people to solve the problems that plague mankind rests on this image of Intellectual Man equipped with the methods of science, or Scientific Man.

The Freudian image of Psychological Man is not clearly distinct from the image of Scientific Man. It stresses self-awareness as a special feature, but Freud was reared in the materialistic scientific traditions of the nineteenth century, and his early training was centered in the biological realm. As a psychological practitioner he continued to think of himself as a scientist; he conceived of the psychotherapist as an objective, scientific observer, and he believed that the mature person was one who had achieved the objectivity of the true scientist. Thus, both as a model of what the human being is and as a model of the ideal person, Freud's Psychological Man is actually an extension of Scientific Man. So the myth of Intellectual Man remains with us, but with important shifts in the primary focus of attention and intellect—from the physical world without to the nature of the human being himself.

BASIC ASSUMPTIONS ABOUT HUMAN NATURE

The aspect of human nature that we emphasize in our quest for understanding will probably limit the features we choose in forming a picture of the ideal person. The basic assumptions we make about human nature—the attributes that we consider inherent in human nature in general—will also affect the ideal image. We have noted some of these assumptions, at least implicitly, in our treatment of basic perspectives.

Some of the possible assumptions have to do with whether the human being has the potential for understanding and mastering himself and the world around him. In the Middle Ages it was widely assumed that the human potential was very limited. Saint Augustine saw people as essentially helpless and limited in their capacity for understanding: they might intuit but could never fully comprehend the divine plan, and they were in need of God's grace. In the Renaissance man

9

was considered much more capable of standing on his own feet, of relying on his own powers, of solving problems without divine aid. This attitude has prevailed into the present scientific era, and in the minds of many people it has often been carried to the extreme of according the human species virtually unlimited capacity (given appropriate scientific progress) for understanding all things.

A related issue is whether the human being is regarded as inherently rational or irrational, whether his actions generally reflect reasoned choices or whether they are essentially the product of forces that lie outside rational control. Also related is the issue of will—whether the human being is seen as capable of truly autonomous choice or whether his choices are simply the inevitable products of the external and biological forces operating upon him. Still another issue is whether the human being is viewed as an experiencing subject or person or as an object, something to which we might apply the same modes of observation, analysis, and conceptualization that we apply to inanimate objects. Various combinations of positions are possible on these issues, and the combinations that seem logically simplest may not be the ones that are actually most common.

A somewhat different issue concerns the values we attach to basic human nature. People may be viewed as essentially good, essentially evil, or neither. The positions on this question have usually been tied to assumptions regarding the intrinsic motive forces in man—whether man is inherently selfish or inherently altruistic. Essentially the same issue may be handled in a manner that is more or less ethically neutral. Thus, one might take the position that all human action is ultimately aimed toward one's own pleasure, gratification, or need satisfaction, without questioning whether this is or is not a desirable state of affairs. From such a standpoint, anything that appears to be a "higher" motive—any action designed to benefit others—represents a kind of enlightened selfishness based on the wisdom (most likely unconscious) that we can best meet our own needs by meeting those of other people. It is because this wisdom is generally correct that we *learn* the higher motive and continue to express it after learning it. Alternatively, we might assume either that we natively possess some higher motives or that once we have learned such higher motives they

10

can become "functionally autonomous"—they can continue to operate even though they no longer serve as avenues to personal pleasure or satisfaction.

Many other assumptions can be made about basic human nature, but those we have just considered are among the most important ones that underlie various models of the ideal personality.

THE NATURE OF THE HUMAN CONDITION: WHAT IS WRONG?

Sometimes the ideal state is viewed simply as the full development of qualities already present in rudimentary form in all people. This would be true of the Renaissance view, for example. Perhaps more often the ideal state is viewed as the solution to a problem common to the mass of humanity. Even the Renaissance ideal of the fully developed intellectual man can be seen as a correction for human ignorance, but in the Renaissance people tended to see human ignorance as a problem that would inevitably vanish as man continued to seek knowledge and understanding.

Usually the problem of mankind is not viewed simply as a lack that can be remedied by further development. The more likely view is that human development up to the present has led us to a situation or condition that now needs to be eliminated, perhaps a condition that did not originally exist. The problem may be viewed in terms of inauthenticity, i.e., a tendency to act and think in ways that run counter to our essential nature, so that we are in effect lying to ourselves and others about what we are and what we want and need. Our error may be manifested in a failure to express basic parts of our nature or in a tendency to indulge in false expression or overassertion of certain parts (e.g., what some philosophers and theologians would see as the sin of pride, or hubris).

From the time of Karl Marx to the present, the problem has often been identified as <u>alienation,</u> but alienation takes many forms and the word itself has many shades of meaning. The focus may be on alienation from oneself. This is akin to inauthenticity, since it implies a fail-

11

ure to experience all parts of oneself as true parts of the totality of one's being. The idea of alienation from others shifts the focus to the social realm. Other writers have stressed alienation from God or from nature.

Closely related to the idea of alienation is the idea of experienced individuality, or individual separateness, as a source of difficulties. This idea appears in many systems of thought, and many solutions have been offered for it. Some systems view the problem as one of inner conflict, or conflict between different parts of the individual. This notion has been common since Freud, who saw man's most basic conflict as one between his instinctual or biological needs and needs implanted by society. Since Freud viewed the opposition of instinct and society as inevitable, he felt that only a partial solution to the conflict, involving awareness and balance, was possible. Later writers have stressed many other forms of inner conflict and have suggested other possible kinds of solution.

Some writers see society itself as the source of problems. Thus, Marx identified a psychological problem, that of alienation, but he traced this in turn to particular features of the contemporary social system, and he looked accordingly to changes in the social system for a solution to the problem.

PRESCRIPTIONS FOR AN IDEAL CONDITION

We have seen now that there are several possible aspects of human nature to which we can attend, there are many possible assumptions we can make about the inherent attributes of people, and there are many ways of identifying the basic problems in the human condition. In each case, our choices will affect any decision we make about the ideal condition. Yet for any combination of choices there is still a range of possible attributes that we may regard as part of the ideal and there are many views we may hold regarding the appropriate pathways for moving toward the ideal.

I think it is possible to identify a number of basic models or prototypes of the ideal mode of being and living that have underlain most of the thought given to the issue. Before attempting to do this, however, it may be helpful to make a few general observations. There are three or four basic perspectives that one can assume with respect to the whole problem of human betterment. One, directed toward the present psychological potentials of individual people, defines the ideal condition solely in terms of attributes of an individual condition that is attainable. In this approach there are two alternative assumptions of major importance. One may either assume that the ideal condition is attainable by everyone, given the proper circumstances, and hence regard it as a universal goal toward which everyone should strive, or one may assume that the optimal condition is possible only for some, in which case it would be inappropriate to regard it as a universal goal, for only those individuals with the necessary constitution can achieve it. Plato's notion of the philosopher-king might be such an ideal model.

According to another perspective, the ideal condition is not actually attainable by anyone, at least at the present stage of human development. In this case the optimal state might be identified with the nature of a divine being and regarded as a goal of future evolutionary progress, requiring either further biological development or psychosocial evolution that will fundamentally change the nature of human society. Nietzsche's Superman might be a case in point.

Still another perspective is directed primarily toward the social environment, generally presuming that the personal mode of being is highly dependent on that environment. Individual variations in need and constitution tend to be ignored, and it is assumed that appropriate revisions in the social system will benefit everyone. The present state of society is viewed as the primary source of a failure on the part of people in general to live in the ideal way. For the most part, in this book we shall be concerned with approaches that focus on psychological attributes rather than societal prescriptions.

Given a focus on a psychological goal, there are a number of basic ways in which concepts of this goal can vary. The goal may be viewed as the end product of a long course of development, or it may be viewed as something that can be manifested by almost anyone at any time. On the whole, Western traditions tend toward greater future

13

orientation than Eastern traditions and are more likely to be concerned with long-term developmental products, but there are many exceptions to such a generalization.

Concepts of the goal also vary in the extent to which the ideal state is viewed as a fixed or constant condition, a state in which one lives "happily ever after" once it is reached. If the desired goal is in fact seen as a psychological state, say euphoria, it would seem foolish to prescribe it as a fixed condition, since the human organism does not appear to be designed to maintain any specific state indefinitely. If the ultimate fixed condition is identified in terms of psychological traits, the problem is not so great, since we usually define a trait in terms of modes of behavior and experience that are recurrently manifested rather than continuously present. An alternative is to identify the ideal condition in terms of growth processes rather than in terms of an end state. In this case, any state that is manifested at a given time—whether we label it ecstasy, sleep, depression, or psychosis—may be viewed as valuable, provided the individual is not stuck in the state and is able to learn from the experience of it. Such a view would take into account the fact that many of our states are subject to natural cycles of fluctuation.

MODELS FOR THE IDEAL PERSON

In identifying the specific attributes of the ideal person, we obviously have a vast range from which to choose, but there are several modes of variation that are rather conspicuous. Some concepts focus on the modes of experience of the individual, while others place greater emphasis on modes of action or expression. Some focus on the individual's relationship to himself, or the relationships among parts of the individual. Others are concerned more with his relationship to other people. Still others are concerned with the individual's relationship to something beyond the personal realm—to God, to nature, to the universe.

To consider specific models of the ideal that have been important, we can start with those that emphasize awareness or understanding.

These have been prominent in Western thought. This kind of model can be traced at least as far back as classical Greece. It appears again in the notion of the successful intellectual man of the Renaissance. To some extent, in continental Europe the artist has been revered as a special subtype of Intellectual Man, a subtype that emphasizes creativity as much as awareness. In recent times, the scientist image has gained importance, and, as we have noted, the image of Psychological Man, the self-aware being, may be regarded as a twentiety-century derivative of this line of thought.

Other models stress efficient action rather than awareness, and these too have ancient roots. The hero of ancient times, in myth, legend, and life, was a doer of deeds that required strength, cunning, and boldness. The warrior, the conqueror, and the man who claimed political power in ancient times were representatives of the hero model. In the Middle Ages the knight became the representative of the model, and the image underwent a bit of transformation through the development of codes of chivalry. The knight, of course, was essentially an armed and mounted warrior of noble rank who earned the status of knighthood by possessing the necessary physical requisites and mastering the arts of warfare. In the twelfth and thirteenth centuries, however, knighthood began to be associated with certain ethical ideals that represented a fusion of military and Christian values. These ideals included piety, honor, valor, and loyalty (to one's lord, to God, and to the lady to whom the knight had pledged his devotion). Complementary virtues of feminine grace and chastity were idealized for women. The knight model is the foundation for many standards of gentlemanly conduct that have persisted in succeeding centuries; many of its elements persist in the image of the cowboy hero developed in novels and films of the American West.

Religious traditions furnish still different models, notably those of the prophet, the mystic, and the saint. The first of these emphasizes wisdom or insight. The second emphasizes devotional states, experiences in which one is close to the divine, and perhaps an awareness that is not or cannot be expressed in profound utterances. The image of the saint is a still more conspicuous ideal model in Christian tradition. It contains some of the features of the mystic, in that the saint is regarded as having a close relationship with the divine, but it is more in terms of deeds and effects on other people that he (or she) is judged to be saintly. The saint inspires a sense of awe and performs deeds that seem to require divine help or guidance. He also manifests a faith or commitment so deep that he will accept great suffering or martyrdom for the sake of his ideals and humanity. A great love of people and of God is often seen as a central attribute of the saint.

Love or relatedness may be stressed without any of the other features of the religious models. Thus, we may regard the humanitarian, the altruist, the individual devoted to the welfare of mankind, as another distinct model.

There is yet another species of model that we might call the natural person. Such models appear in many forms and are less simply identifiable with a particular tradition. Exemplars appear in the writings of Rousseau and others who see our basic problems as ones imposed on us by civilization. In many humanistic traditions, the ideal person is viewed as one who develops his natural abilities and dispositions and overcomes social barriers to free experience and expression. The model may emphasize harmony with nature, spontaneous expression, or a natural mode of awareness. Many ideal concepts that stress the actualization of human potentials incorporate the basic idea of a natural-person model.

Another quality that appears in many ideal concepts is autonomy. This is an element in some types of the hero image, in models that stress creativity, and in Nietzsche's concept of the Superman. One finds it in the heroes of Ayn Rand, as well as in the ideals of many people who reject her philosophy.

There are still other qualities that appear in recent concepts of the ideal condition. The idea of adjustment, in the sense of a stress-free relationship to the world or to certain parts of ourselves, does not appear to have received much emphasis until modern times. This may tell us something about the contemporary state of our society. Also relatively recent in the West is the concept of inner harmony. At least this idea has not been so salient in models of the past. It now takes many forms. It may be articulated as freedom from subjective distress, as self-consistency, as a balance of inner forces, or as some kind of overall integrity of self-experience and expression.

Thus, the extant models of the ideal person or ideal condition encompass a wide assortment of qualities. Apparently there is no single idea that runs through all the models. I believe, however, that nearly all the ingredients of our concepts of the ideal condition can be reduced to five basic modes of human fulfillment:

1. *efficiency*—efficient functioning in either the intellectual, social, or physical realm.
2. *creativity*—production or realization of original form or original experience.
3. *inner harmony*—absence of conflict, a cooperative functioning of all parts of one's being.
4. *relatedness*—orientation toward positive interaction with others.
5. *transcendence*—participation in a realm of being that extends beyond individual being, an experienced dissolution of one's separate individuality.

These modes have been expressed and combined in various ways in the ideal models noted above. Thus, the hero and Intellectual Man models stress forms of efficiency, and the artist embodies creativity. The mystic epitomizes transcendence, while the ideal of the saint usually combines transcendence with relatedness. The image of the prophet may combine transcendence with efficiency. In the chapters that follow, we shall consider in great depth the evolution and elaboration of such models, and we shall examine their traditional and contemporary expressions. In the final chapter, I shall treat the five modes of fulfillment at greater length and offer some concluding thoughts about them.

TWO

TRADITIONS IN WESTERN THOUGHT

Having considered some of the basic emphases that are possible in concepts of optimal functioning, we shall attempt to get an overview of the historical development and interplay of these ideas in Western thought in order to make sense of the array of contemporary ideas about the optimal personality. Before we launch into a historical summary, however, a few general observations merit consideration.

Any historical account written in terms of prominent individuals or movements will tend to oversimplify, to exaggerate differences, and to yield a conceptual structure that is far better defined than the underlying human events that the account is supposed to represent. It is like a photograph taken on high-contrast film through a lens that transforms all shapes to simple geometric forms. In this chapter, I shall make no pretense of having captured the total spirit of any one period nor of having isolated all the important streams of influence. I can only point to what I see as some of the conspicuous thinkers and movements of the past that seem linked in vital ways to the present. None of the thinkers is an accurate mirror of his own time in Western culture, and none of the movements comes close to being a miniature representation of the complex total spirit of a period. Thus, the Renaissance is of major importance for our purposes, but the awakening that it involved in European thought was actually felt by only a small cultured segment of society. For the great masses of people, the period was not greatly different from the centuries that immediately preceded it.

One reason no movement or individual can fully represent a period, of course, is that every period is characterized by conflicting

18

forces and trends. We often think of forces and counterforces in human thought as operating in sequential fashion—a major theorist is followed by another who reacts against his views. But any thinker or fashion in thought that attracts much attention is almost bound to generate contrasting lines of thought that appear in close temporal conjunction. Any important movement tends to be accompanied by opposing countercurrents that are also a part of the prevailing cultural climate.

It is tempting to reduce our account of the history of Western thought to a simple dichotomy, to say, for example, that it represents the interplay of two opposing traditions—perhaps one traceable to classical Greece, the other to early Judaic thought, or perhaps one traceable to Aristotle and the other to Plato. While there is some merit in such dichotomies, historical analysis does not yield very simple polarities. We do not find just a shifting back and forth between two extremes; we find various kinds of interplay between opposing ideas and various kinds of cross-fertilization. Hence, the basic alignments of one period do not match those of another.

It is possible to describe a great deal by dichotomies if we are willing to deal with a number of them in combination, and it is possible to recognize several polarities that are useful for an understanding of patterns and traditions in Western thought. An important polarity is that involving an emphasis on the intellect as opposed to an emphasis on feeling, emotional experience and expression, or on direct experience (perhaps of a mystical character). Another is the dichotomy of extraversion versus introversion—whether attention is directed primarily to the material world or directed inward. We also find significant alternations between an emphasis on authority (particularly that of the Church and ecclesiastical leaders) as a regulator of ideas and an emphasis on individual self-reliance.

These polarities combine in all possible ways, and correlations between them shift over time. Thus, the Renaissance combined a new emphasis on individual self-reliance with an extraverted thrust that fostered scientific activity and exploration. At another time we might find the extraverted orientation accompanied by a dogmatic insistence on authority. There seems to be a tendency for new ideas to arise with a

19

spirit of increased freedom of experience and thought. But if the new ideas persist, they tend to become bound in forms that are increasingly regarded as ultimate truths; they then provide the basis for new orthodoxies which in turn must be overcome. Today's heresy is often tomorrow's dogma.

One final general observation has to do with the shifting role of the basic disciplines that we call theology, philosophy, and science. We have come increasingly in the twentieth century to think of these as separate domains of thought. Yet historically they are so intertwined that a history of any one of them would have to cover much of the same ground as a history of the others. This is especially obvious if we go back to that long period known as the Middle Ages, when nearly all of the important scholars were to be found in the Church and theology and philosophy were essentially indistinguishable. It was during that period that the Church exercised maximal influence and was in fact the dominant influence on thought in the Western world. From the Renaissance on, the relative influence of the Church has steadily declined, while the role of independent disciplines that we may generally call science has steadily increased. Finally in the twentieth century we have arrived at an era in which developments in science have a profound influence on the entire society and an impact on thought that is comparable to that of the Church when the Church was at the height of its power. Science has become the dominant religion of the Western world.

EARLY GREEK PHILOSOPHY

Plato and Aristotle were the major figures of the classical period in Greek philosophy and perhaps the major figures in the entire history of Western philosophy. Plato, a pupil of Socrates, is often viewed as the most important seminal figure in the idealistic tradition in philosophy. A central doctrine in his writings is his theory of forms. He believed that the physical world revealed to us by our senses has only a partial or relative reality because it is always changing, it is constantly in flux. A basic reality must be fixed. For Plato this meant that only the

20

forms or ideas that underlie the physical world are completely real. They are the immutable archetypes that underlie the changing facade of temporal events. While this reality is not immediately revealed to the senses, the human intellect can penetrate to it by reason.

By exercising the intellect, we arrive not only at intellectual truth but at moral virtue as well, for Plato believed that the supreme form was the idea of the good, whose function in the realm of ideas he likened to the function of the sun in the material realm. In *The Republic* Plato established the metaphor of man, in an uninstructed or ignorant state, as a prisoner chained inside a cave in such a position that he can see only the shadows of things against the inner wall. Limited to a world of two-dimensional shadows, he must be led out into the sunlight before he can perceive the real world. In Plato's view, the ordinary individual is like the prisoner in that he does not grasp the hidden reality of forms. It is the philosopher's task to lead him to this reality and ultimately to a vision of the highest good. One can move toward the "sun," or the highest good, through a study of the dialectic, a method of inquiry and logical analysis that leads from the particular idea to the more general and universal.

According to Plato the ideal individual is, above all, one guided by reason. Such an individual is virtuous and deals in a just way with other people, but it is his reason that enables him to do so. Within himself he functions harmoniously, his appetites and passions given appropriate direction by reason. Because just action depends on reason, the just state is one which is run by men governed by reason. In *The Republic,* the first important utopian treatise, Plato argues that the just state must be run by men who, through their study of the dialectic, are able to understand the relationship of all things to the good. The state is destined to be plagued with political evils "until philosophers are kings or the kings and princes of this world have the spirit and power of philosophy."

Aristotle was a pupil of Plato and shared many of the basic attitudes of his master. Yet in many respects his basic temperament and outlook were different, and his work pursued a much different course. He is a forerunner of more empirical and realistic modes of thought in philosophy. While Plato aspired in his youth to be a poet, Aristotle had

21

a greater inclination toward natural history. While Plato sought certainty in the realm of abstract ideas, Aristotle was more fascinated with facts and sought information of a scientific nature. He regarded form as more closely bound to matter than Plato did, and except for God, the divine or pure form, he insisted that form could not be viewed as having a separate existence of its own.

Like Plato, Aristotle stressed the importance of reason. He argued that the goodness or virtue of a thing lies in the realization of its specific nature. Man's unique quality is his reason, and the highest good for the human being is to exercise and develop this capacity. Well-being in general is not reached through the pursuit of pleasure but through a more rationally directed life of contemplation.

Carl Jung once suggested that we could understand the history of Western philosophy in terms of an interplay between thinkers oriented to the inner realm of experience and thinkers oriented to the outer, material world of objects.[1] He regarded Plato and Aristotle respectively as the prototypes of the introverted and extraverted classes of philosophers. Another way to look at the matter is to note that there are three modes of understanding that are stressed in early Greek thought: direct observation of the material world, intuition, and logical or rational analysis. Aristotle emphasized the first, and Plato emphasized the second, while rational analysis assumed great importance for both men and for early Greek philosophy in general.

Comparing the outlook of early Greek philosophers with the attitudes of scholars in other periods, we could say that the Greek spirit places heavy emphasis on the cultivation of the human mind. Of course, Aristotle and Plato believed that education should deal with the total development of the individual, that it should nourish all his potentialities—physical, moral, and spiritual, as well as mental. In the moral realm we find the idea of moderation. Aristotle felt that irrational impulses, unchecked by reason, led to extremes. The man of reason would tend to approximate the "golden mean," displaying the virtue of courage, for example, rather than the extremes (or vices) of cowardice or foolhardiness. He would display temperance rather than either insensibility or intemperance, and liberality rather than meanness or prodigality.

Closely related to the emphasis on the development of the mind

22

was a humanistic outlook, an emphasis on man as the being of utmost value and greatest potential. But it was not just mankind in general that was valued in Greek thought, but the individual who developed his potential to its limits. There was a great respect for the individual will and an encouragement of individualism and competition both in the intellectual realm and in the physical realm. Of course, if a thinker became too influential and was viewed as a threat by a head of state, he might be subject to violent suppression (as in the case of Socrates), but on the whole the Greek spirit was characterized by a strong individualistic pride, or hubris—a defiance of fate, an effort to emulate the gods. Prometheus, the Titan who stole fire from heaven and gave it to man in defiance of Zeus, was for the Greek people the greatest hero of mythology.

In the period following the death of Plato and Aristotle and leading to the beginning of the Christian era, we find much evidence of the continuing influence of these two men, but we also find many new ideas emerging through the work of the Epicureans, the Stoics, the Skeptics, and the Neo-Pythagoreans. The emphasis on human reason persisted. In the writings of the Stoics we find this expressed in the concept of Logos, a divine power that was universally manifested. In the human being, it was held to be manifested primarily in reason, or in the ability to recognize reality and to think. For the Stoics the ideal man was the *logikos*, the wise man or man of reason. The *logikos* was also in a sense the natural man, since he exercised the function most basic to his nature. In Stoicism, the equivalent of the Christian idea of salvation would be the attainment of wisdom.

Another idea introduced by the Stoics is the concept of *apatheia*, a state of wisdom that is so highly developed that the individual is no longer concerned with pleasures, pains, and the satisfaction of the vital drives or desires. This differs from later Christian concepts of asceticism in that it implies a transcendence of bodily concerns rather than acceptance of self-punishment. The Greeks recognized that their defiance of the gods was likely to have tragic consequences, but they did not think of this in terms of sin. Hence, punishment at the hands of fate might be inevitable, but it was not something to be willingly sought and accepted.

There was also a mystical stream of thought in the Platonic and

23

Neoplatonic traditions that continued into the Christian era. In this stream, there was less emphasis on individualism. The goal of human existence was seen as maximal participation in the divine realm. To an extent, the individual could achieve this end in mystical states in which he lost his sense of bodily separateness. Our existence in the flesh was itself seen as a separation from the divine realm, however, and the ultimate goal of life was seen as the cessation of our temporary bondage to the body and a union with the One, or with God.

Early Greek thought thus yielded a rich assortment of ideas regarding the ideal person and ideal mode of living. Taken as a whole, it shows a conspicuous emphasis on the mode of efficiency—on the development of the individual's intellectual and physical capacities, but particularly on the development of reason. The models that stress efficiency also stress individualism. Among the many competing influences, however, the mystical tradition placed primary emphasis on the mode of transcendence.

EARLY CHRISTIANITY AND THE MIDDLE AGES

Christianity introduced many new elements into Western thought. For the most part, it may be viewed as a blend of Judaic and Greek traditions. As such it was not unique, since there had been increasing cultural exchange among the people around the Mediterranean over a period of centuries, and such philosophers as Philo, outside the Christian sphere, sought to reconcile aspects of Judaic and Greek thought. Essential to the emergence of Christianity was the widespread anticipation among Jews at that time that a messiah would appear, as well as an anticipation that a new aeon was soon to begin in which the whole world would be transformed and its many ills removed. Judaic thought also brought with it a view of man as a fallible creature tainted with original sin.

From Greek thought Christianity borrowed the concept of Logos but altered it a bit. As in Stoicism, Logos was understood in terms of a divine power, but not a power manifested in reason. Logos was viewed as the manifestation of the divine, or the self-manifestation of

24

God, present in Christ in a unique way. Jesus as the Christ was seen as the fulfillment of essential human nature. The Christ image, or the messiah as conceived in Christianity, represents the ideal of human fulfillment, and it is an image that does not emphasize reason so much as love, faith, and participation in a divine realm that cannot be grasped by human reason—a combination of the modes of transcendence and relatedness. While the individual human being cannot hope to attain the perfection represented by Christ, it is assumed that he can approach full humanness through the Christian way of life. Where Logos is construed in terms of knowledge or understanding, it tends to be construed in a less intellectual way than in Greek thought. Thus, according to early theologians like Clement, living according to the Logos is equated with participation in the realm of love and faith. In its highest form this participation leads us to a knowledge of God, but knowledge in the sense of direct acquaintance rather than in the sense of rational analysis or theoretical formulation (*gnosis* rather than *episteme*).

The terms most often used to refer to the goal of life from a Christian standpoint are *salvation* and *grace,* and these represent a marked departure from the Greek ideal. The concept of salvation involves redemption or rescue from the consequences of sin, either sin one has committed himself or the orignal sin of Adam for which all mankind bears a burden of guilt; through salvation one is permitted to partake of eternal life with God. In Christian theology salvation is generally regarded as a function of grace, the free favor of God. Doctrines of grace vary considerably and divide over such questions as whether grace is given universally or selectively and whether the individual can do anything to earn it. A common element, however, is the idea that the individual is quite dependent on God for this gift—hardly so self-sufficient as some of the Greeks believed—and incapable of doing anything that would fully pay for such a glorious gift.

In the earliest period of the Christian era, many doctrines and doctrinal controversies arose. Some of these concerned the nature of Christ, and some concerned the conditions for grace. The notion of asceticism appeared in this early period (in the writings of Terullian, for example) as a means of securing grace. The basic rationale appears to

25

be that if we punish ourselves, God will not need to punish us. As we have noted, asceticism resembles the Stoic concept of *apatheia* in that it entails a denial of bodily needs, but it differs in so far as this self-denial is viewed in terms of punishment rather than detachment and its aim is not wisdom but salvation.

In the early centuries of the Christian era the most important theologian, apart from Saint Paul, was Saint Augustine, who was born A.D. 354. Augustine acquired considerable knowledge of philosophy before he embraced Christianity; his writings clearly show the influence of Plato and Neoplatonism. Like Plato, Augustine was an introverted intuitive thinker and he sought certainty in a world of inner experience. He believed that God could be known, though not totally comprehended, through immediate experience, and the reality of God was for him more certain than the reality of the material world.

Like other early Christians, Augustine de-emphasized reason. For him, the most important faculty was the will, and both will and God for him had the quality of love: will involves a striving for reunion with God, and this striving or desire for reunion is love. Reunion fulfills man's most basic nature, but this basic nature is distorted by sin, which separates us from God. Augustine regarded pride, or hubris, as an important ingredient of sin. In a state of hubris we turn from God to ourselves and attach undue importance to our individual resources. Thus, a quality that the Greeks regarded as a concomitant of our strivings for the ideal condition was viewed by Augustine and other early Christians as a quality that led away from the ideal. Concupiscence, the endless pursuit of sensual gratification, is also seen as an aspect of sin and a consequence of attaching undue importance to one's individuality, a consequence of pride.

Augustine took a rather dim view of man's potential and worth in his present state. Man has will, in the sense in which Augustine used the term, but he lacks true freedom. Furthermore, he is unavoidably corrupt by virtue of original sin and wholly dependent on the favor of God for salvation. Augustine did believe that everyone who was baptised as a Christian would be accorded grace, but there were other theologians at the time, notably Pelagius, who credited the human in-

26

dividual with greater freedom to make decisions and to determine his own destiny.

After the disintegration of the Roman Empire, the Church became the main unifying force in Western culture and began to acquire much of the power that had been wielded by the Roman government. In the philosophical or theological writings of that time, the Middle Ages, we can discern two main traditions. One is a mystical tradition that stresses immediate religious experience. This is broadly speaking a Platonic tradition, and it is marked by the great influence of Augustine. The other is a more rational, empirical tradition, which at least in method owes much more to Aristotle. Without question, the outstanding medieval figure in this tradition is Saint Thomas Aquinas.

Important figures in the mystical tradition include Bonaventura, Bernard of Clairvaux, and the Franciscans. Saint Francis himself is certainly one of the most inspiring individuals in the entire history of Christianity and has often been viewed as the man who came closest in living his own life to following the path of Christ. He was a man of great humility who committed himself to a life of poverty. He was a man of intense religious fervor who constantly displayed a great love for all fellow beings, not only people but plants and animals, indeed the whole of nature. Perhaps no other man better exemplifies the qualities that have come to be associated with the ideal of saintliness. In a traditional sense, of course, the Virgin Mary is regarded as the chief saint, but as her image has evolved in Christian thought, she has come to represent a somewhat different model of saintliness, perhaps one that more simply emphasizes receptivity to the will of God. Francis exemplifies at the same time a close contact with the divine, or with the totality of nature, and an active concern for the welfare of other beings, a union of the mystical ideal and unselfish love. As a historical influence on Church traditions, he founded an order that stressed active charity as a monastic pursuit, rather than the contemplative life that had characterized the spiritual descendants of Augustine. He also introduced a new attitude regarding our relationship to nature that has influenced Christian thought ever since.

If we think of Christianity as a religion whose guiding ethic is un-

27

selfish love, there is probably no other historical figure who more clearly embodies this ideal. Its occasional focus on this ideal is one of the major contributions of Christianity to human civilization, and to the extent that we value this ideal we may say that Saint Francis represents what is best in Christianity and what was best about the Middle Ages. It is no secret, of course, that the practices of Christians have often diverged far from this ideal and that some of the bloodiest wars in history have been fought in the name of Christianity. The historical facts prompted Gilbert K. Chesterton to remark: "The Christian ideal has not been tried and found wanting. It has been found difficult; and left untried." [2]

A somewhat later product of the Platonic or Augustinian tradition is professed in *The Imitation of Christ*. Although its authorship has been disputed, the work is usually attributed to Thomas à Kempis, who lived about two hundred years after Francis. For many, this book represents the ideal Christian life, one imitative of the life of Jesus. Its essential orientation is one that stresses a mystical devotion to Christ and disparages reliance on the human intellect. It was evidently intended as a body of advice for monks, and it offers rather detailed recommendations for all areas of life. The reader is advised to lead a life of humility and to avoid seeking riches or other worldly gratifications. The importance of ample solitude and quiet contemplation is stressed, and one is cautioned against getting involved in too active a social life. Undue familiarity with other people is discouraged, yet the importance of dealing with others in a spirit of love or charity is emphasized. Good deeds should be done in a spirit of charity; otherwise, they lose their meaning. Above all, however, the book tells us that we can achieve happiness by turning to God and seeking closeness with God. Unhappiness results from fixing one's love instead on earthly things and from cultivating a desire for the pleasures of the flesh. Thus, the optimal condition as pictured in this work is essentially the mystical ideal.

The influence of Aristotle was not strongly felt in the Christian Church until fairly late in the Middle Ages, but in the thirteenth century there appeared the greatest of the scholastic philosophers, Saint Thomas Aquinas. Like his teacher Albertus Magnus, he was a moder-

28

ate realist and a student of the writings of Aristotle, whose methods and distinctions he applied to the problems of Christian theology. Since the thirteenth century, the Thomistic view has been an important element in Catholic thought; in this century it is represented by such neo-Thomists as Étienne Gilson and Jacques Maritain.

Unlike the mystics, Thomas stressed the importance of the human intellect as the means to knowledge and certainty. He sought to prove the existence of God by logical argument. He regarded reason as the supreme faculty, the faculty most distinctly human, and the faculty that should naturally dominate over the will and the emotions. He believed that only the active intellect survived the body at death.

His prescription for an ideal mode of life inevitably stressed reason and self-control. He defined virtue as the stable disposition of a rational will to act rightly and do well. In identifying the cardinal virtues, he chose those that were common to the writings of Aristotle, Plato, and the Stoics—temperance, fortitude, prudence, and justice. He saw all of these, however, as expressions of Christian love and inseparable from this cardinal Christian virtue. For Thomas, the exercise of reason accompanied by faith in God seems to be an essential combination. Brotherly love for other people and the other important virtues are deemed to follow from this.

Often in Christian thought an emphasis on rational self-control has been linked to a strenuous avoidance of pleasurable satisfactions and a tendency to regard emotions as dangerous and in need of repression. This does not appear to be Thomas' position. He apparently did not regard the emotions as particularly dangerous, and he disavowed the excesses of some of the ascetics. Rather, he simply shared with many of the early Greeks the view that reason should be in charge of things.

The ultimate goal of life for Thomas was a state of loving union with God. He believed that this state of ultimate peace and happiness was not possible until after death, and on this issue he clashed with some of the mystics of the Franciscan order. For Thomas, it was important to cultivate the moral and intellectual virtues that are part of a scrupulously Christian life, but he thought it was a vain hope to believe

29

that one could attain complete peace in one's earthly existence by doing this.

In Thomas Aquinas we find an interesting blend of Christian and Greek ethics. Despite the fact that Greek thought had influenced Christianity from the outset, the development of the intellect had not been stressed by theologians and the humanistic thrust of Greek thought was replaced by an insistence that God, not the insignificant individual human being, was the ultimate measure of all things. In viewing man's intellect as his most essential feature and regarding the cultivation of this faculty as an ethical obligation, Thomas recaptured an important element of the Greek outlook and combined it with the Christian ethic of love.

It was in the same period that medieval codes of chivalry and knightly conduct were developed, also stressing a combination of Christian virtues—faith, hope, love—with virtues derived from older traditions, including courage, wisdom, and moderation. Despite knighthood, despite Thomas Aquinas, and despite the Platonic influence in the ancient and medieval Church, however, there was little evidence at any time in the Middle Ages of the spirit manifested in the cultured class of early Greece. By and large, people did not look for fulfillment of their human purposes and destiny in their present lifetimes. The optimal condition, the goal of human existence, was generally regarded as something to be found in an afterlife. Thus the important thing was to lead a virtuous life in the hope of eventual rewards after death. At its best, this outlook inspired acts of benevolence and kindness that might have seemed out of place in the individualistic climate of early Greece. It also enabled people to endure great hardships and deprivations. Perhaps from the standpoint of a social reformer, people with such a view of life would be too inclined to accept oppression and brutal realities, trying to find symbolic meaning in them rather than doing whatever was necessary to change their earthly lot. In any case, the period of the Middle Ages has often been pictured as one in which the social system remained fairly static. Status, social, and work roles were rather rigidly fixed, and people abided by the dictates of what they regarded as divinely established authority.

30

THE RENAISSANCE AND THE REFORMATION

With the Renaissance the dominance of the Church began to decline, both in the political realm and in the realm of intellectual activity. The Renaissance began in the fourteenth century in Italy and reached its height there in the fifteenth and sixteenth centuries; elsewhere in Europe we might date it from the fifteenth to the middle of the seventeenth century. It was a period marked by many new developments in literature, in science, in philosophy, and in the arts. The scientific method was propounded in early forms by Francis Bacon and others. It was an age of exploration and discoveries and an age marked by new economic and political developments. New nations emerged in Europe. There began an economic revolution in which commerce and credit assumed an importance they had not had in the economic life of the Middle Ages.

With the Renaissance came a new spirit of individual expression, a return to the individualism of classical Greece. There was less appeal to authority in matters of thought, morality, and taste, and a greater tendency to assume that the individual could best make his own independent decisions. This meant that much of the morality of the Middle Ages was abandoned. With a loss of the repressive elements of that system of morality, there came an increased freedom to explore all kinds of experiences as well as an increased expectation that individuals would and could rely on their own resources. Humility, compassion, kindness, and altruism were often viewed less as Christian virtues than as signs of weakness of character.

The Renaissance also brought a renewed stress on the development of all the potentials of the individual—his powers of observation and his intellectual and creative powers. There was a widespread feeling that the laws of nature were almost within the grasp of the human mind, that people had the potential for doing almost anything, and that with an increase in knowledge the human species could assume full mastery of the world. This attitude was an important spur to the development of science. In such an age, the ideal condition was no

31

longer seen in terms of grace but in terms of the maximal development of the intellectual and creative resources of the individual in his present life. The man who best epitomized the Renaissance ideal was Leonardo da Vinci.

During the Renaissance, scholarship began to flourish outside the Church, and many changes began to occur within the Church itself. The Reformation was prompted to some extent by the spirit of the Renaissance. It began with protests against the authoritarianism of the Church, with objections to many of its doctrines, and with cries of outrage against the economic abuses of some of the more corrupt men who held positions of power in the Church. The reformers varied among themselves, of course, and from the Reformation there emerged several forms of Protestantism and a number of distinct, independent churches. Three of the leading figures in the Reformation who laid the foundations for subsequent varieties of Protestant thought were Martin Luther, Huldreich Zwingli, and John Calvin.

Martin Luther was the first to raise a storm of protest in the Church. From his study of the Bible he concluded that the all-important elements in religion lay in the experience of the individual—his faith in God and his search for a close relationship to God. He believed that the Church placed too much emphasis on its own authority, and he objected to the absolute power of the Pope. For the Church to insist on submission of the individual to papal authority as a condition for salvation seemed to him a gross distortion of the word of the New Testament. Initially he sought to reform the Church from within, but his repeated attacks on the papacy ultimately led to his excommunication.

For Luther, the most important element in the Christian life was faith. His studies revealed to him a loving God who freely dispenses grace, and faith consists of accepting this God and accepting the fact that one is accepted by him. Beyond this basic acceptance of God and God's will, such things as allegiance to the Church, the performance of rituals, and the belief in particular doctrines are of no consequence. They are not preconditions for grace. Faith for Luther implies love of God, and by accepting his grace we can enter into a loving relationship with him. Conversely, sin is to be understood in terms of

32

unbelief or failure to accept God's acceptance, and its basic consequence is the despair of being separated from God.

In principle, Luther's view of man is that of a very limited creature, whose capacity for understanding and for accomplishing good is insignificant compared to the power of God. Paul Tillich expresses the Lutheran position in this way: "I know that I do not do anything good, that everything seemingly good is ambiguous, that the only thing which is good within me is God's declaration that I am good, and that if I accept this divine declaration, then there may be a transformed reality from which ethical acts may follow." [3] This is reminiscent of the Augustinian view of man. Yet it is difficult to examine Luther's own life, with his assertion of faith and his defiance of an ancient institution of which he had been a part, without concluding that Luther himself was a man of great courage who possessed tremendous confidence in his own ability as an individual to ascertain the truth.

The leading Protestant reformer in Switzerland was Huldreich Zwingli. Like Luther, Zwingli opposed the authority of the Roman Church and was led to his own position by his study of the Scriptures, also ultimately formulating a doctrine of justification by faith alone. Zwingli's idea of faith, however, seems to place less emphasis on direct experience of God, and his descriptions suggest that his experience of faith lacked the emotional intensity of Luther's. Unlike Luther, he did not experience a religious crisis in his own life. He was more inclined to quibble with the dogma of the Church on purely intellectual grounds. In comparison, Luther's outlook was more mystical, more concerned with immediate personal experience, and less concerned with intellectual doctrine or intellectual interpretation. Zwingli's outlook was more rational and humanistic (placing more emphasis on the rational powers of the human individual).

Zwingli was a bit more in tune with the spirit of the Renaissance and with the spirit manifested in the economic system that was emerging in Europe. Luther felt in closer touch with the whole of nature and would have preferred to return to a simpler kind of society. The views of both Zwingli and Calvin were fairly compatible with those of a scientific and industrial society that seeks to transform nature for human purposes.

33

John Calvin had a less intellectual approach to religion than Zwingli, but he apparently saw little possibility of the kind of close relationship to God that Luther emphasized. Unlike Luther, he had little to say about love, either the love of God or God's love of mankind. He apparently viewed God less as a loving force than as something rather austere, mysterious, unapproachable—even horrifying, for he could deal out a horrible fate that one could do nothing to prevent. Central to Calvin's theology was the doctrine of predestination. According to this doctrine, some people are elected by God for eternal life, while others are foreordained for eternal damnation. All is well for those in the former group, but since mankind cannot influence the will of God, there is nothing one can do deliberately to earn grace and avoid the fires of hell if that is one's assigned fate. From a human perspective, God's will is totally irrational, and we cannot hope to understand it.

On the other hand, it is possible to know whether or not an individual has been elected for salvation. The marks of election are essentially the qualities of a good bourgeois citizen. They include faith in God and the other virtues that Calvin regarded as the ingredients of a proper and moral Christian life. Thus, we might generally assume that the people whom Calvin regarded as good Christians were the ones most likely to secure grace, but superficial marks can be misleading. If we are not foreordained for grace, we cannot earn it just by leading the proper life. Presumably those who are elected for grace are more genuinely virtuous than those who are not, and merely acting virtuous is not enough. On the whole, Calvin tended to describe human nature and the human situation in rather negative terms. He viewed people as naturally inclined toward sin and in need of restraint, and as prone to hypocrisy; hence, they can readily assume the guise of righteousness when in fact they are inwardly sinful. The world, too, is described in negative terms, for Calvin tended to see it as a place of exile. Like many medieval Christians, he regarded the body as the prison of the soul, a valueless shell that we temporarily inhabit.

Calvin's formula for right living, of course, was not designed to enhance our enjoyment of the world. Whether or not we are among the chosen, it is important for us to try to lead the true Christian life. As he described it, this is not a life of love but one of self-denial, calculated to overcome our human weaknesses. The qualities that he stressed included thrift, industry, sobriety, chastity, temperance, and responsibility. Thus the faithful person does not seek pleasures in the present. He works hard with an eye to the future, but a future that is also not meant to be enjoyed. Calvin had much in common with the early ascetics of the Christian Church in his emphasis on self-denial and avoidance of pleasure. Although his brand of asceticism was not intended as a formula that would ensure grace, it was presumably a formula followed by those elected for grace, and it was a formula calculated to make the world a more godly, though perhaps not joyful, place.

Calvin looked with favor upon the capitalist economy that was developing in his time, and he encouraged increased trade and production of goods. He felt that a system in which people invested money and struggled for future profit was consistent with the good Christian life, though he disparaged the use of money or profit for mere self-indulgence. The constant struggle and effort were all-important. It is the Calvinist brand of Protestantism, with its emphasis on industry and future-orientation, that Max Weber referred to as the Protestant ethic.[4] It is in a sense the spirit of capitalism, an attitude that serves the purposes of an investment economy and fosters the growth of such an economy. This is not to say that the Protestant Reformation was a cause for the emergence of a capitalist economy, for that economy started before the Reformation. There is reason to believe, however, that a Calvinist outlook spurred more rapid industrial development in the countries where it flourished. At the same time, it seems probable that the outlook of John Calvin himself was strongly affected by the economic situation of the period in which he lived.

Calvin was born in France and spent his life on the Continent, but his doctrines found their expression in England in Puritanism, which had its beginnings in the latter half of the sixteenth century. Like Calvin, the Puritans extolled qualities that were conducive to economic success—self-reliance, frugality, industry. Many of them took an even dimmer view of basic human nature than Calvin had, and they insisted even more strongly on self-denial and self-discipline. They believed people were essentially sinful by nature and that they could only achieve good by extreme effort, rigorous discipline, and constant self-examination. They considered hard work a religious duty. They condemned profanation of the Sabbath, blasphemy, fornication, drunkenness, playing games of chance, and participation in theatrical performances. From a modern perspective, the Puritan way of life was rather grim, but Puritanism exerted an influence on the weltanschauung of the English-speaking people that is still felt today. The Presbyterian and Congregationalist denominations had their roots in Puritanism, and the Puritan idea of congregational democratic church government is one that has strongly affected political developments in the Western world.

LATER TRENDS IN WESTERN THOUGHT

In later periods developments in science and industry had an increasing impact on Western thought. In the first half of the sixteenth century, Copernicus had laid the foundation for a revolution in our views of man's place in the universe. Early in the seventeenth century Galileo clashed with ecclesiastical and political authorities over his defense of the Copernican heliocentric system and was forced to recant. Yet the experimental researches of Galileo and others and the writings of such men as Francis Bacon in defense of scientific empiricism signaled a turning point in Western thought. Scientific truth could no longer be dictated by dogmatic authority—unless, as has sometimes happened, the authority was himself an established scientist. Scientific method, in any case, became a widely respected avenue to truth. Thus, by the latter half of the seventeenth century the Western world was ready to accept Isaac Newton. Newton made bold contributions to many areas of physical science, and the world was particularly impressed with his laws of gravitation and motion. His work gave hope to the possibility that the complex workings of the universe might be understood in terms of the operation of a set of relatively simple natural laws that could be disclosed through the methods of science. While Galileo had been viewed as at least a borderline heretic, the world was ready in

36

Newton's time to see him as a new kind of hero, the prototype of Scientific Man.

Nature and Nature's laws lay hid in Night:
God said, Let Newton be: and all was Light.[5]

The eighteenth century is often characterized as the period of the Enlightenment, an age marked by great confidence in human reason and belief in natural law. There were important precursors to the Enlightenment in the seventeenth century—the discoveries of Newton, the rationalism of Descartes and Pierre Bayle, the empiricism of Francis Bacon and John Locke, the writings of Spinoza. The eighteenth century was marked by the contributions of such philosophers as David Hume and Immanuel Kant. Kant captured some of the spirit of the age in his essay "What is Enlightenment?" where he offers this definition: "Enlightenment is man's release from his self-incurred tutelage. Tutelage is man's inability to make use of his understanding without direction from another. Self-incurred is this tutelage when its cause lies not in lack of reason but in lack of resolution and courage to use it without direction from another. *Sapere aude!* 'Have courage to use your own reason!'—that is the motto of the enlightenment."

The vital ingredients of the eighteenth-century outlook captured in this definition are rationalism and autonomy. The individual, in Kant's view, can achieve great understanding if he assumes the responsibility of thinking for himself. Kant recognized that we could maintain a certain comfort and security if we relied on authority and let someone else do our thinking for us, and he stressed the importance of abandoning this kind of security. Through the exercise of unfettered reason, in the view of the philosophers of the Enlightenment, it was believed that people could not only answer the riddles of the physical universe but could also achieve a clearer comprehension of human nature and human society and then act on that knowledge for the betterment of mankind.

The Enlightenment was also marked by increased tolerance of diversity in all realms of thought—religion, politics, philosophy. John Locke had written on the importance of tolerance and was often

37

viewed as its leading advocate. In retrospect, we are not likely to see Locke as an ultraliberal, since he did believe in the legal suppression of both Catholics and atheists. Perhaps the twentieth century merely seems more enlightened to us, however, because the issues posed by formal religion are no longer so focal. The people of this century seem a bit more concerned with political heresy and deviance in the realm of sexual behavior. This makes a direct comparison of two periods difficult. In any case, writers of the eighteenth century frequently advocated tolerance and attacked restraint of various kinds on freedom of thought and action. Like the leaders of the Renaissance, they encouraged a kind of individualism.

There was also a kind of optimism in the eighteenth century, resting on a faith in the harmony of natural or unregulated events. In sharp contrast to the Calvinists, the major writers of the Enlightenment believed that if everyone just followed his own natural tendencies and sought his own happiness things would work out well for everyone. A common will would emerge, and the result would be a more widespread enjoyment of the riches of life.

The Enlightenment was never a unified movement, and there were countercurrents to some of its main features. The Romantic movement in philosophy and the arts began to emerge in the latter part of the eighteenth century. It contained much of the same individualistic spirit found earlier in the century but represented a revolt against rationalism. The Romantics exalted the emotions and the senses over reason and intellect, and they had a higher regard for the creative artist than for the scientific thinker. Within this movement there was a stress on imagination and fantasy, on religious mysticism, on symbolism, and on beauty in nature and art. Some of the Romantics displayed a nostalgic longing for what they saw as the spirit of the Middle Ages.

The optimism and faith in natural harmony of the Enlightenment were a part of Romanticism too. Inspired by some of the writings of Rousseau, the Romantics advocated a return to nature and a belief in the natural goodness of man. Particularly in the arts, they displayed interest in the "noble savage," in the "simple peasant," and at times in the violently self-centered "hero." In these images they saw a refreshing counterbalance to the molded, conforming products of society. In effect, for them the model of the optimal condition was the Natural Man, the individual who has not been contaminated by society or who has managed to free himself from its constraints.

Rousseau himself believed that both science and the arts had failed to contribute to the morality and happiness of mankind but had instead fostered immorality and insensitivity. He apparently believed that people had earlier lived in a condition that was much more ideal, more suited to human needs, because it was a more direct expression of basic human nature. He recognized, of course, that it was not possible to return to such a state but believed that useful political and social reforms were possible. His writings served as a source of inspiration for the leaders of both the American and French revolutions.

Many of the intellectual figures in the American Revolution—Thomas Jefferson, Thomas Paine, Benjamin Franklin, John Adams—embodied essentially the same spirit found in the mainstream of eighteenth-century thought in Europe. The Declaration of Independence enumerates the oppressive acts of the British government and proclaims "that all men are created equal, that they are endowed by their Creator with certain inalienable rights, that among these are life, liberty, and the pursuit of happiness." This is an eloquent expression of the idea that the greatest good for all comes when people are free to express their natural tendencies and structure their own society without coercion. The primary author of this document was Thomas Jefferson, who has come to represent a new ideal in the realm of the Political Man. Like Plato's philosopher-king, Jefferson was a man of great intellect, but he epitomizes a democratic ideal, for he believed that the best political system was one in which the educated masses all had a voice in their government and democratically elected their leaders. As a prototype of a democratic ideal, Jefferson is not the sort of man who has a natural right to the powers of a king but the sort of man who is ideally chosen for leadership in a political democracy.

Western thought in the eighteenth and nineteenth centuries was also shaped by developments in the economic realm. The Industrial Revolution in England is usually dated from the middle of the one century to the middle of the other. For much of northern Europe and the

United States, this was a period of transition from a stable agricultural and commercial society to a modern industrial society, a society in which factories grew large and relied increasingly on complex machines rather than on simple hand tools. It was a period marked by many inventions and technological innovations that were bound to affect social life in general. Increasingly coal was used as a source of energy in place of wood, and many uses were found for steam power. People began to concentrate in cities. In many areas of production the independent craftsman became outmoded; instead, many workers were employed by a single factory owner, and problems that had not existed in an earlier economy began to arise in the relationship between capital and labor.

The writings of Adam Smith were influential in the latter half of the eighteenth century. This was still early in the Industrial Revolution, and Smith did not foresee all the problems that would arise with increasing industrialization. Representing an application of the spirit of the Enlightenment to the realm of economics, he believed in freedom of action, and for him this meant a laissez-faire economy. The greatest good for all would be achieved if everyone were free to pursue his own self-interest in the economic realm, and both laborers and entrepreneurs would benefit from a competitive free enterprise system.

Smith's industrial-age philosophy stresses a kind of individualism that links it to other expressions of the Enlightenment. Of course, Smith's focus was on economic self-interest rather than on self-reliance in the intellectual realm. Like other writers of the eighteenth century, however, he manifested great faith in the natural harmony of unregulated events, and his outlook was but one more expression of a stream of thought, traceable to the Renaissance and perhaps earlier to classical Greece, that finds the highest good in the development and expression of the powers of the individual human being.

THREE

WESTERN THOUGHT IN THE MODERN ERA

DEVELOPMENTS IN SCIENCE

For our purposes, it is convenient to think of the modern era as the period from the middle of the nineteenth century to the present. This is a period in which developments in science have not only greatly affected Western views of mankind and the universe but have had a tremendous impact on our society as a whole. The first major scientific achievement of this period was Charles Darwin's theory of evolution, a summary of which was first published in 1858.[1] According to Darwin all living forms evolve, and higher organisms gradually develop from lower organisms through the operation of a principle of natural selection, whereby those variations within the species that have greater survival value are preserved and those that have less survival value are eliminated (through the death or nonreproduction of the less fit). The basic elements of the Darwinian position have been generally accepted by biologists, with the expansions and modifications permitted by scientific knowledge that has since accumulated.

Like the earlier revolution brought about by Copernicus and Galileo, evolutionary theory basically affected our ideas about the nature of the human species. It put us in a less distinctive position within the total realm of animal life, suggesting that most of the differences be-

41

tween human beings and other animals can best be described in quantitative terms. If we accept the Darwinian view, it seems more questionable that man's essential nature can be understood in terms of some unique attribute that is totally absent in other forms of life. Such issues were a cause for grave concern within the Church for decades and remained matters for public debate well into the present century, although only a few literalists and fundamentalists now seem interested in carrying on the debate. Western thought as a whole has absorbed the evolutionary view of mankind.

The idea of human evolution was not altogether new with Darwin, but after the publication of *The Origin of Species* the idea enjoyed increased popularity. It was extended to the psychological and social realms by such writers as Herbert Spencer. Whatever novel elements it may add to our understanding of man, it is consistent with an emphasis on progress that has long been prominent in Western thought. More than people of other cultures, Westerners—perhaps in particular those of Northern European extraction—tend to feel that the things of real importance lie at some ill-defined time in the future and that our present situation and activities are worthwhile only if we are making progress, if we are effecting the changes required to move us closer to the ideal future condition. This is an attitude that has often appeared in Christian thought, but it was best articulated by Calvin and lies at the core of the Protestant or Puritan ethic. From such a perspective, of course, the ideal present condition for any individual is progressive change. The ideal condition may be viewed as a fixed state only in some future that never quite arrives.

Evolutionism as a social philosophy has been adopted by many writers. A good example would be Julian Huxley. Huxley is himself a biologist and the grandson of Thomas Henry Huxley, an evolutionary biologist of the nineteenth century. Julian Huxley is concerned not only with evolution on a biological level but also with what he regards as cosmic evolution and psychosocial evolution.[2] The last of these underlies the development of human culture. From Huxley's standpoint, we make useful progress to the extent that we make changes that permit greater fulfillment of human potentialities. Through psychosocial evolution we have acquired great ability to control and utilize the physical world around us. Further progress requires an increase in our understanding and in our ability to control and utilize the forces within ourselves. We can advance the course of psychosocial evolution on a species-wide or society-wide level, but we can advance it also within our own individual lives.

For Huxley, two important conditions for progressive cultural change are an increase in knowledge and the interpenetration and interaction of different cultures. Huxley's evolutionary humanism is multifaceted, but it seems on the whole to place fundamental emphasis on belief systems based on accurate knowledge. He is concerned with our human potential for all kinds of experience, not just the experience directly afforded by scientific awareness, but he evidently sees scientific knowledge as a key to progress. It is the knowledge we need to solve practical societal problems and to provide the conditions for individual fulfillment.

The work of Darwin has had still more direct effects on psychology, for it is in the modern era that psychology has emerged as a separate scientific discipline and ceased to be regarded primarily as a subdomain of philosophy. Some of Darwin's work was essentially psychological in character, and he is one of the scientists of the nineteenth century who strongly influenced the development of the new science. More broadly, biology as a whole and to some extent the other natural sciences influenced the development of psychology, because in attempting to build a science, an empirically based psychology, psychologists tended to view the biological and physical sciences as models. This meant not only patterning methods after those used in the natural sciences, but adopting much of the metaphysical base common to those sciences in the nineteenth century. Eminent early contributors to experimental psychology were such men as Hermann Helmholtz, Gustav Fechner, and Wilhelm Wundt, who had received earlier training in the natural sciences.

Within philosophy there had been two main traditions in the treatment of psychological issues—an empiricist tradition that flourished in England, represented by Locke, George Berkeley, and David Hartley, and a rationalist tradition, more idealistic in orientation, that flourished on the Continent and was marked by the strong influence of Leibniz

43

and Kant. The former tradition was more conducive to the development of an empirical scientific psychology and clearly exerted the stronger influence in its development. Though the people influenced by this tradition tended to employ introspection as a method, they usually showed less interest in capturing the totality of human experience than in analyzing it into elementary components. Thus, for them human consciousness was to be understood in terms of combinations and sequences of elementary ideas governed by principles of association. Features that pervade this tradition include an emphasis on direct observation as the essential means for establishing truth, an elementaristic emphasis in both method and theory, and an essentially mechanistic orientation with respect to the nature of human consciousness.

The empiricist tradition and the traditions of the natural sciences have had a strong influence on both of the dominant streams of twentieth-century psychology—psychoanalysis and behaviorism. At the same time, we see within psychology in this century a rather exaggerated effort to secure some of the prestige that the Western world has accorded to science, manifested both in a preoccupation with methodology and in a concern with the language in which observations, hypotheses, and conclusions are stated. The net result is a pronounced inclination on the part of Western psychologists to view people in a rather detached manner and to attempt to understand them in the way that a natural scientist would seek to understand a physical object. Simultaneously, there is a tendency for Western psychologists to take the ideal of the true scientist as a model for their own behavior and then to extend this model to people in general, so that they tend to think of the ideal person as an efficient processer of information about the physical and social environment.

We shall deal with the views of contemporary psychologists in more depth in later chapters. There are other developments in science as a whole that we must consider briefly, for they are a crucial part of the cultural context that is shaping and will continue to shape thought in psychology. The twentieth century has witnessed a vast mushrooming of knowledge in the natural sciences. The dramatic advances in atomic physics and molecular biology are only a small part of the total increase in scientific information. Some of this growth has been made possible by new instruments, such as particle accelerators and the electron microscope. An increase in public financing of scientific research has also contributed to it. Whatever the sources and reasons for the growth, it has had consequences that raise totally new issues for mankind. We have seen the development of atomic weapons, made possible by scientific research, and we have seen these weapons stockpiled in quantities sufficient to obliterate all life on this planet. As biological researchers continue to unlock the secrets of life contained in the cell, the prospect of extensive genetic manipulation looms as an increasingly feasible possibility. Eventually we shall be in a position to direct human biological evolution, to create the kinds of people who are most desirable.

Unfortunately the kind of methodology that can give us this creative power cannot tell us what kind of person is most desirable. As we have seen, that is a very old question to which many answers have been given, and it is not in the nature of the question that a definitive answer can be furnished by empirical science. The point here, of course, is that in the twentieth century science has amassed knowledge whose application can obviously have staggering, even terrifying, consequences. This fact is affecting the image of Scientific Man in the Western world. It has shown us that this is indeed an image to be reckoned with and to be respected, but in the eyes of many people it is becoming an image to be feared. If this modern sorcerer has the power to solve all our problems and bring us to salvation, he also has the power to lead us to total disaster.

Science obviously has a major role to play in our society, and it is going to affect our lives in profound ways and shape our views of man, nature, and the human situation in still further ways, but it is hazardous to forecast the future and predict what form the changes will assume. Science itself is not an inanimate thing. Individual scientists are people, and many of them are very much concerned with the issues created by their work. Their concern may lead to some changes in the prevailing philosophy of science. We have already seen many such changes in this century. In physics, the strict determinism of the nineteenth century has given way to a probabilistic determinism. Biol-

45

ogy is less mechanistic than it was a half-century ago when Jan Smuts issued his plea for holism.[3] Perhaps the really profound changes are yet to come.

INDUSTRY AND TECHNOLOGY

Science is not the only element in our culture that has made for rapid changes in the modern era. There is an individualistic trend in the Western world that has been clearly evident ever since the Renaissance. In the Renaissance it found expression in an emphasis on an all-around development of the potential of the individual for experience and expression. Later the emphasis narrowed and the individualism found primary focus in the material or economic realm. The cultivation of individual sensitivity became less important, and there was an increased interest in competition and acquisition in the business world. The capacity for understanding and aesthetic appreciation became less important than the shrewdness or cleverness that yielded monetary achievements. Of course, this is not an exclusive focus, for the achievement motive is conspicuous in many areas of life in the Western world.

In any case, it is evident that a form of individualism entered into the commercial developments that were in progress during the Renaissance and still more conspicuously in the Industrial Revolution that was to come later. By then economic competition had become an established way of life that many writers, including Adam Smith, saw as very beneficial. By the middle of the nineteenth century, the Industrial Revolution had wrought effects that were regarded by many people as very detrimental. Thus, Henry David Thoreau saw people crowded together in cities under miserable conditions they felt powerless to control. "The mass of men," he said in *Walden,* "lead lives of quiet desperation." His own solution was to retreat to a solitary life in the woods, where he could be in closer touch with nature, and when necessary to refuse to abide by the dictates of society.

At about the same time, Karl Marx also painted a very grim and more elaborate picture of the industrial society in which he found him-

46

self.[4] The root problem as he saw it was the capitalist system, with its division of labor and its emphasis on private property. In such a system money acquires undue importance, because the older values appreciated by the individual artisan have been lost. We work only to obtain money and come to value ourselves and others in terms of the money we possess. Even if we did not view ourselves in monetary terms, we would still find ourselves within this system in a labor marketplace in which we are treated by employers as commodities, spurred to produce and valued in terms of how much we produce. According to Marx, a system that operates in this way is basically dehumanizing.

He saw other evidence of its dehumanizing effects in the gross mistreatment of workers in the factories of his day—women and children required to work long days in crowded and unsanitary conditions, a lack of concern on the part of management for the safety of workers in mines and in factories with dangerous machinery, and generally a subordination of the human needs of workers to the desire of owners for profits. According to Marx, everyone is dehumanized in this system, for it encourages the basest impulses in both employers and employees and does not permit the full humanness of either to ripen.

The concept of alienation has enjoyed popularity among social scientists over the last few years, and it is often viewed as a very recent phenomenon. Perhaps in some forms it is recent, but few modern writers have given as comprehensive a treatment of alienation as Marx did over a century ago. He spoke of three forms of alienation. First there is alienation from work. The worker in the capitalist industrial society experiences his work and the products of his work as something external to himself. He is treated as an appendage to a machine and enters mechanically into one stage in the process of production, and the result is a product that he cannot appreciate as his own and in which he can take no pride. Thus, he inevitably regards the work itself as distasteful, something that he does only to achieve a necessary monetary reward. By virtue of the same process, the worker experiences alienation from himself. Since the product of his labors is perceived as something alien, the worker cannot fully realize his own creative powers. In effect, he gives away some of his own power to the

47

object that he produces in the course of production. Finally, there is alienation from other people in this system, for the system is one in which people seek to use and exploit one another for personal gain, rather than seeking genuine relationships.

The ideal solution for the ills of this society, as Marx saw it, lay in a socialist system in which private property and classes would be eliminated and the sexes would enjoy social equality. No group would exploit another group, and people would share more equitably the fruits of their labors. With the elimination of competitive rifts, of class conflicts, and of the division of labor, the sources of alienation would be eliminated. Everyone would then have maximal opportunity to develop freely and fully. Marx was very critical of the Church, referring to religion as "the opiate of the masses," a drug used to facilitate exploitation. Yet Marx himself was clearly a product of Judaeo-Christian tradition. He experienced many difficulties in relating to people himself, but his social philosophy was one that attached greatest value to love and community, qualities that were central to at least the early forms of the Christian ethic and qualities that run counter to the individualistic strain in Western culture.

Whatever the benefits that have accrued from continuing "progress" in Western society, a number of other writers have suggested that some psychological problems have grown increasingly severe. Rollo May, alluding to the basic theme in W. H. Auden's poem "The Age of Anxiety," suggests that anxiety has become more pervasive, intense, and overtly manifest than it ever was in earlier periods in our history.[5] He believes that this situation stems from the fact that social prestige based on individual competitive success has become the dominant goal in our society. This is a goal that is evident not only in the economic realm but in our schools and families and in our sexual and love relationships as well. A peculiar property of the central value that we have adopted is that it tends to generate interpersonal hostility and isolation that lead to anxiety, which in turn leads to increased competitive striving. Abram Kardiner has suggested that this kind of striving has no satiation point.[6] Hence, our frantic efforts to achieve may tend to increase whether they lead to success or to failure.

May and a number of other writers see the contemporary problem as the product of a trend that began in the Renaissance. The ordinary citizen of the Middle Ages presumably tended to think of himself as a member of a group—a family, a village, an institution, a people—and derived a sense of security from that identity, however bleak his circumstances may otherwise have been. He strove for salvation. In the Renaissance, the goal of salvation began to be replaced by the goal of self-realization. There was a greater emphasis on the capacity and power of the individual, a stress on personal creativity and achievement. The Renaissance spirit placed a high value on the individual, but on the strong individual, not on the single person as such. For some, this new spirit meant a new sense of freedom and strength. They welcomed the opportunity for individual exploration and expression. They even welcomed the solitude and isolation from the community that this might entail. A spiritual individual of the Middle Ages might have relished solitude as a condition for spiritual attainment, an opportunity for coming into closer contact with God. The greatest representatives of the Renaissance spirit, Leonardo and Michelangelo, relished solitude for a totally different reason—it gave them an opportunity to realize fully their creative powers and to exercise their own intellects without undue contamination from without and without having to share their creative successes with anyone else. Michelangelo wrote, "I have no friend of any kind, and I do not want one. Whoever follows others will never go forward, and whoever does not know how to create by his own abilities can gain no profit from the works of other men." [7] The notebooks of Leonardo da Vinci describe even more forcefully the good fortunes of a man who is totally alone.

If the sense of isolation that was now possible was enjoyed by some, it certainly added to the discomfort of others. Many of the recent effects of the individualistic spirit in Western culture could not have been anticipated in the Renaissance. The spirit was initially accompanied by the attitude that its expression would yield benefits for the social group as a whole, and this idea was certainly reiterated in the eighteenth century notion of harmony. In many ways, this expectation has been validated in the economic, political, and intellectual realms. Thus, the material circumstances of life have obviously improved over the centuries in the Western world. The individualistic

49

spirit, however, has been transformed in ways that are not so beneficial.

Basically the kind of individualism introduced by the Renaissance was competitive, and this aspect has increased in the course of time, reinforced, then contaminated, by the competitive processes of commerce and industry. As a result, the idea of self-realization in all phases of creative activity tended to be replaced by achievement in the economic realm. More and more, Western society came to be characterized by competition for wealth, and competition in other realms has tended to focus on securing the marks of success. It is not so important now simply to realize one's own capacities for experience and creative expression as it is to be recognized as an individual who is better than others. Such an emphasis is more disruptive of the sense of community than was the individualism of the Renaissance, and it is more likely to lead to interpersonal hostility and make us feel isolated. When we recognize, furthermore, that the spirit of the Renaissance was probably really felt by only a segment of the society at that time but that the striving for individual competitive success is now a very pervasive feature of our society, it is not difficult to see why some would say that this is the age of anxiety. Rollo May states the essential issue confronting people in our time in this way: "How can interpersonal community (ethical, psychological, economic, etc.) be attained which, integrated with the values of individual freedom, will liberate the individual from the sense of isolation and concomitant anxiety inhering in excessive individualism?" [8]

Excessive individualism and competitive striving, of course, are only a part of the problem that people now experience in our society. There has been a host of economic, technological, scientific, and political developments in the past few decades that have caused many of us to become increasingly alarmed about the direction in which our civilization seems generally to be headed. As we noted in the first chapter, Drucker felt in the 1930s that the people of the Western world had lost faith in the image of Economic Man and no longer saw either capitalism or socialism as a solution to their problems. They were ripe in Italy and Germany for the emergence of fascist states. World War II ensued, bringing a major upheaval in the lives of Europeans and to a lesser extent in the lives of Americans. Since the war there has been recurrent concern in this country over the prospect of a movement in the direction of totalitarianism. We have witnessed the creation of loyalty oaths, the political witch-hunts of the McCarthy era, and extensive prying by the government into the private lives of citizens in the name of national security. George Orwell's *1984*, written in 1949, depicts in fictional form a possible end-product of such a trend, a state in which the government has achieved a high degree of thought-control over the people it governs.[9]

Whether or not we are moving in the direction of a political system in which we will be subject to the kind of manipulation that Orwell describes, there is little doubt that there are elements in our way of life that are conducive to the progressive evolution of a highly complex social system in which any sort of participant democracy becomes impossible. A basic ingredient of Western individualism is an effort to achieve. The individual enters into a competitive struggle not only with other people, whom he seeks to surpass, but with nature as well. Both tend to be treated as objects to be mastered. In no other culture has there ever been such an emphasis on the conquest of nature, and this emphasis has led to great material progress. Such scientific and technological activity in the West, and particularly in the United States, has not only refashioned our style of living; it has transformed the social system in which we live. According to Alvin Toffler, technological development in our society has reached a point at which it might be said that we are passing from the industrial age into an age of superindustrialism.[10]

Further considering the social consequences of superindustrialism, Theodore Roszak speaks of the present condition of our society in terms of technocracy, a social system that is basically operated by a regime of experts.[11] Those in ostensible positions of government turn increasingly for guidance to experts who in turn appeal to scientific forms of knowledge. This is essentially the system that results when a highly industrialized society becomes organizationally integrated. Such a system has its benefits, but the individual citizen inevitably loses power of decision. He has no means of exerting control over the institutions that control his life.

51

Charles Reich uses the term _corporate state_ to describe the present situation in our society.[12] He makes less reference to technological and scientific experts, but otherwise he is describing much the same system, in which all institutions—government, business, industry, educational institutions, etc.—become thoroughly interconnected and the individual's initiative and decision are lost to the total organization.

If the new complex society operated in a way effectively designed to maximize the benefits for everyone, perhaps it would make people feel more secure than they have in the past. Unfortunately, there is too much evidence that it can function in a very irrational manner. Perhaps the clearest evidence for a sizable segment of the American populace was the Viet Nam war. Under a succession of four presidential administrations, the United States became progressively involved in a war in which it supported an exploitative military regime in South Viet Nam in what was initially a civil war between that government and the rebel force known as the Vietcong. More and more people began to wonder whether American involvement could be justified on moral, political, or intellectual grounds. During the 1960s we became aware that the United States, relying heavily on airpower and the use of napalm bombs in Viet Nam, might well be responsible for the destruction of hundreds of thousands of civilian lives in a distant part of the world. With increasing vigor young people began to protest involvement in Southeast Asia, and thousands refused to be conscripted to fight in such a war. The antiwar movement reached its peak in 1967 and 1968 and was probably an important factor in President Lyndon Johnson's decision not to run again for office. Yet at a time when many were hoping that the war would be brought to a halt, Johnson was succeeded by another president who extended active military engagement for an additional four years, increased the bombing, and expanded the war to neighboring areas of Indochina. Over a fourteen-month period in 1969 and 1970 the Air Force engaged in a total of 3,630 bombing raids in Cambodia that were not reported to the American public. Yet the military moves of the Nixon administration evoked little active protest. The antiwar movement may have been instrumental in removing Johnson from office, but his departure was followed by a series of events that apparently convinced many people that public protests were essentially futile, that their best efforts could not divert the society from its irrational course.[13]

Of course, mankind has been plagued for thousands of years by bad political decisions and by actions of government that have disastrous consequences, but burgeoning technology adds a new dimension to the irrationality of the social machine. Technology can be devised for destructive purposes, and once devised it can prove to have destructive effects that were not intended by its designers. The dramatic examples are in the realm of weaponry. Atomic weapons can wreak devastation on a scale that nobody envisioned before the present century. In addition, it appears that a fair amount of government funding has gone into the development of weapons of chemical and biological warfare that have essentially the same potential for massive destruction as atomic weapons. When we realize what a minute amount of money has been spent in comparison by governments to finance research into constructive solutions to human problems, we can hardly avoid wondering whether we really have an optimal society.

Another fruit of advanced technology is the ecological crisis. No one really has a clear overall picture of the extent of this crisis, but it is evident that our efforts to subdue nature and bend it to our own purposes have introduced novel hazards. It is conceivable that a propellant substance used in aerosol cans may do unforeseen damage to the outer layers of our atmosphere. It is possible for an insecticide applied to one species of insect to create a chain of effects that affect many forms of animal life remote both phyletically and geographically from the small creatures for which it was intended. In recent years we have drastically increased the pollutants in our oceans, streams, and atmosphere, and this pollution can render the planet less habitable for humans as well as other forms of life. Our increasing use of fossil fuels has a host of undesirable effects on the air we breathe, while the introduction of nuclear energy as a substitute may bring still more serious hazards. It is possible that in some efficient supertechnological society of the future the problems created by technology will be solved as rapidly as they are created. Meanwhile we live in a world in which technology has produced effects that threaten the continued existence

53

of life on this planet. Whether we dwell on this fact or try to avoid thinking about it, it is bound to affect our views on the optimal mode of living.

Yet another feature of contemporary living on which Toffler has focused attention is the increased rate at which we must experience novelty or change. Not only are technological advances continuing; they manifest an accelerating rate of increase. The same is true of scientific knowledge. Most of the scientific knowledge we possess has been acquired in this century, and it has been said that 90 percent of the scientists who have ever lived are alive at the present time. In addition to the advent of atomic weapons and the beginnings of other uses of nuclear energy, we have seen spectacular innovations in our means of communication and transportation and in industrial methods. We have seen the development of space travel, which not long ago seemed a feat for future centuries. The applications of electronic computers to business, industry, and research have been mushrooming, but we have witnessed only the beginning of the computer age.

Accelerating change is not confined to the realms of scientific knowledge and technology. Toffler finds evidence of such change with respect to the movement of people from one location to another, in interpersonal relationships and contacts, in organizational structures, and in language. In short, we live in a world characterized by increasing novelty and multiformity in all features. We experience increasing diversity with respect to manufactured products, subcultures, and life-styles. One result is that we face greater and greater pressure to make choices that people have not had to make in the past. Some of these choices—particularly those pertaining to life-styles and to groups with whom we identify—relate closely to our experienced identities and cause us to suffer identity crises. Toffler believes that the basic effect of the contemporary condition of heightened change, novelty, and diversity is a form of distress that he calls "future shock."

It has become abundantly evident in recent times, then, that the individualistic spirit that began to emerge in the Renaissance is a sword with two edges. This spirit has brought industry, invention, and discovery and has led us to the age of modern technology. People have widely assumed in the past that the innovations yielded by the individ-

54

ualistic spirit would tend generally to redound to the benefit of the society as a whole, and there is much to support this view. Yet by the same token we now live in a society in which the hazards and the rapid change produced by technological innovation are a new source of distress.

There are several ways in which we can seek to cope with this distress. We can try to dampen it or tune it out by repression and denial. We can try to avoid thinking about it. We can let others do the thinking and just follow as automatically as possible. We can condemn the society and try to drop out of it, but this has become virtually impossible, for it is in the nature of this society that it will make its effects felt all around the globe. The hippies attempted to drop out while remaining clustered in cities like San Francisco and New York, but the surrounding society viewed them as parasites and reabsorbed them. The path of activism offers still another alternative. One can battle for power and seek to reform the ways of government, industry, and technology.

The problems posed by the modern technological society, however, are not problems of simple political reform. They are not the sort of problems one can solve by throwing a few rascals out of office, by deposing a president, or by writing a new constitution. There is a growing awareness in our society that there is something very fundamental in the underlying outlook that needs to be transformed. People involved in the counterculture and antiwar movements of the 1960s and people concerned today with the ecological problems we now face have raised many questions about the individualistic spirit that leads us to strive for mastery in both the social and natural realms. Pointing to the growing threats to our natural environment, they suggest that instead of trying to conquer nature, we should recognize that we are a part of a delicate ecosystem that cannot tolerate unrestrained tampering. To survive, we must learn once again how to live in harmony with the rest of nature, instead of striving to change it.

A similar reasoning would seem applicable to the realm of international affairs. Perhaps people have always tended to think of mankind dichotomously, in terms of *us* and *them*, the ingroup and the enemy. In past centuries the line of division was drawn around tribal

55

groups or villages; it is only in very recent times that it has circumscribed a nation or a group of nations. Now we tend to draw the line between two hemispheres. The exact location of the line is subject to fluctuation, but the ancient attitudes persist. On the other side of the line lies the enemy. If we do not consider it our right to conquer the enemy, we do assume that it is his intention to conquer us. Hence we must be on guard lest we be attacked. If we arm ourselves, it is strictly for defensive purposes. If he arms himself, employing much the same logic, we assume it is because he intends to attack. In an age of nuclear weapons, this way of looking at the world can pave the way to the ultimate holocaust. We are more likely to survive if we can learn to think more in terms of mankind as a totality.

It is possible that we are on the verge of moving into an era in which the individualistic spirit will no longer be such a dominant motif in Western culture, at least not *the* dominant motif. A growing awareness of the hazards that accompany this spirit has already begun to affect our thinking about the ideal mode of living. One consequence is a widespread suspicion in our society that Eastern modes of thought may contain much wisdom that is lacking on our own traditions, and we see increasing references to Hindu and Buddhist ideas in the literature on human personality.

CONTEMPORARY RELIGIOUS THOUGHT

While the Church was displaced long ago as the primary institution serving to shape our conduct and our attitudes toward the world, religion continues to be one important factor in our experience. Religious thought both influences us and reflects changes that have occurred in the rest of society. The Judaeo-Christian stream of thought remains a major source of our views regarding the optimal mode of living, and it may be illuminating to trace this stream along with developments in science and industry into the present.

Much of what we can observe in the realm of religious thought can be summarized in four points:

56

1. The major older traditions continue in one form or another. Thus, both mystical and rationalistic approaches are still in evidence.
2. There has been an overall tendency to de-emphasize universal ethical precepts, apart from the most fundamental ones, and to show greater respect for individual choice.
3. Scientific thought, from Darwinian theory to psychiatry, has been gradually absorbed by the Church and by religious thinkers, and to a great extent religious thought has come to reflect the scientific view of the world.
4. In recent years religious leaders have shown an increased concern with contemporary social issues, or at any rate an increased tendency to assume roles that involve active efforts to influence social processes in society at large.

Several contemporary religious thinkers have views on the optimal condition that merit our specific attention. The ones we shall consider here are Martin Buber, Paul Tillich, and Pierre Teilhard de Chardin. These three cannot be said to typify the present stage in Western religious thought, but they represent three distinctive viewpoints that have commanded widespread attention. Each of these men is clearly a joint product of the modern era and of ancient traditions.

Martin Buber A Jewish philosopher of religion, Buber lived from 1878 to 1965. His writings reveal most strongly the influence of Jewish mysticism, but he studied the mysticism of China and India and of medieval Christianity as well. He was influenced by the Christian existentialism of Kierkegaard, and his own unique blend of all these influences has in turn had a great impact on contemporary Christian thinkers.

We cannot properly discuss Buber's ideas without referring to Hasidism, the Jewish tradition that most strongly affected his thinking. The term *Hasidim* referred originally to an ancient sect who resisted the incorporation of Hellenistic ideas into Judaism. It has been subsequently applied to the adherents of Hasidism, a mystical movement founded in Poland in the eighteenth century by Baal-Shem-Tov in reaction to the sterile rationalism and academic formalism that characterized most rabbinical thought and practice at the time. Hasidism is basically an active, not a contemplative, mysticism; its adherents do not seek an ecstatic experience of union with God, but instead seek experience through loving action and joyous religious expression involving music and dance.

Baal-Shem himself believed that purity of heart was more important than anything that could be achieved intellectually, and he aroused the antagonism of the Talmudic scholars of his time. Unlike many other mystics, he disdained asceticism and had an accepting attitude toward the pleasures of the senses. His life was marked by great humility and by many acts of kindness. Both in thought and in deeds he appears to have been comparable to Saint Francis.

Much of Buber's work was devoted to an interpretation of Hasidism and of the leading figures in the movement.[14] In keeping with this mystical tradition, Buber did not feel that he could provide a theological doctrine concerning the nature of God but could only point the way to a means of experiencing God. He felt that the problem of our relationship to God is inseparable from that of our relationship to our fellow men—we can communicate with God and love God only if we can communicate with and love other people. The fundamental problem of our time, according to Buber, is an inability really to communicate with either God or our fellow men.

In his best-known work, *I and Thou*, Buber considered a unique characteristic of the human species—the ability to assume either of two attitudes toward our surroundings. We can regard our surroundings as It, viewing them as things that we can observe with detachment, or we can relate to these surroundings more intimately as Thou. Both attitudes are necessary. It is only through the I-Thou relationship that true relating occurs. In this orientation, we are living in the present moment. Genuine love can occur only between an I and a Thou, and this love implies that each feels a responsibility for the other. To the extent that we negate the other person, that we deny his full being, he becomes for us an It. Through the I-It orientation we withdraw from the immediate present. We can process remembered events of the past and anticipate future events. We can order, describe, arrange, and use people and things for our own purposes. It is essential that we be able to do this, and yet the It world is a lifeless world of which we do not experience ourselves as being a vital part. Buber wrote, "Without It, man cannot live, but he who lives with It alone, is not truly man." [15]

Normally the two orientations alternate, and the I-Thou at least cannot last for long. In one moment, we experience the immediacy of relationship with another being. In the next moment, we remember what has just happened, the event becomes describable, and the person becomes a quantity of attributes about which we are thinking. The remembered Thou is now an It. True encounter is always very brief, but it can recur.

In the course of a lifetime we tend to experience a progressive increase in the It world. The history of the species also shows this trend. We have learned to deal more and more with a material world that we seek to analyze, control, and use. We may experience a threatened loss of security in occasional moments when an experience of the Thou breaks through. To the extent that we seek to do everything via the I-It orientation, we tend to lose our capacity for relatedness. This not only affects our experience of other people, it affects our experience of ourselves. It leads to a kind of alienation from the self. The I in the I-It is not the same as the I in the I-Thou. The I in the I-It is an I with no intimacy, no mutuality; there is only action from the I upon the It, and no experience of reciprocity. The experience of one's full humanness requires the mutuality of the I-Thou. Buber believed that in the course of experiencing the relatedness of I-Thou, the consciousness of the I grows clearer, reaching a point where "the I confronts itself for a moment, separated as though it were a Thou."

We live in a society that stresses the I-It. Thus, Buber's value for us may lie in his calling attention to the importance of the I-Thou, even though he stressed the necessity of both attitudes. He dealt with the two orientations not only in the context of the relationships between individual persons, but in the context of the broader society and in the context of religion. In general, in the social realm he felt that both relationship and separateness are necessary. One must be able to identify and to empathize with others, but one must also be able to depend on the significance of his own individuality. Going exclusively to the one extreme, however, may lead to a kind of perpetual symbiosis, an annihilation of one's individual self, while going to the other extreme

59

tends to imply the excesses of pride and self-admiration. On a societal level, Buber warned against the extremes of collectivism and separatism. In the one, the individual relinquishes responsibility for being an individual person; in the other, we see a loss of concern for the well-being of others. For Buber, the ideal would be a kind of "utopian socialism" that is conducive to more meaningful relationships among people. He felt that the Kibbutzim of Israel approach this ideal.

Buber believed that in relating to other people we are, in effect, relating to God, for God is the eternal Thou, the Thou that cannot become an It. Obviously in religious doctrine, which concerns itself with the nature of God, God is treated as an It, but God can be experienced only through direct relationship. As a mystic, Buber tended to regard the dogma of organized religion as a major cause of its spiritual decline. It should be noted that for him the experience of God implies the full duality of the I-Thou orientation. He rejected the religious orientation that stresses absorption into God, or union with God, as the ultimate goal. He also rejected a religious outlook that stresses man's helpless dependence on God, since this denies the strength and vitality of the I.

In this book, we are primarily concerned with contemporary views of the optimal mode of living. Buber's significance for our purposes lies in that fact that he was the most salient exponent of a model that combines mysticism and relatedness. There are many novel features in his presentation of this model, but the model itself has ancient roots in both Jewish and Christian thought.

Paul Tillich There are many parallels between the ideas of Buber and those of Tillich, though the sources and the language of expression are a bit different. By birth and training Tillich was a Lutheran, but his work reflects broad erudition and he draws ideas from existentialism, from modern depth psychology, and from the entire history of Christian thought. He taught theology and philosophy in Germany, but because of his opposition to the Nazi regime he was dismissed, like Buber, from a teaching post at the University of Frankfurt in 1933. He thereupon accepted an invitation from Reinhold Niebuhr to come to

New York and join the faculty of the Union Theological Seminary. He remained in the United States until his death in 1965.

Tillich regarded anxiety and despair as important elements in the human condition.[16] He defined anxiety as the state in which a being is aware of its possible nonbeing, and he distinguished three types of anxiety. One is the anxiety of fate and death, or ontic anxiety, which threatens one's ontic self-affirmation. The second is the anxiety of emptiness, loss of meaning, or meaninglessness, which threatens one's spiritual self-affirmation. The third is the anxiety of guilt and condemnation, which threatens one's moral self-affirmation. Despair is a more extreme condition, an ultimate state that cannot be exceeded because it is a state without hope.

Noting that this has sometimes been called the age of anxiety, Tillich argued that there have been other periods in which anxiety was very prominent, but that the character of it has changed. The three forms tend to accompany one another, but one may be more evident at a given time than the others. At the end of the ancient period in Western civilization, ontic anxiety was the predominant form. At the end of the Middle Ages, moral anxiety was predominant. At the present time, spiritual anxiety is predominant. Thus, we are plagued with alienation, rather than with guilt or with the imminence of death.

Anxiety is inevitable because awareness of being presupposes awareness of the possibility of nonbeing. Our being includes many things besides material life—it includes all those elements in our lives that contribute to a sense of meaning and a sense of worth. We can attempt to reduce anxiety by reducing awareness, or by relinquishing a part of our being. Neurosis is a way of avoiding nonbeing by avoiding being. The neurotic attempts to gain a greater feeling of security by affirming a reduced or more limited self.

The course that Tillich preferred is in some ways the opposite of the neurotic path. It is the course of courage. He defined courage as self-affirmation in spite of nonbeing. Courage cannot and does not eliminate anxiety; rather it takes the anxiety of nonbeing into itself: one accepts the inevitability of anxiety as a consequence of being and chooses to be. There are two sides to self-affirmation. One may affirm the self as an individualized self, and one may affirm one's being as a part of something else, as a part of a group or a larger whole. In the Middle Ages the emphasis was on the latter. Individualism implies an emphasis on the former. The Renaissance and the Enlightenment focused on this type of courage.

There has been a recurring emphasis on the courage of individual self-affirmation since the Renaissance, and we see this emphasis on the part of many contemporary existentialists. In collectivist societies on the other hand the existence of the individual is subordinated to the existence and the institutions of the group, and the stress is on the courage to be a part. The democracies of England and the United States at their best have involved a synthesis of individuality and participation, a balance between liberalism and democracy, an enduring tension between the courage to be as oneself and the courage to be as a part. (Tillich felt, however, that modern America has become conformist, that it places the greater emphasis on participation in the group.) If either form of self-affirmation is overemphasized, to the exclusion of the other, something is lost. In collectivism there is a loss of the individual self. In the extreme of individualism sometimes seen in existentialism there is a loss of the world.

For Tillich, the ideal form of courage is one that unites both forms of self-affirmation by transcending them. Such courage, he said, must be rooted in a power of being that is greater than the power of oneself and the power of one's world. This is the power of being-itself. Tillich speaks of God as being-itself, as the ground of being, and as the God above the God of theism. Thus, the courage rooted in being-itself is an integral part of the religious life, though not necessarily a part of much that passes for religion. Tillich noted that in relation to being-itself, either a participant form of courage or an individualized form may be accented. If participation is dominant, the relation to being-itself has a mystical character. If individualization is dominant, the relation to being-itself has a personal character. Much of the history of Christianity can be understood in terms of movement between these two forms of courage.

Tillich believed, however, that both poles in religious experience can be accepted and transcended and in this case the relation to being-itself has the character of faith. He felt that this kind of faith was manifested by Luther and other leaders in the Reformation. Tillich was careful to distinguish his use of the word *faith* from other common uses. Faith for him is not a mere belief in the incredible, or a blind allegiance, or a leap to dogmatic certitude. Since faith rests on courage and requires awareness, it presupposes doubt and skepticism. It takes anxiety and despair into itself rather than removing them. It requires what Tillich called the courage of despair, an acceptance of uncertainty.

Pierre Teilhard de Chardin In Teilhard de Chardin, too, we find a blend of modern scientific thought with Christian tradition. Perhaps more than any other religious thinker Teilhard attempted to draw insights from the natural sciences. In his work we find a remarkable effort to synthesize the products of rationality and scientific method with the products of faith and mystical revelation. Like Tillich he was concerned with the polarity of individualization versus participation, and he foresaw an almost inevitable reconciliation of the two extremes—a higher synthesis. If he can be said to accent either pole, it is the pole of participation, for his ideal is one that stresses love or relatedness, but the realization of this presupposes for him a perfection of individual consciousness.

Teilhard's life provided a unique preparation for the sort of grand synthesis that he attempted. Born in France in 1881, he grew up at a time when much controversy still raged over the issues posed by evolutionary theory. As a child he developed a strong interest in nature that led to a lifelong career in paleontological research. The basic issues of religion also concerned him throughout his life. He came from a devout family and was ordained as a priest in 1911. In 1922 he received a doctorate from the Sorbonne. The evolutionary ideas expressed in his early writings began to arouse a bit of suspicion within the Church, but he encountered still more direct opposition when he addressed his writing to theological issues. In the face of this opposition, he devoted most of his time to scientific matters. Yet his major works reflect a brilliant effort to achieve a new synthesis of Christian and scientific thought.

Basically Teilhard endeavored to apply the idea of evolution on a cosmic scale.[17] He believed that this principle operates on many levels, from the inorganic to the spiritual, and that different levels have assumed primary importance at different stages in the overall evolution of the universe. He propounded a basic law of complexity-centricity that governs the formation of new entities. According to this law, there are two complementary processes, one involving the union of various elements on a given level, the other involving a diversification. Darwinian theory assumes the operation of such a law in the biological realm, since species evolution requires both the emergence of trait variation and the consolidation of a species through the processes of natural selection. According to Teilhard, the law operated long before life appeared in the universe, and through its operation first atoms were formed, then molecules, then megamolecules, then living cells, then successively higher forms of life. At each level, the creation of a new entity was followed by the emergence of variety: various kinds of atoms, various molecular compounds, various forms of life and species. Each stage in the total evolutionary process has yielded an entity that is more "complex-centered" than any prior entity—i.e., a new unity that is more complex than anything existing before.

Teilhard believed that mind or consciousness is present at all levels, that it is coextensive with matter. It assumes primary importance in the evolutionary process, however, only at the human level. Indeed, at this level morphological evolution has ceased to be important, while consciousness has become self-conscious and become capable of transcending the immediate physical reality in time and space. Teilhard also argued that mankind has achieved maximal diversification. The human species is divided by race, culture, and ideology. Having encircled the globe, mankind cannot become increasingly diversified; as the human population grows, as the speed and ease of transportation increase, and as long-range communication becomes more convenient and more efficient, mankind must become increasingly consolidated in one way or another. It is possible for new schisms to develop, and it is possible for totalitarian systems to emerge that will impose a coercive unity on people from without. The development that Teilhard regarded as both more likely and more desirable, as well as more consistent with the total evolutionary process, is one in which mankind will become more harmoniously united by the force of love. At the human level, evolution has shifted from a primary focus in the biological realm to a primary focus in the psychic realm. The next step is a shift from an emphasis on the development of individual consciousness to an emphasis on social evolution, a movement toward a new unity that transcends the limits of the individual being.

The ultimate goal of evolution, as Teilhard saw it, is not simply a harmonious world-culture, for he thought in terms of a blending of minds that is difficult for us to grasp fully at our present stage of development. We are moving toward an ultimate point of convergence that he spoke of in terms of superconsciousness, hyperpersonality, or simply Omega. He viewed Omega as essentially equivalent to God or Christ. God or Omega is at the same time the goal of evolution, something that is in formation for us, and something that is already implicit in everything that is. Love is the essence of Omega. Like consciousness, love assumes particular importance at the human level. One might characterize evolution beyond this point as a movement toward pure love-consciousness.

Since Omega, or God, is already implicit in everything, it serves as a guiding force, operating by the radiation of love-energy, in the evolutionary process. This would seem to make Omega an absolutely inevitable end point, but it is not, since at the human level we have reached a stage where the entity that has emerged, the self-conscious human individual, has the power of choice and is responsible for his own future. From this point on, evolution requires our active and willing participation. We must recognize Omega not simply as a possible goal, but as the desirable goal. To the extent that we perceive unification with others as involving a loss of individuality or a loss of freedom, we may be inclined to resist it, but Teilhard insists that union by love serves to differentiate individuality further rather than erasing it and that true freedom is possible only if we accept our salvation through love. Teilhard's evolutionary thesis is, of course, a way of construing the Christian idea of salvation. In stressing man's participation, his cooperation in a mututal effort with God, Teilhard is expounding a traditional theological doctrine, but certainly in a very new guise.

We should note that in expounding this doctrine, Teilhard was really speaking simultaneously about the course of our individual lives and the future course for the entire species, and indeed the future of the entire universe. The problems of the individual reflect the fact that mankind has achieved a reflective self-centered consciousness. This achievement, the "original sin" of egocentric self-consciousness, was an important and necessary step in evolution, but clinging to it can serve as a barrier to further development. To fulfill ourselves as individuals, we must learn to relate to the totality of mankind.

Teilhard had more to say, however, about the development of mankind as a whole, and he pointed to a future when we shall all transcend the present level of human development. In fact, he pointed to a future that lies totally beyond the material realm. He assumed that *Homo sapiens* can continue to exist as a biological species for only a limited time, and that the material world as we know it is destined for ultimate extinction. His evolutionary theory focuses on a process of progressive "complexification," but he recognized that in basic ways the physical universe is going in the opposite direction—it is gradually deteriorating through an irreversible process of entropic decay. In our ultimate union at Omega, at the apex of the "cone of time," we shall experience rebirth on a purely spiritual plane. Teilhard asks, "Is it not conceivable that Mankind, at the end of its totalisation, its folding-in upon itself, may reach a critical level of maturity where, leaving Earth and stars to lapse slowly back into the dwindling mass of primordial energy, it will detach itself from this planet and join the one true, irreversible essence of things, the Omega point?" [18]

THE MENTAL HEALTH PROFESSIONS AND THE CONCEPT OF MENTAL HEALTH

So far in this chapter, we have examined the modern era in terms of innovations in science, industry and technology, and religious thought. In each of these spheres we have seen modern expressions of ancient traditions. The developments in science, industry, and technology are an outgrowth of trends that we can trace to the Renaissance, and they have wrought major changes in our society. Modern religious thought has still older roots, but it also reflects the growth of scientific knowledge and contains a response to the conditions of modern society.

This book, of course, is centrally concerned with views regarding the ideal person and the ideal mode of living. We have seen that the traditions underlying scientific and religious thoughts contain a variety of pertinent prescriptions and that the societal changes brought about by science and technology set the stage for a reexamination of many of our traditional ideas about the ideal life and lend a certain urgency to the issue. Increasingly, however, people look to psychology and to the so-called mental health professions for answers to questions about the ideal mode of living. Most of the remaining pages of the book will be devoted to ideas formulated by psychologists and psychiatrists. To establish proper historical perspective, however, it is essential that we briefly consider at this point the mental health professions and the outlook on the human condition that generally characterizes them.

Psychiatry, the other mental health professions, and psychological theory as we know it are all features of contemporary Western civilization. They reflect Western traditions, and they represent a Western mode of dealing with the problems of life. Our current thinking about the ideal mode of living tends to be couched in such terms as "mental health," and we tend to view this concept as the embodiment of modern enlightenment. Yet this concept is not the product of a recent discovery or of a startling scientific breakthrough. As a way of looking at the desirable conditions of human living, it can best be understood as an outgrowth of the traditions we have already examined and as a response to the contemporary problems of our society.

Psychiatry is largely a product of the modern era, though many of its roots within the medical profession can be traced to earlier periods. Perhaps its existence as a distinctive specialty can be traced to the Enlightenment, when major efforts were first made to develop classifications of mental disorders. With the appearance and growth of the mental health professions, many forms of socially deviant behavior and experience that had previously been a concern of political authorities and of the Church came to be viewed as somehow analogous to diseases of the body. Much of what has happened since the advent of

67

these professions can be understood as a function of the interplay of two basic consequences of the role that these professions have assumed in our society. One consequence is that the deviant forms of behavior and experience have come to be regarded as legitimate objects of scientific investigation. The other is that under the sacrosanct authority of professionalized science, our society has found a new and culturally distinctive way of dealing with—to some extent, condemning and disposing of—individuals who violate its norms of conduct, by disguising ethical judgments as scientific truths.

As medicine began to embrace deviant behavior as a part of its domain, physicians naturally tended to extend their customary habits of thought to this new realm. They assumed and sought material or somatic causes for the conditions they were observing. It had long been known that traumatic damage to the central nervous system could lead to psychological aberration, but there was no evidence of such damage in most individuals judged to be insane. The discovery in the latter part of the nineteenth century that one form of psychosis involved a syphilitic infection of the central nervous system, however, gave renewed hope that an organic basis would be found for many other kinds of extreme mental disturbance. Many conditions were long subsumed in medical diagnosis under the rubric *neurosis* on the assumption that some yet undetected condition of the nerves would eventually be found to underlie them.

In some cases, the assumption of underlying organic pathology led to useful discoveries, but the medical disease concept came to be applied rather freely to all kinds of conditions remote from the traditional domain of medicine. To some extent, the use of the disease concept was simply a matter of social expediency. Thomas Szasz notes that in the latter part of the nineteenth century, hysterics were often suspected by physicians of imitating illness in an effort to cheat and fool doctors.[19] The physician who wished to spare his hysteric patient from such condemnation had one obvious recourse—to insist that the patient was "really ill." By doing this, he legitimized the problems of the hysterics (as well as other "neurotics"), and he legitimized his own activity in treating the patient and accepting a fee for his services.

Whatever the reasons for applying the disease concept to hysterics, it has come to be applied to many conditions that bear far less resemblance to physical illness as psychiatry has embraced an expanding sphere of behavior. Thus criminal behavior, juvenile delinquency, and behaviors regarded by teachers as disruptive of the classroom routine have come to be regarded as medical problems and are often subject to labeling in terms of disease categories. Such terms as *moral amentia* and *constitutional psychopathic inferior,* which suggest an inherent deficiency in the individual, have been applied to people whose behavior might have proved more understandable if its social context had been taken into account. There has been an unfortunate tendency for the disease label to be applied in a way that simply legitimizes society's condemnation of the individual whose behavior is not currently deemed socially acceptable. We are justified in disapproving of him because the medical profession says that there is something wrong with him. Of course, social fashions change, and disease labeling may change with them. In recent years, for example, homosexuality has become increasingly accepted in our society as a variant of the predominant life-style, and in 1974 the American Psychiatric Association officially declassified it as a mental disorder.

Incidentally, the literature on homosexuality provides a good illustration of the extent to which medical labeling of behavior tends to be a pseudoscientific enterprise. To identify a behavior pattern as a disease is to say that it is "really pathological," but how do we determine this? This research evidence indicates that homosexuality is not appreciably correlated with other patterns of attitudes and action that are agreed to be pathological, but it does not follow that homosexuality per se is or is not a form of psychopathology in its own right. On the whole, investigators who have pursued this question have tended to confirm whatever assumptions they made at the outset, since the ultimate criterion for classifying a behavior as pathological is the fact that we consider it undesirable or unacceptable.

Diagnostic labeling is subject to fashion within the professional world itself. Thus, such labels as passive-aggressive personality, early infantile autism, hyperkinesis, and minimal brain dysfunction have been fashionable in recent years and have often been applied to individuals a bit different from the ones for which the labels were originally devised. Fashions are also evident in the treatment realm. In this century, a variety of psychotherapies and a variety of somatic treatment methods have enjoyed periods of popularity.

Through the influence of Freud and others, of course, the psychodynamic view in psychiatry has become increasingly influential, and there has been less overall emphasis on assuming and seeking organic pathology. Yet under the influence of material-scientific and medical tradition, psychiatrists have tended to resort to somatic treatment methods even with conditions regarded as essentially "psychological." Electroconvulsive shock treatment has been applied on a scale that seems truly alarming when we recognize how little is known about its mechanism of operation, apart from the obviously destructive consequences of shooting a strong electric current through a mass of delicate brain tissue. Fortunately, the still more drastic surgical procedures, such as prefrontal lobotomy, have not been employed on so large a scale. In very recent years, psychoactive drugs have come into wide use as a preferred treatment method. Frequently these various somatic treatment methods have been recommended as an adjunct to psychotherapy; more often, they have been employed as the sole form of treatment and justified on the ground that they do in fact produce behavioral changes. Since the behaviors are regarded as symptoms or ingredients of a disease, it is assumed that we are doing something of benefit to the patient when we employ any procedure that serves to eliminate the symptoms. The individual to whom the somatic remedy is applied, however, often perceives himself to be invalidated as a person in the modern psychiatric hospital, where mechanical procedures are employed to alter his behavior but no one appears to be interested in communicating directly with him and in understanding what he is experiencing.

A recent application of a physical remedy to the behavioral realm that has received increasing attention is the use of drugs to treat hyperkinetic children. Commonly the hyperkinetic child is initially identified by the classroom teacher, who refers the child to a physician, who in turn prescribes the drug. There is a widespread assumption in such cases that the hyperkinesis has an organic basis, but there is greater reason to suspect that much of what is perceived as hyperkinesis—abnormal restlessness and overactivity—is simply behavior that is incorrectly channeled from the standpoint of the public school system, activity that continually comes to the attention of the teacher because it is not the activity that he or she has requested. It appears that the society in which we live is becoming not only a psychiatric society but also a society in which drugs are employed to deal with just about everything.

Recently there has been a growing dissatisfaction with the widespread over-application of the disease model. Many social scientists and mental health professionals have expressed such dissatisfaction, as well as a few psychiatrists, including Thomas Szasz and R. D. Laing. In *The Myth of Mental Illness,* Szasz argued that disease labeling often amounts to a kind of pseudo explanation and tried to show that in the case of hysteria a more systematic account was possible if we interpreted the symptoms in terms of such things as social communication. More recently he has argued that we have erred profoundly in treating drug abuse and drug addiction as an essentially medical problem.[20]

Laing's work has focused more on schizophrenia, and he has decried the tendency to regard this as a disease comparable to somatic illnesses. In some of his writings he has argued that schizophrenic behavior is best understood not as a condition of the individual but as a locus within the total pattern of communication and relationships operating in a family.[21] In more recent writings, he has treated schizophrenia somewhat more as an individual condition, but he has insisted that it represents a stage in a natural healing process, a psychic voyage that can lead the individual to a higher level of sanity—quite possibly a level that exceeds that of the surrounding society.[22] Laing believes that we should permit the individual to go through this experience and, if possible, guide him on the trip. To treat his situation as a disease with symptoms we must eliminate by drugs, shock, or behavioral manipulation does more harm than good.

If the disease model is inappropriate for most of the problems handled by psychiatrists and other members of the mental health professions, it is certainly inappropriate as a way of conceptualizing human personality in general. Yet it is undeniable that a large part of

71

our contemporary thinking about the nature of people has its roots in the clinical setting, where efforts to account for psychopathology preceded efforts to build more comprehensive systems of theory. Hence, in a subtle way the disease concept figures in a great deal of our thinking with respect to the nature of people, with respect to the nature of the human situation, and with respect to what people should or should not be.

More broadly, we can say that most of our ideas about the desirable human state have obvious roots in Western traditions, particularly those traditions associated with the growth of science and with the Jewish and Christian religions. Our ideas also reflect the current state of our superindustrialized society and our efforts to cope with the products of this society. The burgeoning mental health professions are themselves both a product of our traditions and a response to the conditions that these traditions have yielded in our time, since they represent an effort to deal scientifically with the problems created by a scientific industrial society.

In later chapters we shall examine the ideas of leading theorists in greater depth, but here we may attempt to identify some common elements that pervade most contemporary thought about the optimal mode of living. The terms most frequently employed to label the ideal condition are *adjustment, normality, maturity,* and *mental health. Adjustment* usually implies the achievement of a harmonious relationship with one's environment. It may also imply an inner harmony, or freedom from internal conflict. These two conditions are usually regarded as interrelated, since some of the internal forces are products of social conditioning. In general, we think of a well-adjusted person as someone who manages to meet his own needs while coping effectively with the physical and social demands of his environment and who is characteristically free from feelings of distress. This is certainly a very popular idea in our time. Writers make fortunes by publishing books that promise to tell us how to achieve "peace of mind." The drug industry has found a rich and eager market for tranquilizers and antidepressants. Drugs that are more potentially destructive but more readily available, such as alcohol and aspirin, have long been widely used to relieve anxiety and depression. Several generations of advertising and slang have impressed on us the importance of being nonchalant and debonair, of "playing it cool," of avoiding being "uptight" or getting "freaked out," and when things get too disturbing of taking a "Bayer break."

Surely this emphasis on adjustment is symptomatic of a society in which people frequently feel themselves at odds with the world around them and in which they often experience anxiety but can neither trace it to a well-defined threat from without nor imagine a well-defined course of action that would alleviate it. They feel out of joint and sense that something is wrong somewhere inside or in the way in which they relate to the world outside. Under these circumstances, we can hardly avoid thinking that it would be better to be "adjusted." We want a condition in which things run smoothly and we are not troubled by such negative emotional states as anxiety, depression, or anger.

Obviously adjustment is in some sense a desirable condition, but whether it corresponds to a situation that we can properly regard as ideal surely depends on how we achieve it. The means most readily available all entail some loss of effective functioning. We can consume manufactured remedies, we can confine our lives within very narrow limits to avoid stresses, or we can cultivate a style of chameleon conformity, trying to bend with all pressures from without and to fit smoothly into all situations. In other words, we can simply reduce our capacity for feeling, limit our contact with the world, and limit our self-awareness. If on the other hand, we wish to funtion fully, we certainly have to recognize that life contains problems. If we respond to them more sanely and directly, we are likely to experience anger when we encounter the destructive actions of others, guilt when we recognize our own failures to act appropriately, and anxiety when faced with grave uncertainty. Distress is an inevitable part of living, but we may succeed in keeping it within tolerable limits if we seek effective ways of coping. If our world has gone so badly awry that reasonable adjustment is no longer possible, perhaps we need a few maladjusted people who will try to change it.

The term *normality* is often used in much the same way as the term *adjustment*. More strictly the term implies approximation to a norm or standard. The norm may be a statistical one. In this sense, the

73

normal individual is simply a typical or average member of the population. Or the norm may be one formulated on nonstatistical grounds. In this case, *normality* tends to carry much the same meaning as *mental health*. In its most distinctive uses, the term implies that it is desirable to behave and experience in conformity with the standards of conduct and experience that are generally accepted in our society. If a person does this, he will act and experience in much the same way as most other members of the society. Such a pattern is conducive to social adjustment, and it is subject to the same observations we have made regarding adjustment as a desideratum. In every society, of course, the conforming individual tends to be accepted, while the nonconformist is viewed with suspicion, fear, or hostility. So normality is universally acceptable, although it means a different pattern of functioning in every society. In our society, it may involve incorporating the conflicting standards of individualism and love that are both basic to our view of the world, thereby entailing some internal contradiction.

There are obvious objections to statistical normality as a concept of the ideal mode of living. It is easy to think of common modes of behavior that could stand modification. Improving our society will involve changing the actions of many of the people in it. Furthermore, it is easy to think of desirable modes of functioning that are statistically quite abnormal. The most valuable creative contributions to the world have been made by very atypical people.

In practice, the term *maturity* is usually applied to many of the same characteristics covered by *adjustment* and *normality*. The distinctive feature of this term is that it has developmental implications. Maturity is something that we attain by growing up and by learning to function in the ways appropriate for adults. It would be possible and useful to identify features of human development that are common to people in all cultures, but what is deemed appropriate adult behavior is obviously subject to cultural variation. Those qualities that are regarded as desirable, normal, or healthy in our society are likely at the same time to be the qualities that we associate with maturity. These include the acquisition of an acceptable social facade, the cultivation of skills for social interaction, and the learning of various societal roles—in short, learning how to fit smoothly into the social environment. They may also include certain qualities of wisdom or judgment that increase with experience and that enable the individual to cope effectively with many situations.

There is a marked tendency in our society to think of maturity in terms of the expression of needs and emotions. We tend to think of the mature person as someone who is emotionally reserved or restrained, who can tolerate a great deal of frustration and delay in need gratification, and who can devote a lot of time and effort to tasks that will yield rewards at a distant point in the future. We ascribe immaturity to the individual who demands immediate gratification, who is very intent on seeking pleasure and avoiding pain, and who expresses his emotional reactions immediately and forcefully. It is considered more mature to sit down for long hours and write books like this than just to run around and have fun. We tend to think of people in other societies as being somewhat backward and immature because they lack the future orientation that is so characteristic of our way of life, and we think that if we could simply export some of our achievement motivation, they too could enjoy the fruits of cultural progress. In other words, our notion of maturity embodies many of the ingredients of the good industrial citizen and owes much to the Protestant ethic. Personally, I am well aware that being saturated with the Protestant ethic enables me to function fairly well in the professional world, but I should certainly hesitate to prescribe this code of living for everyone else. It has already created too many problems in our society.

Of the four terms I noted above, *mental health* is the one whose usage has increased most conspicuously in recent years. This is the term most clearly tied to the medical disease model, for it implies an absence of mental disease. It is also the term that has the most scientific ring to it. We are likely to assume that whatever is said in the name of mental health ensues from careful investigation. On the whole, the qualities ascribed to the mentally healthy person are the same as the qualities that have been labeled adjusted, normal, and mature. They may include an absence of distress, an ability to relate well to other people, a capacity for tolerating a delay of gratification, and emotional control. There is a growing tendency to include spontaneity, as the hazards of over-control become more evident. Sometimes

75

Christian love and concern for other people are stressed. Sometimes more individualistic values are stressed—autonomy, environmental mastery, creativity. It is difficult to secure a comprehensive picture of the meaning of this term, because despite its scientific appearance, it is a term that has actually been defined in many ways, and there is little current agreement on what constitutes the essence of mental health.

Thus, *adjustment, normality, maturity,* and *mental health* are all highly value-laden terms that are applied to a range of qualities that are currently considered desirable in our society. My intent here, however, is not to expose these as worthless concepts that need to be discarded but simply to illuminate the function they actually serve. It is important to brush aside any scientistic aura that such terms have acquired and penetrate to the cultural climate that underlies them.

Each of these terms has a somewhat variable meaning, and their meanings overlap to some degree. They are all used to denote conformity to the adult role expectations of this society. These expectations themselves encompass an array of values derived from both the love-oriented Judaeo-Christian traditions and the more individualistic traditions of Western culture. The greater weight seems to be attached to these values associated with the individualistic stream that underlies the development of science and technology (which in a broad sense includes both modern psychology and medicine). Thus, mental health (and maturity, normality, and adjustment) may be attributed to the individual who displays intellectual competence, realism, independence, emotional self-control, perseverance, and productivity. These are the values of a future-oriented and achievement-minded industrial society. The love ethic is also apparent in many definitions of mental health, but usually in a rather dilute form—in the guise of social concern and the ability to relate successfully to others. Thus, our current concepts clearly show the imprint of older traditions.

To the traditional values are added some elements that reflect the contemporary state of our society. These elements include such ideas as frustration tolerance, stress tolerance, and an ability to withstand the hazards and rapid changes of modern life without either becoming too disorganized or experiencing too many disturbing emotions. In the terms of the five modes of human fulfillment I have described, I would say that contemporary mental health concepts stress a combination of efficiency, relatedness, and inner harmony.

At the moment, of course, I am trying to deal in a very global way with notions of the ideal person and ideal mode of living espoused by members of the mental health professions, and in a short space I can only try to capture the common core of these notions. It is my thesis that this core contains no surprises for the shrewd historian. In the thinking of various individual psychologists and psychiatrists, however, we can find many novel ingredients and novel transformations of traditional ideas. We shall consider a number of these individual theorists in later chapters.

FOUR

TRADITIONS IN EASTERN THOUGHT

In the preceding chapters, I attempted to show that our modern Western views on the ideal mode of living, even if we cast these in terms of "mental health," rest on traditions whose roots extend far back in history. At the same time, these views can be seen to contain reactions to the contemporary state of our society. Later in the book, we shall consider the views of a number of contemporary theorists in greater depth and see the ways in which each uniquely draws together and creatively expresses elements of the Occidental weltanschauung. We can better appreciate those elements in Western thought that are distinctly Western, however, if we examine some systems of thought that have arisen in a different cultural setting. For this purpose, we shall turn to the East and consider those systems embraced by the terms *Hinduism* and *Buddhism*.

It might be better still to make a comparative study of systems of thought throughout the world, but such an undertaking is a bit beyond my means and not altogether essential for the purposes of this modest volume. Hinduism and Buddhism constitute a logical choice to the extent that they contain views of human nature, of the human condition, and of the ideal state that are highly evolved, yet distinctly different from the views that predominate in the West. Indeed, the Hindu-Buddhist tradition has a longer recognized history than any system of thought known in the West, and in the eyes of many it is philosophically more advanced. Be that as it may, it certainly constitutes an important segment of contemporary thought, and it contains views on the optimal mode of living that are quite worthy of consideration in

78

their own right. By virtue of this fact, Hindu and Buddhist ideas are attracting increasing attention in the West and have begun to infiltrate Western psychology. We shall see Hindu and Buddhist elements in the theories treated in subsequent chapters.

On the other hand, Hinduism and Buddhism do present a couple of drawbacks for our immediate purpose. For one thing, if we are interested in comparing "pure cultures," cultures free of mutual contamination, this is not a perfect choice. Probably no perfect choice could be found, for the world is not large enough to permit two literate cultures to exist in mutual isolation for a very long time. There is reason to believe that Hindu thought came to the attention of Westerners as early as the sixth century B.C. and that Pythagoras and some of the Neoplatonists were influenced by it. In recent centuries, of course, the inhabitants of Western societies have shown a pronounced tendency to try to Westernize the whole world and to ensure that their ways of thinking and behaving gain universal recognition.

Another drawback to our choice is that Hindu-Buddhist traditions constitute an extremely complex array of doctrines and practices that have evolved, alternated, and interacted over many centuries. We cannot expect to secure a comprehensive picture of Hindu and Buddhist thought, for that might well be a more difficult undertaking than securing a comprehensive picture of Western thought. It is merely more obvious to us as Westerners that the latter would be virtually impossible. In any case, I make no pretense of being an authority on Eastern thought. I shall simply attempt, as I did with Western thought, to identify some of the most salient ideas that bear on the nature of the ideal person or optimal mode of living.

Having offered this waiver, let me now pose as an authority and make a few sweeping generalizations about Eastern and Western thought. First, we may note a number of parallels. In both cultural milieus there is a great diversity of contrasting and incompatible ideas. In examining the history of Eastern thought, we find as much flux as we do in the West. We also find specific traditions within which doctrines are held constant over periods of centuries. Alternations and interactions of ideas in the East involve essentially the same polarities that we have noted in Western thought, or at least very similar polarities. Thus, rationality, intellectual abstraction, or conceptual elaboration opposes direct experience, intuition, or mysticism. We find also an emphasis on social formalism, ritual and ceremony opposed to an emphasis on naturalism and spontaneity. At some times and places there is strong insistence and reliance on authority; at others, the direct or unique experience of the individual is all-important. There are polarities that involve our relation to the world—acceptance versus rejection of the world of our experience, acceptance versus renunciation of worldly pleasures, and so forth. In addition, it is possible to identify historical sequences in the East that resemble those found in the West. The advent of Buddhism represented a kind of Protestant Reformation within Hinduism to the extent that it entailed a rejection of both the authority and the ritualism of the Brahmin priests. Of course, the two historical developments were separated in time by more than two thousand years and have no direct historical link with each other, but they suggest that similar processes underlie the tides in human affairs in all parts of the world.

Noting the parallels between East and West, we are prepared to recognize that the most conspicuous differences are likely to be relative, but these differences are nonetheless important. Within some of the polarities we have just noted, there are important differences in emphasis. While the polarity of rationality versus intuition is clearly evident in both parts of the world, rationality has been dominant on the whole in the history of the West, while intuition has been more conspicuous in the Orient. There is a cultural difference in the function of authority that arises from this difference. In the West, the authority tends to serve as the source of intellectual knowledge or dogma. In the East, the authority is more often a guide to spiritual enlightenment, one who facilitates intuition rather than one who imparts information. Although the Eastern master is less authoritarian in the sense that his role is highly dependent on the experience of the person that he guides, his authority in some ways tends to be more absolute. This is generally true of the guru in Hindu culture. Hindus usually maintain that one must have a guru, or guide, to achieve enlightenment and that one's submission to the guru is a permanent submission. Buddhists depart from this position to varying degrees, maintaining in gen-

80

eral that the guru is important in the early stages of one's development but is ultimately dispensable; indeed, once one has achieved enlightenment—once one has realized fully one's own Buddha nature, or overcome the illusion of individual separateness—it would then be inconsistent to experience that nature as something that is simply "out there," projected onto another being to whom one must turn for guidance. This is a way of construing the oft-quoted aphorism, "If you meet the Buddha on the road, kill him." Perhaps the Hindu extreme is not to be found on a large scale in the West, but it may be approximated within certain religious orders of the Roman Catholic Church.

One of the most conspicuous differences between East and West has to do with individuality. On the whole, this is emphasized much more heavily in the West. Westerners rather consistently view the individual as a separate entity and see the optimal condition as one in which the individual is fully developed, whatever form this development may take. If they stress the good of the society or the group over that of the individual, they still see the society or group as composed of separate entities. Hindus and Buddhists see less separation. They are more concerned with the unity of the individual with the whole of nature and inclined to regard the experience of individuality as an illusion. The East-West contrast that we see here is linked to the one involving intuition and rationality, for rational thought is necessarily analytic or separative, while in intuition and mystical experience separate entities tend to merge in larger unities.

Differences with respect to the conception of individuality are accompanied by differences regarding mankind's relation to nature. In its analytic and separatist orientation, the West has tended to see man as something essentially different from the rest of nature and to see nature as a domain to be conquered. It is for this reason that science and technology are largely Western enterprises. Hindu and Buddhist culture attach much more value to achieving harmony with nature and tend to view that harmony as both the natural and the desirable condition.

The culture that fosters the growth of science and technology is also the culture that places a premium on material progress. An orientation toward the future and a concern with progressive change in con-

81

ditions on earth and with advancement in the present lifetime are characteristic of the West. In the East, particularly in Buddhist culture, there is more emphasis on the immediate present experience of life.

Albert Schweitzer saw the basic difference between Western thought and Indian thought in terms of affirmation versus negation of the world and of life.[1] World and life affirmation implies seeing the world and our life in it as something to be valued, preserved, improved, and perfected. Negation would imply a view of our life in this world as meaningless and sorrowful. From the standpoint of negation, we would tend to disparage attempts to improve conditions in the world and would instead look forward to a cessation of this existence. Schweitzer contended that both attitudes are present in the West as well as in the East. Negation was evident in Neoplatonism and in much of early Christianity, while affirmation was strong in earlier Greek thought, as it has been since the Renaissance. The affirmative orientation evident in early Indian thought was superseded by a negation of the world and life that has prevailed up to the present time and that is particularly evident in Buddhism and Jainism. Schweitzer's contention is that affirmation is predominant in the West while negation is predominant in India, and that a better balance is needed in both parts of the world. We need an orientation that embraces both the mystical world view of India and the progress-oriented ethical outlook of the West. This seems to me an interesting way of characterizing the difference between East and West, though Schweitzer's concepts appear to be over-inclusive. Lumping together all the features that are embraced by the terms affirmation and negation can mask some of the subtle combinations found in both parts of the world.

Perhaps this is just another way of saying that it is difficult to find a simple and concise, yet accurate, way of characterizing the basic cultural split. If one is willing to forego the search for a single pair of adequate terms, D. T. Suzuki's description may be useful:

> The Western mind is: analytical, discriminative, differential, inductive, individualistic, intellectual, objective, scientific, generalizing, conceptual, schematic, impersonal, legalistic, organizing, power-wielding, self-assertive, disposed to impose its will upon others, etc. Against these Western traits those of the East can be characterized as follows: synthetic, totalizing, in-

tegrative, nondiscriminative, deductive, nonsystematic, dogmatic, intuitive, (rather, affective), nondiscursive, subjective, spiritually individualistic and socially group-minded, etc.[2]

HINDUISM

For many of the religious, philosophical, and cultural developments of Asia, India has served as a wellspring, particularly those traditions of India embraced by the term *Hinduism*. Hinduism is not a unitary system of thought, and it has not remained in a constant state throughout its long history. It has grown and changed gradually over a period of several thousand years. Its oldest written texts are the Vedas, which are still considered the most sacred Hindu scriptures. They were produced over a period of centuries; the most recent date from about the tenth century B.C., while the oldest were probably first recorded before 1500 B.C.

The Vedas represent a mixture of the religions of the Aryan tribes that invaded India in that early period and the religions of the people who were already dwelling in the subcontinent when the Aryans appeared. They contain hymns, prayers, and an assortment of other prose and verse formulas. Their theological content is varied. There is reference to a variety of gods, but some of the later Vedas suggest a more pantheistic outlook, an idea of a divine ground from which the gods evolve and to which the personality or soul of the dead person goes after the body has perished. Some hymns exalt the drinking of Soma, of rising above the world in a state of intoxicated ecstasy and enjoying the community of the gods. The Vedas contain many elements that foreshadow later developments in Hinduism, as well as many elements that ceased to play any essential role in later Hindu thought.

The foundations for modern Hinduism were laid in the period from 1000 B.C. to 500 B.C. During that period, Brahmin priests evolved a system of ritual and doctrine known as Brahmanism that is expounded in two bodies of writings, the Brahmanas and the Upanishads. These writings were intended to provide interpretations of the

83

Vedas, but in many respects they contain a system that supersedes the Vedic religion. Like the Vedas, they do not really provide a unitary system of thought, but they do contain more elaborate expositions of ideas that have become central to Hindu thought. Most fundamental to Brahmanism are the concepts of Brahman and Atman and the notion of the identity of these two.

In the Upanishads we find several uses of the word *Brahman.* The Brahman is construed in some places as a divine person, in others as the highest spiritual being that unites all forms of perfection in itself, and elsewhere as something still less personal, an absolute substance devoid of specific attributes. Although the concept evolved from an ancient idea of Brahma as a creator god, *Brahman* has come to mean something essentially impersonal—a cosmic principle that underlies all being, the spiritual ground of the entire universe, or perhaps one could say the mind of the universe. *Atman* on the other hand refers to the individual being or soul. It is difficult to define it in a more precise way than this, but it is clear that Atman is not to be confused with the self-concept or the object of ordinary self-reflection, the object of "ego consciousness." It is not consciousness per se, but it is a common ground or principle that underlies all of our experience, whether in waking consciousness, dreams, or dreamless sleep. In one Upanishanic dialogue, it is defined in much the same way as Kant's *pure ego,* and it is held to be something that cannot be realized by the intellect but only through a more intuitive or mystical kind of understanding.

The Brahman is still further beyond the reach of the intellect, and is generally held to be essentially indescribable and unknowable. After all, what we do basically when we describe something is to link it by verbal analogy to something else that we regard as obvious, self-evident, or familiar, and it is in the nature of the Brahman that it cannot be reduced in this way to anything else. We inevitably introduce some kind of distortion whenever we attempt to describe it. Yet the Brahman constitutes the ultimate basic ground of all our experience. According to Brahmanic doctrine, the goal of our development is to realize first the individual ground of our existence, the Atman, and then to realize the identity of Atman and Brahman. In some Brahmanic writings, union with Brahman appears to be treated as a goal that is experienced to some extent in sleep and in ecstatic states but is finally achieved fully at death. The more sophisticated view central to Vedanta philosophy, however, is that the identity of Atman and Brahman is an enduring reality whether we recognize it or not. That is, we are never really separate from the universal soul, and our perceived individuality is merely an illusion. Hence, our goal is not to achieve union but rather to realize that it exists.

According to Vedanta philosophy and much of Hindu and Buddhist thought generally, the world in time and space as we experience it, including ourselves as separate entities within it, is illusion, or maya. Maya in this sense refers not to the physical or material world but rather to the phenomenal world, the world as we sense it and conceptualize it, a variable, changing, and pluralistic realm that masks the true unceasing oneness. Alan Watts construes maya as the world conception of a culture.[3] In effect, he suggests that the illusion is not so much a matter of the way in which we naturally experience the world as it is the traditional way of perceiving and understanding that we acquire as we grow up in a particular cultural setting. Hence, to be liberated from the illusion is to transcend the experiential biases of one's own society.

One of the great paradoxes of Hindu thought is that alongside the Brahmanic doctrine we have just considered there appeared a doctrine of reincarnation that is logically incompatible with it. This doctrine is of slightly later origin, but it is also rather central to Hinduism. According to earlier Brahmanic teachings, the individual soul appears new in the world in a given lifetime, comes but once, and then returns to eternal union with the Brahman. According to the later doctrine of reincarnation, or samsara, the individual soul goes through a cycle of rebirths. The quality of the soul and of its rebirth at a given time is governed by the principle of karma. Karma in this context refers to the aggregate consequences of all past actions, whether good or bad. If the reincarnation doctrine is taken literally, it requires the individual soul to have an independent reality that can persist beyond the individual lifetime. This would be inconsistent either with a doctrine that holds that the individual soul exists in a separate form during a single lifetime only or with a doctrine that holds that the individual soul is actually an illusion.

85

To the extent that the reincarnation doctrine was taken literally, it required a modification of other Brahmanic theses. The individual soul had to be granted an independent existence that could persist through a series of lives. The soul could ultimately attain salvation, or *moksha,* after accumulating sufficient merit and compensating for its misdeeds. This is is a view that is held by many Hindus and Buddhists, perhaps by the majority of them, but it apparently is not generally held by the more serious scholars among them. If we accept the idea that our individual separateness is an illusion, then we cannot take reincarnation as a literal fact. The multiplicity of our lives can only be construed in terms of the multiplicity of the roles and relationships into which we enter in this lifetime while guided by a sense of our individual separateness. Watts claims that this is the view most often held by Hindus and Buddhists who have achieved enlightenment.[4]

Of necessity, the way in which the ultimate goal is conceived by a Hindu depends on the view he assumes with respect to these doctrines. If he accepts reincarnation as a literal fact, then the ultimate goal is the release of the individual soul from samsara. If reincarnation is not taken literally, then the goal is likely to be taken as a state of enlightenment, or *samadhi,* attainable in the present lifetime. The goal is essentially the same in both cases to the extent that it involves a loss of experienced separateness and a sense of oneness with the universal soul, but the conditions for reaching this end are obviously subject to divergent interpretations.

Hinduism is not a unified body of thought, though there are some central themes that permeate it. There are varying philosophical positions within it, and there are a number of systems for interpreting the Upanishads. To a great extent these different systems are viewed as complementary paths leading to a common goal, but there are important practical differences among them. Some systems stress clear thinking and logical argument, while others de-emphasize the role of the intellect and stress intuition or mystical states. Still others place an emphasis on ritual or on ethical conduct.

Most of the practical routes to the achievement of *samadhi* are considered forms of yoga. The term *yoga* implies a fairly definite set of practices for achieving *samadhi,* which one learns and practices under the guidance of a guru. The practices vary considerably. The ones best known in this country are forms of hatha yoga that focus on the purification and control of the body. In other forms of yoga, more attention may be paid to the achievement of understanding, to engaging in selfless action, to expressing in action one's love for mankind or for a particular god, or to concentrative forms of meditation.

Taken as a totality, what does Hinduism have to say about the optimal mode of living? Undoubtedly all the cardinal virtues recognized in the Western world assume their place somewhere in Hindu culture, and a variety of paths of life are considered desirable by various Hindus. In places we find an emphasis on love, charity, compassion, and nonviolence that resembles an important theme in Christianity. Some Hindu practices indicate an asceticism or renunciation of the sensual realm that also has its counterparts in Christian tradition. On the whole, there is less stress on the intellect, on individualism, and on material achievement than we find in the Western world. The holy man is valued more than the practical man of action, and the goal of an experienced mystic union with all being assumes an importance that it has never been accorded in the West.

It is worth noting that Hindu thought leads to a view of the stages of life that is somewhat different from that which is familiar in the West. It has often been noted that people of advanced years are held in greater esteem in the Orient. Western societies—most notably that of the United States—place a premium on youth. We tend to value the mental and physical accomplishments that are possible in the early adult years, while Eastern societies are more inclined to value a wisdom that is acquired over a longer span of life. In the Upanishads, there is reference to four stages in the life of a man: the early years of schooling, the stage in which he functions as a father and head of household, a stage of retirement in the forest, and a stage of wandering when the world is completely renounced. It is assumed in this kind of division that in the first half of life one must perform certain necessary duties in the world. In the second half, one is then free to seek the more important goal of spiritual liberation. The only major theorist in the West who seems to have incorporated such an idea into his system is Carl Jung.

87

MODERN INDIAN THOUGHT AND SRI AUROBINDO

As Hinduism has continued to attract attention in the West, a number of Indian leaders and thinkers have begun to exert a discernible influence on Western thought. Perhaps the Hindu who has had the greatest impact on the West is Mohandas K. Gandhi. As the legal defender of Indian settlers in South Africa and later the champion of the Free-India movement, Gandhi was unquestionably one of the most significant social leaders of this century. His ability to employ spiritual power as a political weapon, through the application of nonviolent resistance, has served as an inspiration to social activists in other parts of the world. For millions of people, both in India and in the West, Gandhi embodies a kind of saintliness—a saintliness involving love and spirituality, but at the same time effective social power rather than quiescent contemplation. In some respects, Gandhi represents a departure from Hindu tradition. Hinduism is basically very socially conservative, for it has served among other things to legitimize and preserve an elaborate caste system in India. Gandhi not only advocated an end to British rule in India; he advocated an end to many ancient social practices, particularly those pertaining to the lowest caste, the so-called untouchables.

In the realm of thought and spiritual practices, perhaps the most important figure in modern Hinduism is Sri Ramakrishna, who lived from 1836 to 1886. Ramakrishna brought to Indian thought an element of universalism. He became a devotee of the goddess Kali early in life and acquired a thorough understanding of Hindu doctrine, but he also studied Islamic, Judaic, and Christian thought. He concluded that all religions are equally valid ways of approaching a relationship to the eternal and universal and that the quality of one's life is far more important than one's particular belief system. In general, the followers of Ramakrishna stress active benevolence rather than quiet contemplation or the espousal of elaborate doctrines. The monks of an order devoted to his teachings are dedicated to lives of chastity, poverty, and charity, suggesting an Indian counterpart to the Franciscan order of the Roman Catholic Church. Perhaps his most important follower was

Vivekananada. Vivekananda met Ramakrishna when he was a young man and devoted himself thereafter to Ramakrishna's teachings.

Among those who seek spiritual enlightenment in India today, there are two streams of influence that seem to be especially prominent. One is that represented by Ramakrishna and Vivekananda. The other is based on the teachings of Aurobindo Ghose, more commonly known simply as Sri Aurobindo. The work of Aurobindo seems to me to merit more extended consideration, for it is surely one of the most sophisticated modern attempts to conceptualize the goal, or the ideal mode, of our existence within the framework of the Hindu view of man and nature. Aurobindo's position is an evolutionary position that takes the findings of modern science into account without being bound to them. In many respects, it constitutes an Indian parallel to the Christian evolutionism of Teilhard de Chardin. Aurobindo's most basic ideas are set forth in a monumental work entitled *The Life Divine.*[5]

Aurobindo spoke of a cosmic evolutionary process in which life evolves out of matter and mind out of life. The progression is not an accidental one, as he saw it, for in each case the higher form is implicit in the form from which it emerges. Thus, matter in a sense is a form of veiled life, while life is a form of veiled consciousness or mind. The human species is in the forefront in the evolutionary process, and at the human level we have reached a point of transition from unconscious to conscious evolution. Still higher levels of development lie beyond. They involve the realization of our individual spiritual nature as well as the spiritual ground of the universe.

The evolutionary process is held to be twofold. On the one hand, there is the visible process of physical evolution, involving a succession of finite and mutable forms. At the same time there is an invisible process of soul evolution in which the individual soul, which is considered eternal and immutable, moves in a succession of rebirths through ascending grades of consciousness and form, manifesting itself with increasing directness. Ultimately its identity with universal spirit becomes apparent. Thus, in Aurobindo's work we have an evolutionary viewpoint that incorporates both of the basic doctrines of Hinduism.

At our present stage of development we tend to rely heavily on reason or intellect, but it becomes increasingly apparent that reason

89

can provide only a limited kind of understanding. The next stage in our development, clearly evident in a limited number of people, requires a shift from mental being to spiritual being. The spiritual person has far greater intuitive understanding, is less bound by his conscious ego or intellect, and is more aware of his true self or soul. The shift cannot be achieved through an intellectual process; it requires spiritual realization and experience, through access to processes not subject to direct conscious control and manipulation. There is still another level to be reached beyond that of spiritual being—the level of the supramental or gnostic being.

Aurobindo spoke of three phases of transformation leading to the supramental level. The first is the psychic phase, in which the soul of the individual emerges and begins to assume more active direction of experience and action. The individual has a greater sense of effective guidance and mastery, and he begins to encounter a spontaneous influx of spiritual experiences of all kinds. The truth of being and of nature is experienced more directly since it is immediately available to the soul in a way that it is not to the intellect. The second phase is the spiritual phase, in which by a further opening of our vision we see "an Infinity above us, an eternal Presence or an infinite Existence, an infinity of consciousness, an infinity of bliss—a boundless Self, a boundless Light, a boundless Power, a boundless Ecstasy." [6] This is followed by the final phase of supramental transformation.

Aurobindo also spoke of a series of levels in the ascent from ordinary human intelligence to "Supermind." These include the Higher Mind, the Illumined Mind, the Intuitive Mind, the Overmind, and then the Supermind. In both sets of descriptions, he was characterizing a progression that leads away from our present emphasis on conscious ego-centered reason and control, wherein we become increasingly open first to parts of our being that are inaccessible to conscious reason and then to a universal force or spirit that transcends the bounds of our individual being. The ultimate condition, of supermind or gnostic being, is one in which we achieve full integration with universal consciousness and our entire life, our consciousness, and our action are governed by the universal will.

It is clear that this goal is far different from the ego-centered notion of the powerful superman that tends to be popular in the West. Yet the gnostic being, as conceived by Aurobindo, does not lose individuality or uniqueness, nor does he lose freedom. He enjoys ultimate freedom, for being fully in tune with nature he experiences all action as spontaneous and free at the same time that it is naturally ordered. He transcends the experiential limitations of the ordinary ego-centered individual, and he transcends the limitations imposed by the weight of social sanctions. He is "beyond good and evil" in the sense that he has transcended the need for societal standards of conduct by realizing more directly the operation of the highest divine law of nature.

"This, then, would be the nature of the gnostic Person, an infinite and universal being revealing—or, to our mental ignorance, suggesting—its eternal self through the significant form and expressive power of an individual and temporal self-manifestation." [7] Elsewhere, Aurobindo said:

> The gnostic individual would be the consummation of the spiritual man; his whole way of being, thinking, living, acting would be governed by the power of a vast universal spirituality. All the trinities of the Spirit would be real to his self-awareness and realised in his inner life. All his existence would be fused into oneness with the transcendent and universal Self and Spirit; all his actions would originate from and obey the supreme Self and Spirit's divine governance of Nature. All life would have to him the sense of the Conscious Being, the Purusha within, finding its self-expression in Nature; his life and all its thoughts, feelings, acts would be filled for him with that significance and built upon that foundation of its reality. He would feel the presence of the Divine in every centre of his consciousness, in every vibration of his life-force, in every cell of his body. In all the workings of his force of Nature he would be aware of the workings of the supreme World-Mother, the Supernature; he would see his natural being as the becoming and manifestation of the power of the World-Mother. In this consciousness he would live and act in an entire transcendent freedom, a complete joy of the Spirit, an entire identity with the cosmic Self and a spontaneous sympathy with all in the universe. All beings would be to him his own selves, all ways and powers of consciousness would be felt as the ways and powers of his own universality. . . . The gnostic individual would be in the world and of the world, but would also exceed it in his consciousness and live in his Self of transcendence above it; he would be universal but free in the universe, individual but not limited by a separate individuality. The true Person is not an isolated entity, his individ-

uality is universal; for he individualizes the universe: it is at the same time divinely emergent in a spiritual air of transcendental infinity, like a high cloud-surpassing summit; for he individualises the divine Transcendence.[8]

BUDDHISM

Buddhism originated in the thought of a man named Siddhartha, or Gautama (his family name), who came to be known as the Buddha. Gautama lived in the sixth and fifth centuries B.C. It is said that he was born into an aristocratic Hindu family, grew up in luxury, married, and had a son, but that his father took great pains to shield him from the misery of the world. At the age of 29, however, Gautama went out of the palace one day against his father's orders and was confronted with the spectacle of human suffering. He resolved to leave his wife and home at night and to seek an understanding of the riddle of life. For six years he tried a variety of paths in quest of enlightenment, including asceticism and self-mortification, but failed to find the insight he was seeking. He finally sat down under a tree and vowed not to move from the spot until he had found enlightenment. On the forty-ninth day his efforts were rewarded, and he proceeded to teach his ideas to others.

Whatever the amount of historical truth in this legend, it is clear that Buddhism arose on the foundation of Hinduism but that it represented a departure from some aspects of Brahmanism. Certain Hindu doctrines were retained, in particular the principle of karma and the concepts of transmigration and rebirth. Indeed, the basic concern of Gautama was to find the means of achieving liberation from the misery of the repetitive cycle of rebirths. Such liberation remains the basic focus of all forms of Buddhism, though not necessarily in the sense of a literal end to the cycle of rebirths. Early Buddhism also retained from Hinduism a rather negative view of the world and of worldly pleasures. The world was viewed as a place of ignorance and suffering from which a release was desirable, and the path of wisdom was felt to entail firm restraint of the appetites and passions. Extreme asceticism and mortifications of the flesh, however, were rejected.

92

In other respects Gautama and the early Buddhists departed from Hindu traditions. They de-emphasized the importance of the caste system, which Hindu doctrine had served to rationalize in terms of karma, without going so far as to advocate a total abandonment of it. They rejected the authority and the ritualism of the Brahmins. For them, the Vedas were no longer deemed sacred, and the Brahmanas and Upanishads were no longer considered vitally important. Gautama considered most of the metaphysical speculation contained in those works to be rather useless and uninteresting. His own concerns were more ethical than metaphysical. He hoped to define a path toward liberation, not to define the nature of absolutes.

Gautama's most basic teachings were set forth in the "four noble truths": (1) that all life involves suffering or sorrow, (2) that the origin of suffering is desire, (3) that suffering ceases when desire is eliminated, and (4) that the way to achieve an elimination of desire is to follow the "middle way," the specific technique of which is described in the "noble eightfold path." In a sense, the notion of the middle way implies something comparable to the idea of moderation or the golden mean advocated by early Greeks. It is a course midway between asceticism and self-indulgence.

The noble eightfold path includes: (1) right knowledge or belief, (2) right intention, (3) right speech, (4) right conduct, (5) right occupation or means of livelihood, (6) right effort, (7) right mindfulness, and (8) right concentration or meditation. As specifically interpreted, these eight points provide the foundation for a rather elaborate ethical system that is subject to some variation among Buddhists. In effect, the eight points are a way of stating that one should do good and avoid self-indulgence and actions harmful to other beings. Thus, "right effort" implies keeping the mind free from evil and devoted to good. "Right intention" entails resolving to renounce sensual pleasure and to refrain from harming other living creatures. The third and fourth points—right speech and right conduct—have been interpreted in terms of a code of conduct known as the "five precepts." In these, one is advised to abstain from the taking of life, the taking of what is not given, all illegal sexual pleasures, lying, and the consumption of intoxicants (because they tend to cloud the mind).

93

Gautama's disciples and Buddhist monks since have generally led rather austere lives, pledging themselves to poverty and chastity and vowing to refrain from killing, stealing, falsehood, and strong drink, adhering rather strictly to the eightfold path. The basic purpose of this mode of living is to achieve nirvana, a state of blissful detachment in which the conditions that lead to rebirth no longer exist. Westerners tend to regard Buddhism and its goal of nirvana as an escape from life. Sigmund Freud saw it as an effort to regress to a state of infantile or intrauterine unawareness. Albert Schweitzer viewed the Buddha's basic teaching as an extreme form of world and life negation, for he construed the four noble truths as stating that all suffering springs from the will to live and that it can only be ended by extinguishing the will to live.[9]

These appear to be misinterpretations on the part of Westerners who attach greater importance either to individuality or to active involvement in the world than Gautama did. It is clear, however, that Gautama saw the desired goal in terms of a detachment from the world and that the means toward that end also involved detachment. Indeed, detachment is more central to the eightfold path than it may appear to be at first glance, for both the avoidance of harm and the avoidance of sensual pleasure involve this. By remaining chaste, one avoids becoming too attached to the world. By not harming, one avoids becoming needlessly involved in the suffering of the world. Love and compassion do play a role in early Buddhism, but not a very central role. While Gautama proscribed the infliction of harm on others, he did not prescribe active charity. He was more concerned with the achievement of an inner perfection than with the quality of the individual's relationship to the world about him. As for the purpose of the mode of living that Gautama advocated, the precise interpretation of his teachings is subject to dispute. The interpretation of nirvana as an end state has varied and has undergone historical shifts, but on the whole Buddhists have construed it primarily in terms of enlightenment, not in terms of a cessation of life or a loss of awareness.

In Brahmanic doctrine, enlightenment would have meant the realization that Atman is Brahman. For Gautama, it had a much different meaning, for he not only rejected this identity, he rejected the concepts of Atman and Brahman. He regarded both the universal soul and the individual soul as concepts without meaning. He saw the experienced self as an impermanent, constantly changing phenomenon, too subject to fluctuation to be considered an enduring reality.

In general, in Buddhist thought our sense of individual separateness and self is seen as responsible for suffering, and to achieve enlightenment is to see beyond this imaginary reality and to experience the universe devoid of the perceived separateness that we have imposed upon it. From this standpoint, to say that desire is the cause of suffering is to say that we experience suffering because we perceive ourselves as being separate from the rest of the universe and become overly concerned with the needs and status of these split-off entities. We bring about an end to suffering when we realize that this is all an illusion.

It is interesting to note that the theme of a pervasive human suffering runs through many traditions in both the East and the West. In general, it is assumed that the suffering is not an inevitable part of life per se, but rather a consequence of our experienced individuality or separateness. Thus, Adam and Eve eat of the fruit of the tree of knowledge and acquire a self-awareness that sets them apart from all other creatures. For this loss of innocence, for this presumption, they must pay a price. In Greek mythology, Prometheus brings to mankind the power of creative transformation, of seeing in darkness, of awareness. For this transgression, he is bound to a mountain peak where he must endure having his liver consumed daily by a vulture. It was recognized in both Greek and Judaic culture that to dare to assert oneself as an independent, creative, and self-aware being is to claim for oneself a bit of the power of the divine and that agony is certain to follow. Given this state of affairs, the basic question is whether one should accept the pain and assert his will against the gods or humbly seek forgiveness for being a member of a species so inclined toward error.

Western traditions in the main tend to accept individuality as a given, a condition that is ineradicable and irreparable. Starting from this premise, the individualistic traditions tell us to accept our situation as an opportunity. We should become more aware and more creative,

95

we should accept the challenge and take the risks, and perhaps ultimately we shall emerge triumphant in the struggle with nature and be the masters of our fate. Some of these traditions entertain the hope that if we play our cards just right we may overcome our agony. Others say that anxiety and guilt are a necessary price for being fully human and that we should simply accept them as unavoidable. This appears to be the attitude of many existentialists.

existentialists

Much of Christian thought advocates a different course. It generally assumes that God has created the human being as a creature separate from himself and endowed this creature with a will, a capacity, and perhaps even a proclivity toward sin. Given his separateness, however, the human being can minimize his pain by trying to fulfill as best he can the will of God. The proper course may be viewed in terms of making oneself an analogue of God, of trying to be a better approximation to God's image, of leading a life imitative of Christ. Or it may be conceived in terms of seeking a loving union with God and perhaps with the rest of mankind.

Eastern traditions are less inclined to assume the inevitability of individual separateness. In Hinduism, the basic reality is held to be that of nonseparateness. We experience ourselves as separate because we are insufficiently aware. As we approach full awareness of our true nature (the Atman), we discover that we are in fact inseparable from the spirit of the whole of nature. The Buddhist position is a similar one, but it dispenses with some of the conceptual scaffolding of Hinduism. From a Buddhist standpoint, we err when we merely begin to formulate a concept of ourselves as the separate person, the individual, the "I" as distinguished from all else. Our very effort to be individually knowing is itself a form of ignorance and leads to suffering. The suffering ceases when we recognize our individuality as an illusion.

Within Buddhism, there is some variation in the way in which the illusion and the enlightenment that brings it to an end are conceptualized. There are early controversies in Buddhism over such questions as whether everything evident to the senses or nothing evident to the senses was real. In the second century A.D. Nagarjuna introduced a distinction between absolute truth and relative truth that has influenced much Buddhist thought since then. This distinction, much like

96

one Plato had introduced, assumes that absolute reality inheres only in things that are permanent and unchanging. The world of the senses can be viewed as having a relative reality. Our experienced identity or ego would also have at best a relative reality, for according to Buddhist doctrine it is an ever-changing composite formed by the "five Skandhas": the physical body and its senses; feelings and sensations; emotional reactions or volition; perceptions leading to memory; and consciousness. All of these components change as does the "I" that arises from them.

It should be noted that the five Skandhas are bound to a particular physical lifetime. Hence, the sense of ego or identity that rests on them is also so bound and cannot be assumed to pass on into another bodily vehicle. If reincarnation actually occurs, it is only some more abstracted trace that can be subject to transmigration—a force generated by a particular existence or a conscious principle that can be expressed anew in a new life. Strictly speaking, it is rather meaningless to speak of reincarnation with respect to a particular individual identity unless, at the very least, memory is carried over from one lifetime to the next. Lacking this, we are left at best with some element of consciousness that survives physical death. If it survives, we may wonder whether it reappears in another individual form or whether it merely remains as an ingredient of the total mass of human or life consciousness—and we may be tempted to ask whether this is a difference that makes a difference. In the history of Buddhist thought, one can find various interpretations of reincarnation and associated views as to the course of delivery from the cycle of rebirths. An increasingly prevalent view is one in which reincarnation is not taken literally and enlightenment is simply dependent on an insight (which may come in an instant, rather than gradually accruing over a series of lifetimes) into the true nature of reality and our misconstructions of it.

Buddhism ultimately died out in the land of its birth, India, but at one time or another it has managed to influence the lives of people in nearly all parts of the Far East. It spread in early centuries over a large geographic area, interacting in the course of its movement with other cultural traditions and undergoing change. Today it is common to distinguish two main forms of Buddhism: Mahayana Buddhism and Hi-

97

nayana Buddhism. Hinayana, or Theravada, Buddhism is found in Burma, Thailand, Cambodia, Laos, and Sri Lanka—countries along the southern border of the Asian continent. Mahayana Buddhism is found in Viet Nam, Nepal, Sikkim, Bhutan and countries to the north—Tibet, China, Korea, and Japan. Sometimes the Buddhism of Tibet is viewed as a separate third branch, and it is variously called Vajrayana Buddhism, Lamaism, and Tantric Buddhism.

Hinayana Buddhism remains closest to the original form of Buddhism. In contrast to other forms, it places a heavy emphasis on the achievement of individual enlightenment. The ideal Buddhist in this tradition is the holy man who follows the path of the Buddha and arrives at the same goal himself. Early in Mahayana Buddhism another ideal appeared, that of the bodhisattva, the holy man who has experienced enlightenment but who vows to remain in the world and to continue experiencing rebirth until everyone else is ready to enter nirvana. Whether or not this ideal continues to be construed in terms of an actual acceptance of rebirth, it implies a de-emphasis of detachment and a greater emphasis on charity. There is much variation in practice, of course, and charity may involve anything from kindly inaction to very active compassion.

As a result of the influence of other religions with which Buddhism has interacted, various theological beliefs can be found in Mahayana sects—various deviations from the essentially atheistic position of Gautama. In some popular forms of Buddhism, one finds a variety of gods, and nirvana is interpreted in terms of a heavenly paradise. In some sects one can even find the idea of a hell to which evildoers go after death. In general, to the extent that Buddhism has been popularized in countries to the north of India, an emphasis on the rigors of monastic life has been replaced by an emphasis on faith and devotion, often accompanied by beliefs that deviate considerably from original Buddhist doctrine. Even among the sects that show less contamination from popular religions, there is some variation in emphasis. Some sects, for example, stress meditation, while others de-emphasize it and stress rationality over intuitive insight. At least in method, those that stress intuition and meditation are probably closer to early Buddhism.

The most important of these today are the Zen Buddhist sects of Japan.

eg.

TIBETAN BUDDHISM

Buddhism was introduced into Tibet in the eighth century A.D., a period in which the mystic cult of Tantrism had become widespread in India. From Tantrism, Tibetan Buddhism derived much of its ritual and much of its symbolism. Tantric symbolism makes considerable use of sexual elements, such as pictures showing deities in intimate embrace. Although this symbolism is usually understood in the East to have a meaning that is more spiritual than carnal, it has inspired a number of Western faddists to create their own versions of "tantric yoga," incorporating procedures that have no real counterpart in Oriental practices.

The flavor of Tibetan Buddhism was also greatly affected by the Bön religion, which was native to the region and generally practiced before the advent of Buddhism. Some of the elements of this ancient religion—shamanism, sorcery, spirit exorcism, magical formulae, demonolatry, and worship of nature gods—are still found in strong force among people of little education, who are often Buddhists in name only. Though Buddhism has, in effect, been the "state religion" of Tibet for centuries, it has only gradually proceeded to displace competing practices and ideas throughout Tibet, and it has been infused in various areas with a good deal of local coloring.

With the invasion of Tibet by the Communist Chinese, it appears likely that both the native religion and Buddhism are doomed to extinction in that part of the world. It is reported that the Chinese have destroyed monasteries, outlawed Buddhist practices, and either killed many lamas or forced them to leave the country. As a result, Tibet seems destined to lose a rich cultural tradition, but that tradition may now have a better chance to become known and to flourish in the West, for some of the leading figures in Tibetan Buddhism have migrated to England and the United States. Over a thousand years ago,

99

a Buddhist named Padma Sambhava said, "When the iron bird flies and horses run on wheels, the Tibetan people will be scattered like ants across the world, and the Dharma will come to the land of the red man." Perhaps the time has come for the fulfillment of this prophecy.

The principles that are most central to Tibetan Buddhism are those that are common to Buddhism in general, though there are some differences in emphasis. The most basic concept is that of *sunyata* (often translated as *voidness, emptiness,* or *suchness*), or the absolute nature of reality, the reality common to all things, a reality that defies all our efforts to grasp it intellectually. It is empty in the sense that it cannot be understood in terms of any attributes that we attach to it in our efforts to understand it. The realm of phenomenal beings with which we are accustomed to dealing in perception and thought is the realm of *maya,* the realm of illusion. Since Tibetan Buddhists seem generally to accept the distinction between absolute and relative truth, this does not mean to them that the world of our ordinary experience is unreal, but simply that it represents a reality of lesser degree. It is an impermanent reality, but one that is quite lawful. According to Lama Govinda, the body—that changing, perishable vehicle we inhabit—is a product of the mind, but it does not disappear the moment that we recognize this fact. Once the products of the mind take material shape, they obey the laws of matter.[10] Impermanent phenomena are illusory in the sense that they do not represent the most fundamental reality, but they are not hallucinations.

Tibetan Buddhism accepts the Hindu doctrines of karma and reincarnation in a fairly literal sense. It holds that to the extent that we remain in ignorance, clinging to a sense of our individual separateness in the phenomenal world and experiencing desire, we remain caught in the world of samsara, in the repetitive cycle of rebirths. The samsaric world is often represented pictorially in Tibet by the wheel of life, a circle containing an assortment of symbolic pictures and divided into six segments corresponding to different aspects of the illusory samsaric world. We can bring the cycle of rebirths to an end by achieving enlightenment, by seeing through the illusion and recognizing the true nature of ultimate reality. Paradoxically, we are told that although we may not realize it, we are already enlightened. We are all Buddhas in essence and are unenlightened only to the extent that our true nature has not fully unfolded. Perhaps another way of putting this would be to say that enlightenment is something that we only have to permit, not something we have to learn. A somewhat related paradox found in Buddhist thought is the idea that from an absolute standpoint, there is no difference between *sunyata* and *maya* or between samsara and nirvana. All being and all phenomena are *sunyata* according to their true nature. It is only from the illusory perspective of the phenomenal world that one can make a distinction between the absolute reality and illusion.

Be that as it may, the ideal state as seen in Tibetan Buddhism is the Buddhist ideal of enlightenment. The enlightened individual would be one who is fully aware and who thus sees through the illusions of the phenomenal world, including the illusion of his own ego. He would be free from the desires and suffering that arise from ignorance and in full control of his appetites. Although fully in touch with the "true" reality in the "here and now," he would be detached from the world to which others about him cling. As we noted, Mahayana Buddhists add to this ideal of enlightenment the compassion of the bodhisattva. This is of particular importance in Tibetan Buddhism.

Lama Govinda says that three kinds of liberated beings are distinguished in early Buddhist scriptures.[11] The first is the saint, or *Arahan,* who has overcome passions and the illusion of egohood, but who has not achieved the all-pervasive consciousness of perfect enlightenment. The second is the Silent Enlightened One, or *Paccekabuddha,* who has the full knowledge of a Buddha but lacks the capacity for communicating it to others. The third is the Perfectly Enlightened One, or *Sammasambuddha,* who is a saint, a knower, an enlightened one who has attained a full maturing of all his spiritual and psychic faculties, and whose consciousness encompasses the infinity of the universe. The third of these ideal types came to assume a particular importance in early Mahayana Buddhism, because it represented a type of being capable not merely of liberating himself but of carrying many other beings to liberation as well. It came to be associated with the ideal of the bodhisattva, the enlightened being who willingly postpones his own final liberation from samsara in order to facilitate the liberation of all other beings.

The bodhisattva ideal assumes a concrete importance in Tibetan Buddhism that it does not have elsewhere, since the leading figures in the cultural life of Tibet have been recognized as *Tulkus*. A *Tulku* is a specific incarnation of an enlightened being who has taken the bodhisattva vow. According to Chögyam Trungpa, most of us are bound to an earthly samsaric existence because we remain enmeshed in egohood, but in the case of a *Tulku* a different force is involved in rebirth, since no ego or individuality is any longer present in the ordinary sense.[12] For the sake of other beings, the bodhisattva may be reborn in a series of Tulkus. In some cases a *Tulku* may be viewed as an incarnation of an archetypal source of wisdom, rather than of a specific individual person. Strictly speaking, insofar as individuality is an illusion, it is not a specific individual that is reborn in any event, but rather the essence that is realized when through enlightenment individuality is sloughed off. It is said that a great sage may extend his influence over several lines of reincarnations simultaneously, different aspects of his nature being expressed in several *Tulkus*. The most prominent figures in Tibetan Buddhism are the Dalai Lama, who is considered a reincarnation of the bodhisattva Avalokiteshvara, and the Panchen Lama, considered a reincarnation of Amitabha, the Buddha of Light.

Another conspicuous feature of Tibetan Buddhism is a rather abundant pictorial representation of godlike beings, such as Vairocana, the Illuminator, and Aksobhya, the Immutable. To some Westerners this suggests that Tibetan Buddhism is a polytheistic religion. There are gods and demons associated with the Bön religion, of course, that may be credited by some Tibetans with a real existence, but the mythical figures of Buddhism have always been regarded by educated Buddhists as just that. They are understood as symbolic of aspects of our experience. Demons and gods provide a vehicle for the projection of our experiences of torment and of insight. It seems to be understood in Tibetan Buddhism that while we are seeking enlightenment, these images may enable us to experience more fully those parts of our experience that we have not yet fully understood.

It is likely that Westerners have frequently misconstrued the role of myths and symbols in Hinduism and Buddhism, assuming that wherever they find reference to gods, demons, heaven, and hell the people who speak of such things maintain a literal belief in their existence. Alas, it is we in the West who live in a literal-minded society. We have lost much of our capacity to use mythological symbols, to fully experience their meaning. We assume that people who do live with such symbols have failed to represent the world with scientific accuracy when in fact scientific description is not their concern. To criticize a myth or a poem for failing to be a good scientific theory is a bit like arguing that Einstein was a failure because $E = mc^2$ is neither a sonnet nor a palindrome.

We live in a society that disparages indulgence in myths on the part of adults, we preserve a few mythical figures like Santa Claus for the use of children, and we smile indulgently at the excitement of the child's involvement in the myth, but we seek the company of children at Christmas time in order to indulge the child within ourselves without making it too obvious that we need to do that. For many aspects of our experience, we no longer have available myths that we could employ to augment our awareness. Science has become the predominant mythology of our society in the sense that it provides the basic framework for understanding life and the universe about us, but it does not fully meet our need for symbols.

Lacking a generally recognized mythology, we tend to mythologize rather sporadically, particularly in the political sphere. We invest our hopes in charismatic leaders that we imagine to be capable of disentangling the knots of modern society, and we project more disconcerting qualities onto ethnic minorities, people with different lifestyles, and other nations. In this haphazard way, we achieve a greater sense of comfort without becoming any wiser. Perhaps an avowed mythology would provide a more useful vehicle for projecting those parts of ourselves that we have not fully owned, giving us an opportunity to explore their basic nature as we gradually gain a better awareness of their source and locus.

103

TAOISM AND CONFUCIANISM

When Buddhism reached China, it found a fertile ground in which it could take root and develop further. While the more abstract, speculative features of Indian thought could not flourish in China, there was much in the basic spirit of Buddhism that seemed compatible with the Chinese outlook on life. While Westerners have often struggled to achieve control over nature, Chinese traditions have more consistently emphasized the idea of living in harmony with nature. Common to Buddhism and to such native Chinese traditions as Confucianism and Taoism is the idea that man achieves his highest goal, his salvation, his liberation, simply by being natural, or by realizing his essential nature. While this idea is also found in Western traditions, it competes with traditions that assume that our destiny is to rise above nature or that we have no essential nature and are free to create ourselves as we wish, to be "self-made."

An ancient idea that runs through many traditions in Chinese thought is the notion that there are two basic interacting forces or principles governing the universe—the yang and the yin. Yang and yin are said to be variously expressed in such contrasts as heaven and earth, the masculine and the feminine, hardness and softness, warmth and cold, dryness and wetness, good and evil, upper and lower, joy and sorrow, life and death, love and hate, activity and passivity, the positive and the negative, brightness and darkness, steadfastness and changeableness, agreement and opposition, etc. However one seeks to describe or construe the essential nature of the two principles, the important point so far as Chinese thought is concerned is that they are complementary. An overemphasis on either creates an imbalance, and things go awry. The ideal situation is that in which they are permitted to interact harmoniously.

The two major ancient traditions of thought in China, Taoism and Confucianism, both stress the idea of harmony, but there are many basic differences between them. Confucianism is essentially an ethical system concerned with social relationships, and more broadly with the management of society as a whole. It assumes that people are basically social creatures whose natural mode of relationship is one of harmony. For the maintenance of this harmony, however, Confucianism prescribes a system of ritual and etiquette. This is summarized in terms of ten attitudes that ideally govern five basic human relationships. These attitudes include love in the father combined with filial piety in the son, gentility in the elder brother combined with humility and respect in the younger brother, righteous behavior in the husband combined with obedience in the wife, humane consideration in elders combined with deference in juniors, and benevolence in rulers combined with loyalty in subjects. Confucianism assumes certain conventional social arrangements to be a natural state of affairs. Thus it emphasizes reverence for elders and for people in authority, and it presupposes the subordination of women to men. But on the whole it is oriented to the welfare and happiness of all concerned (within the limitations of conventional social patterns) and rests on a principle much like the Golden Rule of Christianity: never do to others what you would not like them to do to you. It must be a very practical and workable system in many respects, for it is likely that no other ethical system ever devised has governed the conduct of so many people over such a long period of time as Confucianism.

To some extent, Taoism has competed with Confucianism, but on the whole the two traditions have coexisted rather compatibly because they are quite complementary to each other. Each provides what is lacking in the other. The Confucian system is concerned with social relationships, while Taoism is more concerned with the individual's relationship to himself and to the whole of nature. Confucian thought tends to be very orderly and rational. Taoism is more mystical and intuitive, more concerned with aspects of our experience and of nature that do not submit to rational analysis.

The most basic concept of Taoism is the concept of the Tao. This word might be translated as "the way" or "the path," but in Taoist thought it refers to the basic way in which the universe functions, the course of natural events. This is viewed as a course that cannot be fully grasped by the intellect, a course that in its essence is not subject to description, but it is assumed to be at least partly characterized by spontaneous creativity and by regular alternations of events that pro-

105

ceed without deliberate effort. The aim of human existence from a Taoist standpoint is to attain and maintain harmony with the Tao. To do this involves basically just letting things happen, not interfering with nature. Perhaps the concept that best captures this idea is the concept of wu-wei, which means something like inaction, or doing nothing.

Thus, Taoism stresses the importance of letting things take their own course, of refraining from deliberate thought or action. From a Taoist perspective, Confucianism may be said to place too much emphasis on deliberate adherence to rules of conduct and to disregard the importance of natural, effortless action. Taoism early served as a sanctuary for people dissatisfied with the ethical system of Confucianism. For the most part, however, the Chinese appear to have recognized for centuries that each system provides things lacking in the other and that together they provide a desirable balance that neither can offer by itself. With respect to their focus, extraverted in the one case and introverted in the other, and with respect to the modes of understanding that they stress, the two systems are somewhat analogous to the Platonic and Aristotelian streams in Western thought. In combination they allow for the interplay of thinkers of varying temperament and outlook.

Confucianism and Taoism together also represent a combination of discipline with freedom that seems to be a common ingredient of Eastern paths of liberation. Many of these paths involve practices that are designed to free the individual from the constraints of conventional ways of thinking and acting. Yet these practices flourish within the confines of social systems and monastic orders that are highly structured. It is widely recognized in the East that without the initial order, the procedure designed to yield freedom would only yield chaos. This is a point often overlooked by Westerners who favor the adoption of Eastern practices.

ZEN BUDDHISM

As Buddhism spread into China, it necessarily accommodated to Chinese ways of life. Mahayana Buddhism became a more practical philosophy in China, one more concerned with the needs of ordinary people. In countries to the south, it often seemed to stress superhuman goals, goals that no ordinary mortal could attain within a single lifetime. In China it tended to be understood more in terms of a harmony and naturalness within the reach of everyone. A variety of new Buddhist sects appeared in China, each reflecting a particular blend of Buddhism with Chinese tradition. Among the more important were the Ch'an sects. (The equivalent Japanese term *Zen* is derived from *Ch'an,* which in turn is ultimately derived from Sanskrit *Dhyana,* or meditation.) Ch'an or Zen Buddhism may best be viewed historically as a blend of Buddhism and Taoism. It now flourishes mainly in Japan, where it has undergone further development. It evidently offers something for which many Westerners feel a strong need, for it is the form of Buddhism that has attracted the greatest attention in the West. A number of books on Zen have appeared in English in recent years and been widely read. The best known are the ones written by Daisetz Suzuki, the most eminent Zen master of our time, and by Alan Watts, the writer who has shown the greatest skill in conveying the ideas of Zen to Westerners.[13]

In Japan, the Zen school of Buddhism has the second largest following. There are a number of sects in Japan that reflect adaptations of Buddhism peculiar to that country. The most popular school of all is that of Shin Buddhism, which provides a bit of color and pageantry lacking in Zen.

The basic precepts of Zen are few and simple. It derives an antischolastic and antitextual bias from Taoism, and Zen Buddhists refrain from elaborate philosophical speculation. One of the most basic features of Zen is its emphasis on naturalness and spontaniety. This involves the idea of *wu-wei,* or nonaction, of simply letting nature take its course. But it also involves the idea of fully participating in whatever we do, including things that entail intense activity and expression. Inactivity per se is not the aim of Zen. Watts notes that one of the most remarkable properties of the human mind is the capacity for self-reflection, but having this capacity we often tend to be too self-conscious, or to let our self-awareness become a hindrance to action.[14] We reflect in the course of acting and end up wobbling, instead of acting effectively.

107

Zen training is designed to eliminate the blocking of action and thinking that stems from self-reflection and to restore the spontaneity and sincerity of the undivided mind.

Another feature of Zen, one that is more distinctly Buddhist in origin, is its emphasis on recognizing the illusion of the ego. This illusion is seen as responsible for the duality of subject and object, a duality more characteristic of Western thought than of Eastern thought. So long as we maintain this duality, identifying with an idea of ourselves as a well-defined entity separate from the world around us, we regard ourselves as independent agents responsible for constantly choosing between right and wrong courses of action and for choosing actions that will make things better rather than worse. When we realize the true interdependence of all events and recognize the illusion of our separate personal identity, we realize that "choosing is absurd because there is no choice." [15]

In Zen, the idea of the illusion of the ego assumes much greater importance than the Buddhist concepts of karma and rebirth. In contrast to Tibetan Buddhists, Zen Buddhists seem generally to view reincarnation in a figurative sense. They do not think of reincarnation as something that occurs after physical death but as something that occurs from moment to moment as we persist in identifying with a continuing ego that continues to inhabit its present material vehicle.

Similarly, the liberation from the cycle of rebirths is not something that is going to come after a series of lifetimes of struggle. It can come in this lifetime if we let it happen, and it can occur in an instant. The goal of all Zen practices is the experience of *satori*. *Satori* involves an intuitive apprehension of the world in which we see everything free of the structure imposed by our dualistic mental habits. The notion of a sudden awakening that is implied by the concept of *satori* (or the Chinese equivalent *tun-wu*) is evidently not in keeping with Indian traditions, but it appears to make more sense to the Chinese and Japanese. Of course, this does not mean Zen Buddhists regard enlightenment as something easily come by, for a Zen monk may go through years of preparation to achieve satori.

Like the monks of other Buddhist sects, Zen monks lead rather austere lives and follow the rigid discipline prescribed by their masters.

The discipline and austerity are regarded as a means to an end, and asceticism as such is not accorded any particular value. While the Zen master can be very demanding and harsh at times, the Zen outlook is quite nonauthoritarian in many respects. There is little concern with intellectual authority, and the insight that is sought must come from the pupil, not from the master. The function of the master is to facilitate a growth process, and once the growth has occurred his authority is totally dispensable. Ultimately, the monk relies entirely on his own experience.

The monastery is characterized by two basic practices—the use of koan and the meditational practice of *za-zen*. Stressed particularly by the Rinzai school of Zen, the koan is the practical feature that most clearly distinguishes Zen from other forms of Buddhism. It is essentially a rational problem, puzzle, or riddle that the student is asked to solve, but which admits of no rational solution. There are perhaps hundreds of such koans in actual use in Zen monasteries, and they assume a variety of forms. Probably most readers will have heard by now of such examples as "What is the sound of one hand clapping?" or "Has the dog a Buddha nature?" It is fairly easy to concoct examples that better fit the dilemmas and ways of thought of the Western world: "What is the meaning of life?" "How can I lead a life of eternal happiness and constant progress?" "How can I be a free and spontaneous being while writing systematic works on the nature of the optimal personality?" The koan is designed to challenge the student and to generate doubt by demonstrating the inadequacy of all deliberate analytic efforts to find a solution. It is assumed that insight will generally come when the student has abandoned such efforts. In short, the koan is designed to facilitate *satori* by posing a problem that cannot be solved by the logical modes of thought to which we are accustomed.

Za-zen is essentially a procedure in which one sits cross-legged in quietude and deep meditation. Although Zen meditation differs in some details from the procedures prescribed in other sects, in its basic essentials *za-zen* is employed in Zen Buddhism less for the benefits of meditation as such than as a means for reaching the solution of the koan.[16]

EASTERN WISDOM AND WESTERN LIFE

Elements of Eastern thought can be found more and more in the work of Western writers. We shall find evidence of some of these elements in the work of the theorists treated in subsequent chapters. Alan Watts has done a rather good job of showing us the importance of Eastern ideas. Although he does not believe that we can solve our problems by simply importing Eastern practices wholesale, he feels that we really need the essential insights of Vedanta philosophy and Buddhism. He argues that because of our preoccupation with that illusory product of our customary modes of thinking, talking, and perceiving—the individual ego—we cannot achieve a satisfactory relationship with the world around us.[17] We experience ourselves as lonely temporary visitors in the universe. We feel at odds with the world, hostile toward what is "outside" us. Furthermore, we lack "common sense"—i.e., we cannot make sense of the world in a way on which we can agree. In one book Watts states his basic thesis:

> The prevalent sensation of oneself as a separate ego enclosed in a bag of skin is a hallucination which accords neither with Western science nor with the experimental philosophy-religions of the East—in particular the central and germinal Vedanta philosophy of Hinduism. This hallucination underlies the misuse of technology for the violent subjugation of man's natural environment and, consequently, its eventual destruction." [18]

As Watts sees it, Hinduism and Buddhism basically agree on the importance of overcoming the duality of the ego and the world, though they differ in the precise way in which they articulate this.[19] One stresses the unity of the field, while the other stresses the unreality of the ego. However one describes the Eastern goal of liberation, Watts says it is essentially what we need. Psychoanalysis has performed a valuable service in revealing the fact that most of our behavior arises from unconscious sources, but it has erred in retaining the ego as a weak semi-independent agent. Watts has described in many different ways the liberation that results from overcoming the illusion of the ego or the subject-object dichotomy. He speaks of a "recovery

110

from the split between the soul and the body" and of a restoration of "the 'primary narcissism' not just of the organism by itself, but of the organism/environment field." [20] In the abandonment of the illusion, there is a "shift from egocentric awareness to the feeling that one's identity is the whole field of the organism in its environment." [21] This shift is liberating, for it frees us from the inhibiting sense of personal responsibility for choosing every action that we take. "The point," says Watts, "is not that one stops choosing, but that one chooses in the knowledge that there is really no choice." [22] We accept the natural flow of all events, including our own actions, and proceed to function with total spontaneity.

FIVE

SIGMUND FREUD AND PSYCHO-ANALYSIS

HISTORICAL SETTING AND BACKGROUND

We shall consider a number of modern theorists who hold distinctive views of the optimal person and the optimal condition. To secure a sound basis for appreciating their various positions and for understanding the differences among them, we shall examine the cultural and personal context of the work of each theorist. Each of these people gives a somewhat different expression to Western traditions; at the same time, his thinking reflects his own personal temperament and the accidents of his own individual life history. We must also devote some attention to the total theoretical system of the individual theorist, for in each case we are looking at a notion of the ideal condition that is embedded in a more general conception of the nature of human personality and its development, and the specific notion cannot be fully grasped without reference to that general conception.

We can best begin with Sigmund Freud, for it would be impossible to provide an adequate account of modern psychological thought without referring to Freud. Whether one accepts or rejects any or all of his ideas, no one can reasonably deny that Freud has had a far greater influence on contemporary psychological theory than any other single individual. Indeed, it may well be that his influence on Western thought in general exceeds that of any other person of this century. This is a very sweeping statement, but it is difficult to think of a close competitor for such a distinction. Freud's work has had a noticeable impact on contemporary views of art, literature, religion, and morality. It has affected the working habits of artists, poets, novelists, and the clergy, as well as people in psychology and psychiatry. His impact on contemporary mores has aroused both praise and scorn.

How did this man happen to assume a place of such overwhelming importance in Western thought? One can analyze both the man and his theories in vain for a simple answer to that question. No one trait or idea emerges in analysis to account for the total effect. It is often the case that a particular thinker or social leader assumes a position of preeminence because he happens to be the right person in the right place at the right time. Doing, thinking, or saying the same things at a different time or in a different place, he would receive little notice and pass into obscurity. Like Copernicus and Darwin, Freud has been seen as the leader of a major revolution in our thinking about the nature of man and about his place in the universe. Copernicus removed mankind from the center of the universe; Darwin showed us that the human species is closely linked to the rest of the animal kingdom; and finally Freud demonstrated that we are not the highly rational creatures we like to assume we are, for our actions and thoughts are largely governed by forces of which we are unaware.

The parallels between Copernicus, Darwin, and Freud are remarkable in ways that are commonly overlooked. It is most apparent, of course, that each man advanced an idea that undermined our suppositions about the special importance of mankind. In each case, however, the idea was one that had been uttered before. Copernicus was not the first to speak of a heliocentric universe. The idea of evolution had been widely discussed for more than a century before Darwin's theory was published; indeed, the idea that all species evolve from a common primitive ancestral organism was over two thousand years old before Darwin was born. The idea of the unconscious and the idea of man's basic irrationality espoused by Freud can also be traced to antiquity. At the same time, in the case of each of these three men, there were two conditions that combined to make his contributions

113

uniquely significant. Each appeared at a time when Western society was ready for his idea to assume more general currency (but not necessarily widespread acceptance), a time when that idea could move beyond the confines of limited intellectual circles and enter the thinking of people in many walks of life. Furthermore, each of the three developed his idea in a form that enabled him to have a little more impact than others had had.

Freud was a brilliant and articulate theorist who has exerted a tremendous influence on our thinking, but his most fundamental ideas were not concepts that suddenly burst into view for the first time in his writings.[1] His publications merely imbued them with a fresh importance. But we can better appreciate his work if we recognize that Freud himself was a product and a part of Western culture who was born and reared in the latter part of the nineteenth century. He appeared at a time when science had already begun to assume a dominant position in Western intellectual thought. For Freud, of all human institutions science offered us the greatest hope—religion had outlived its usefulness, and political institutions often worked to our detriment. If we could not afford to place our trust in science, we could not afford to place it anywhere. The predominant outlook in the natural sciences of Freud's day was positivistic, materialistic, and mechanistic. This basic orientation is quite apparent in Freud's writings, particularly the early ones.

At the same time, a countercurrent is evident in Freud's thinking. Outside the natural sciences, Western thought in the nineteenth century was strongly colored by the spirit of Romanticism. Freud claimed that he was inspired to pursue a career in medicine after hearing a lecturer read Goethe's poem on nature. Henri Ellenberger, whose monumental work on the history of the concept of the unconscious traces the roots of many of Freud's ideas, claims that Freud, Jung, and Adler all reflect very strongly the spirit of the Romantic era in their work—more than they reflect the spirit of the Englightenment.[2]

Freud's holistic concern with human experience was in keeping with Romanticism, and there were certainly elements in his basic temperament that resonated with the Romantic view of life, but his was a rather special blend of the nineteenth-century ingredients of Western

114

thought. Like other young people of his time, he had a classical education, studying Latin and Greek and reading the classics of various countries. He had an excellent command of the German language and at one time earned a prize for his literary skills, but he also had considerable fluency in French, English, Spanish, and Italian. He earned a bit of money in his youth by translating works from French and English into German. He read the works of British empiricists as well as those of the more idealistic philosophers who prevailed on the Continent. One of the books he translated was a volume of essays by John Stuart Mill. Combining a thorough grounding in materialistic science with an intense lifelong interest in the humanities, in some ways he was a man specially equipped to bring some of the rays of Western thought into a new focus.

It is possible to link Freud's ideas more specifically to a variety of precursors. Certainly his early work was in keeping with the tenor of the physiological theories of his time, and he was clearly influenced by the most conspicuous biological theorist of the nineteenth century, Charles Darwin. His views on instincts are patterned after those of Darwin, and his attempts to account biologically for the origins of society (in terms of the "primal horde") also continued a line of thought that had been pursued earlier by Darwin and by a number of ethnologists.

There is much less evidence that Freud was directly influenced by Karl Marx, the major social theorist of the nineteenth century. To be sure, there are some similarities between the two men. Both were Jews who had rejected the religion of their ancestors and declared themselves atheists. Both were concerned with the subjective ills wrought by modern society and had grave doubts about the beneficence of that society. Unlike Marx, however, Freud was inclined to look to biology for understanding rather than analyzing society itself. Furthermore, Marx, free as he was from a conventional religious view, still had the zeal and temperament of a religious prophet who wanted to transform society. Freud was primarily interested in uncovering scientific truth, content to assume that whatever he discovered would ultimately yield benefits for mankind.

A more important and direct influence on Freud's thinking came

115

from the philosophers who had dealt with the psychological domain to which Freud addressed himself. These included in particular those philosophers who had dealt extensively with the unconscious—Schopenhauer, Eduard von Hartmann, Nietzsche. Through the work of such men, philosophers for the most part accepted the idea of an unconscious mental life in the latter part of the nineteenth century. Freud knew this, of course, and liked to think of himself as the man who had brought an idea that was current in the realm of philosophy and literature into the province of science. Even this claim can certainly be contested, for at that time the unconscious was also an important concern of Johann Herbart, Gustav Fechner, Hermann Helmholtz, Michel Chevreul, Jules Héricourt, and others who were interested both in building psychological theories concerning unconscious mental activity and in providing empirical demonstrations. What Freud could do better than any of these people was to demonstrate to the world at large the importance of this idea. Even in the area of observation in which he was building his arguments, however, he was preceded to some extent by others, particularly Jean Martin Charcot. A still closer competitor was Pierre Janet, who was making similar observations and building similar theory at about the same time and in some respects in advance of Freud.

Of the philosophers the one who most conspicuously foreshadowed Freud was Nietzsche. Like Freud, Nietzsche had an elaborate concept of the unconscious, which he saw as a source of powerful instinctual forces and of influences both from the individual's past and from the past history of the species—Freud's concept of the id comes at least indirectly from Nietzsche. Nietzsche also had similar ideas regarding inner conflict, repression, and sublimation. In contrast to Freud, he placed more emphasis on aggressive and self-destructive forces than on sexual instincts, but Freud moved closer to Nietzsche's position in his later years. Freud was aware of the scope of Nietzsche's thought and regarded him as a man of incomparable insight into his own inner nature. He was so impressed with the great philosopher that he avoided reading Nietzsche for many years, to preclude too strong an influence on his own work. He wanted to remain an independent thinker, but even while avoiding Nietzsche he must have known that he was reexploring much of the ground that Nietzsche had already traversed.

With respect to other significant features of Freud's work there were precedents. Dreams were an important early focus for him. This was by no means a neglected area of human experience at the time, for throughout the Romantic era philosophers and writers had been interested in dreams and had formulated theories about them. Freud was quite familiar with the major works on dreams and investigations of dreams that had been published during the decades immediately preceding his own work in this area, and his *Interpretation of Dreams* contains a rather extensive review of them.[3] Previous writers had considered a great variety of factors that could influence the content of dreams—past life events, events of the immediately preceding day, stimuli impinging on the dreamer during sleep. Freud took all these factors into account, but his central thesis was the wish-fulfillment doctrine. Even here he was certainly not breaking new ground, however, for it had long been apparent to everyone who thought about such things that we tend to dream of things that we desire. To this bit of proverbial wisdom Freud added the debatable contention that dreams always represent fulfillments of wishes. Thus, his work on dreams does not represent a sudden eruption of novel ideas in Western thought; every major element in that work had been anticipated by other people. Yet it was Freud who managed to weave those elements together into an unprecedented masterpiece of theory construction. He managed at the same time to introduce dreams as a basic tool of psychotherapy. All things considered, *The Interpretation of Dreams* is not merely Freud's most significant theoretical work (as he well recognized) and the most important book ever written on dreams; it is probably the most important single book ever written in the whole realm of psychological theory.

Another conspicuous feature of Freud's work is the emphasis on sexuality. He recognized early the importance of sexual factors in the production of neurosis. Later he proceeded to stress the pervasive influence of sexual instincts in the entire realm of human affairs, saw them as operative from a point very early in life, and propounded a theory of human development that centers on the unfolding of these

117

instincts. Here Freud is often pictured as swimming bravely against the strong tide of Victorian morality, forcing the people of Western society to face the truth about their behavior and their motives, and launching a trend toward greater freedom of action and thought in the sexual sphere. Obviously Freud did stress the sexual side of human affairs more than his contemporaries in medicine and psychology, and he must be considered part of a liberalizing stream with respect to sexuality, but his role as key liberator has undoubtedly been exaggerated. Ellenberger says that what we often regard as the strait-laced Victorian outlook on morality and sex had already died out for the most part before Freud began to publish.[4] By the time that Freud began his work, sexual matters were treated quite frankly in the medical and anthropological literature. A widespread public interest in sexual expression of all kinds was evident in the content of books, journals, and newspapers. There was particularly strong interest in sexual pathology, and the work of such people as Krafft-Ebing had attracted widespread attention. The idea that diseases might represent disguised manifestations of sexual instincts or disturbances in the sex life of the patient was a familiar one in medicine. In the case of hysteria, the primary locus of Freud's earliest writings on psychopathology, the idea was in fact quite ancient.

Freud was inclined to regard himself as a lonely hero fighting against much opposition in his early years, remaining largely unrecognized in his homeland, but this picture cannot be altogether accurate. He managed to establish a very lucrative practice well before the turn of the century, and he apparently had no difficulty getting his writings published. Some of them attracted a great deal of attention. Inevitably any individual who attracts much attention in the world of ideas evokes both praise and adverse comment, and Freud was no exception. Various elements in his writings provoked discussion and criticism, but it is doubtful that his emphasis on sexuality was in itself an all-important point of contention. To write about sex in the latter part of the nineteenth century was a sure way to invite attention, but not necessarily condemnation. For all Freud's complaints about his home, Vienna, it was certainly one of the most cosmopolitan cities in Europe. He was well aware of this, and according to his own observations, in

118

continental Europe generally there was an openness with respect to sexual matters that did not prevail in what he referred to as "prudish America."

THE DEVELOPMENT OF FREUD'S IDEAS

Freud developed his ideas over a long period of time. While there is an overall coherence to his work, his concepts do not constitute one single unified theory. His publications span half a century, and in the course of that period many of his ideas underwent modification and revision.

Freud was born in Freiberg, Moravia, in 1856, but when he was still very small his family moved first to Leipzig and then to Vienna. Except for his final year, he spent the remainder of his life in that city. As a young man he had wide-ranging interests, but he thirsted particularly for scientific knowledge. He hoped to achieve eminence through contributions to scientific knowledge and theory, and the field he chose for a career was medicine. He had no strong interest in the practice of medicine, preferring instead to do research and hoping ultimately to seek a university post. Early in his career he worked in the laboratories of various prominent physiologists—Carl Claus, Ernst Brücke, Ewald Hering, Hermann Nothnagel, Theodor Meynert. He worked on many types of problems. He did histological research. In Claus's laboratory he studied the reproductive anatomy of the eel. More of his work, however, was in the realm of neuroanatomy and neuropathology. One of his early publications was a monograph on aphasia; it deals with a neurological disorder, of course, but it contains seeds of his later psychological theorizing.[5]

Of the physiologists with whom Freud worked, the one who evidently influenced him most strongly was Brücke. Brücke was a very staunch mechanist. He was strongly opposed to the vitalistic doctrines that appeared in the writings of some biologists and philosophers, and he felt that neither living matter nor conscious processes required the introduction of a unique set of laws or principles. Rather, psychological processes were to be understood in terms of physiology, and physio-

119

logical processes were to be understood in terms of the laws of physics and chemistry. Although Freud was to wander far from the domain of Brücke's endeavors, the impact of this early master was reflected in Freud's lifelong commitment to causality, and at least in principle to material causality. Although Freud's interest in physiological reduction certainly lessened over the years, he continued to believe that a thorough scientific understanding of psychological processes required linking them to events in the physiological substrate.

The year 1882 marked an important turning point in Freud's career, for it was then that he left Brücke's laboratory and became a practicing physician. He made this move reluctantly, since it meant abandoning purely scientific work for a career that had less appeal for him. Ernest Jones suggested that his decision at that time to marry and to start a family may have prompted him to follow a course a bit more lucrative than any the academic world could provide.[6] Ironically, the new and unwanted career proved a source of scientific insights and theoretical accomplishments that Freud might not otherwise have achieved.

Another important turning point came in 1885, when Freud went to Paris to study for several months with Jean Charcot, one of the most eminent neurologists of that time. Charcot was employing hypnosis to study and treat neurotics, and Freud was impressed with his work. He was even more profoundly impressed with the man, who seemed to manifest an intellectual brilliance he had never before encountered. Charcot more than anyone else inspired Freud to redirect his primary interest from neuropathology to psychopathology and to become involved with psychological methods of treatment.

From 1885 to 1894 Freud interacted closely with Josef Breuer, another physician engaged in the treatment of neurosis, and together the two men published papers dealing with hysteria. Early in this period Freud employed Charcot's method of hypnotic suggestion in treating his patients. Later, following Breuer's lead, he employed a "talking-out" technique. In this procedure, the patient was hypnotized and then allowed to achieve an emotional catharsis by talking about his life. Freud soon abandoned hypnosis altogether and employed the cathartic procedure without it.

In the course of this work Freud developed new ideas about the nature of the various conditions he was treating. He propounded a theory of anxiety, in which anxiety was interpreted as tension resulting from an inadequate release of sexual energy through normal direct expression. In other theoretical efforts, he explained the symptoms of hysteria and of obsessive-compulsive neurosis in terms of traumatic sexual experiences in childhood. The idea of early traumatic experiences was borrowed from Charcot, but the idea that sexual experiences were of exclusive etiological significance was Freud's own contribution. A little later Freud discovered that the early seductions so often reported by his hysterical patients were essentially fantasy creations of the patients rather than actual events; at that point, he decided that if he wished to understand neurosis it was not so essential to identify a few specific incidents in childhood as it was to understand the maturation of the sexual forces that caused the fantasies to arise.

In 1895 Freud wrote a paper entitled "Project for a Scientific Psychology." [7] The paper represents less an effort to present a completed theory than a program for theoretical work to be done. In it Freud set forth a neurological account of the brain and a theoretical model of the mind and mental processes and sought to relate the two. This was the work of a neuroanatomist who had redirected his energies into the psychological realm but who felt that all events in the newer territory had to be understood in terms of brain processes. The paper might be viewed as a written expression of a life-term scientific goal, and it is clear that it represents a matter about which Freud felt intense enthusiasm at the time that he wrote it. In other papers written in the 1890s Freud attempted to account for psychological processes on a neurological level, but there is little indication of such an effort in later writings. It is as if in making a written declaration of his lifelong goal Freud had freed himself to veer off onto detours that would take him far away from it.

The crowning achievement of that early decade, of course, was the *Interpretation of Dreams,* which was first published in 1900. In this book and in the *Psychopathology of Everyday Life,* which soon followed it, Freud first set forth a systematic account of the operation and expression of unconscious motives. Another major work, *Three Essays on the Theory of Sexuality,* appeared in 1905.[8] In it Freud not only attempted to elucidate the sexual roots of neurosis but also expounded a more general theory of human development in terms of a series of psychological stages.

By this time Freud's work had begun to attract attention in distant countries. A group of interested colleagues gathered around him to discuss theoretical issues, and distinguished men came from afar to talk to him and take part in the psychoanalytic movement. Among those who became involved in the movement during the first decade of this century were Carl Jung, Alfred Adler, Otto Rank, Karl Abraham, Sandor Ferenczi, Hanns Sachs, and Ernest Jones. In 1909 Freud was invited by G. Stanley Hall to lecture in the United States, and he made his only journey to America in the company of Carl Jung.

In the years that followed, Freud developed additional ideas about the overall structure of the psychic system and about the basic instincts. In his early psychological work the conscious-unconscious dichotomy is of major importance. Neurotic symptoms, accidents, slips of the tongue, and dreams are to be understood in terms of unconscious tendencies that run counter to the individual's consciously recognized intentions. In his later work Freud ceased to depict the conflicting forces in the personality as being so neatly aligned with consciousness and unconsciousness. The concepts of *ego* and *id* largely assume the roles in theory previously occupied by *conscious* and *unconscious.*

This change did not constitute an abandonment of earlier views so much as a pronounced shift in emphasis. The id is viewed as an unconscious system, a reservoir of instinctual forces. The ego, however, is not equated with consciousness, for it is both conscious and unconscious. It is to be understood not in terms of consciousness but in terms of the cognitive processes that it employs. While the id operates according to the pleasure principle and is oriented toward immediate gratification and relief, the ego operates according to the reality principle. It utilizes perception, takes the real situation into account, and is responsible for planned and deliberate action. It also has a protective, defensive function, however, and it sometimes operates in such a way as to reduce our awareness as well as to enhance it. In

122

general, it serves to channel our awareness and action in ways that, under ideal conditions, lead to maximal long-term satisfaction. A third agent, the superego, was also recognized by Freud. The superego is the internalized representative of the values of society. It embodies both prescriptions for desirable actions (the ego ideal) and proscriptions for unacceptable behavior (the conscience). In his later writings Freud interpreted psychopathology in terms of the interactions of the id, ego, and superego.

Another relatively late innovation in Freud's thinking was a revised theory of instincts. In early work he recognized only instincts that were concerned either with the preservation of life or with pleasure. He attended more to the latter, since sexuality seemed more germane to his theoretical pursuits than hunger or thirst. By 1920, he had apparently decided he could no longer ignore the fundamental importance of aggressive, destructive forces in the psyche, and he introduced a new classification of the instincts, in which they are seen as obeying either the *eros* principle or the *thanatos* principle. In the first group we have instincts concerned with the preservation of life, with growth, and with pleasure. In the second group are instincts that lead us back to the ultimate quiescence of inanimate matter—to our own inevitable death. Destructive impulses in general are viewed as derivatives of a basic instinctual tendency toward self-destruction.

FREUD'S MATURE VIEWS ON HUMAN PERSONALITY

Perhaps the concepts that come closest to providing the key to Freud's views on human nature are conflict, anxiety, and repression. From his earliest psychological works to the latest ones, he attempted to understand what he observed in terms of conflicting forces within the person. First the conflict was seen as one between conscious and unconscious forces. The unconscious forces tended to be pleasure-oriented. In later work the concern was more with conflict between forces oriented toward immediate gratification or pleasure (the id) and forces representing the dictates of society (the superego), with the reality-oriented ego entering as an additional party that might ally itself with, or oppose, either of the other two parties.

Repression is one basic way of dealing with the tension produced by conflict. By means of repression, an idea is rendered unavailable to consciousness. Most often, the ideas associated with id impulses are repressed, and we thereby become unaware of various sexual or aggressive impulses. As long as repression is successful, we are more comfortable. But in any situation that tends to arouse or strengthen the repressed impulse, the impulse threatens to break forth into expression. As a result, we experience anxiety. (Freud recognized other sources of anxiety, including real-life threats to life and limb, but the anxiety associated with repressed impulses is viewed as especially important for the understanding of neurosis.) To reduce the anxiety, we may employ additional defensive strategies that will serve to reinforce repression or keep the impulse under control.

In Freudian theory there are two basic ways of dealing with human development. One has to do with the transformation of cognitive functions, a progressive movement characterized by increasing control and reality contact—or to put it more concisely, with ego development. The ego emerges from the id and normally becomes stronger during the first part of life. The aim of psychoanalytic therapy is often stated in terms of strengthening the ego. Development also involves the emergence and growth of the superego (which, strictly speaking, was regarded by Freud as a part of the ego). This is an important aspect of development in Freudian theory, but it is considered less central than ego development. In fact, Freud viewed superego development as more episodic (less continuous) in character than ego development, since he ascribed the major contribution to superego formation to one phase of development.[9]

The other way of dealing with development is in terms of psychosexual stages, stages in the evolving expression of the sexual instincts. In infancy and early childhood, we pass through the three basic stages called oral, anal, and phallic. These names represent three sensitive tissue areas, or erogenous zones, in which the child invests interest or energy and from the stimulation of which he obtains sensual gratification. The three stages represent three successive forms of "narcissistic

124

cathexis." That is, they are stages of self-love, in which the child's interest is largely invested in his own body.

In the phallic stage, the child ordinarily manifests an Oedipus complex. In the case of the boy, this entails an experience of erotic love for the mother combined with jealousy or hostility toward the father. In the case of the girl, there is love for the father and jealousy toward the mother. Freudian theory contends that the boy is forced by castration anxiety to achieve a resolution of the Oedipus complex. Being confronted with the fact that some people (women) lack a penis, he fears that he may suffer castration and lose his own valued organ at the hands of his rival for the mother's affections. As a result, he relinquishes his claim and settles for the vicarious satisfaction possible through identification with his father. In the course of this resolution, he introjects a large part of his father's value system. Thus, as Freud said, the superego is "the heir to the Oedipus complex."

In the case of the girl, the awareness of the anatomical difference between the sexes has more to do with the onset of the Oedipus complex than with its resolution. The girl discovers that she lacks the prized organ of the male and feels cheated. Her love contains a strong element of identification with the father, who possesses the organ she would like to possess herself. The girl experiences a less pressing need to resolve the Oedipus complex than does the boy, and she does so gradually as it becomes evident that she cannot usurp the position of her mother.

From about age five until puberty, the child is said to be in a latency period—a period in which sexual energies are largely directed away from any sort of direct expression and no new forms of cathexis, or energy investment, appear. Upon reaching sexual maturity, if all goes well, the individual is ready to enter the genital stage. This stage is characterized by the emergence of "true object cathexes"; i.e., the individual is now able to manifest genuine love for another person of the opposite sex. Presumably, earlier attachments (to parents, for example) reflected the child's dependent condition; he cared for the individual who took care of him. In the true object cathexis, he cares for another person for the sake of that person. As the term *genital stage* implies, the mature relationship has a sexual side, but personal sensual gratification is now just one aspect of a new kind of relationship and is not the all-important goal that it was in the phallic stage.

Freudian theory also assumes that in the case of the female a shift occurs in the locus of erotic gratification. As the use of the term *phallic* indicates, it is not the sexual organs in general that are valued in early childhood, but the penis, and to some extent in the female, its counterpart, the clitoris. In progressing to the genital stage, the female undergoes a shift from the clitoris to the vagina as the primary locus of gratification.

Every facet of the psychosexual theory of development has been subjected to heavy criticism at one time or another. For the purposes of the present book, it is not necessary to review or to extend this criticism in detail, but a few obvious points may be noted here. Probably no Freudian concept has been criticized more often than the Oedipus complex. Most critics would grant that Freud's descriptions fit some individuals, but Freud assumed that they were universally applicable, and there has been much debate regarding the extent to which the concept of the Oedipus complex fits all individuals in our own society or in others.

Freud's formulations are particularly vulnerable as applied to women. His theory assumes that all children discover the anatomical difference between the sexes in early childhood and that both boys and girls conclude from this that it is better to be male. While this may be a likely outcome in some male-dominated societies, it is conceivable, as some writers contend, that "womb envy" comes closer to being a universal phenomenon than does "penis envy." In any case, Freud assumed that in the phallic stage the girl really wants to experience pleasure in the same way that the boy does and that she must settle for an inferior version of the penis, the clitoris. To attain a psychosexual maturity, she must later recognize that she is anatomically designed to receive the male rather than to function in the same way as the male, and she must seek gratification through the vagina rather than the clitoris. To psychoanalysts this implies a qualitative shift in the kind of orgasm sought by the female. The distinction between the clitoral orgasm and the vaginal orgasm seems to run counter to all pertinent biological evidence gathered to date, however. It is also doubtful that it can be supported on psychological grounds alone. From a sheerly subjective standpoint, orgasms may be regarded as subject to considerable qualitative variation in both males and females. There is not much evidence that this variation conforms very neatly in females to a clitoral-vaginal dichotomy.

Altogether, there is much in the psychosexual theory of development that has been construed as demeaning to women. Perhaps it is to Freud's credit that he did not pretend to have a thorough understanding of women. A remark he once made to Marie Bonaparte has been often quoted: "The great question that has never been answered and which I have not yet been able to answer, despite my thirty years of research into the feminine soul, is 'What does a woman want?' "

The concepts of psychosexual development and of psychic structure that we have discussed were all introduced originally to account for psychopathology. Hence, they are the basic concepts through which neurosis and psychosis are understood in Freudian theory. In the perspective of the developmental theory, psychopathology is explained in terms of fixations at the early stages of development. Each of us in the course of maturing continues to have a certain amount of energy tied up in the cathexes that appeared early in life. We continue to have some need for oral, anal, and phallic gratification, and we do not completely outgrow our early emotional attachments to our parents. In the development of the individual who becomes neurotic or psychotic, however, some disturbance in the early years causes an abnormal amount of energy to remain invested, or fixated, in these early orientations. If the fixation is not superficially apparent in the succeeding years of growth, it may suddenly become evident at a much later point in life, when the individual is confronted with a fresh problem and, unable to cope with it successfully, he retreats, or regresses, to the mode of adjustment corresponding to the early fixation. Thus the hysteric is said to regress to the phallic stage, and the obsessive-compulsive to the anal stage. The most profound regression occurs in the schizophrenic, who undergoes a wholesale regression to the oral stage. On the whole, regression tends to be evident in more restricted aspects of behavior in neurotics than in psychotics. The early mode of adjustment may not appear in a very direct form of expression of infantile sexual impulses. The impulse, though strong, has been re-pressed, and the neurotic symptom constitutes a disguised, symbolic form of expression, generally said to represent both the infantile wish and the repressing force that opposes its direct expression.

In terms of the structural concepts, psychopathology may be viewed in general as a failure of ego functioning, since it always entails some loss of reality contact. The ego weakness is clearest in the case of the psychoses, where reality is disavowed and replaced with delusion. In the neurotic, the loss is more selective, and the neurotic may simply ignore or avoid a part of reality rather than deliberately contradicting it. He may simply fail to attend to some aspect of the social world around him, to some part of his body, or to his own feelings. The neuroses are characterized by a conflict between the ego and the id, which results in the repression of id impulses by the ego. The ego is operating in this case in the service of the superego. Freudian theory assumes that psychoses start in essentially the same way, with frustration of id impulses, but that the ego is weaker in the individual who becomes psychotic. Instead of maintaining control and repressing the impulses of the id, the ego gives way to the id and contact with reality is lost. Freud also distinguished a third group of disorders, which he called the narcissistic neuroses, which involve a conflict between the ego and the superego. He viewed these disorders as more closely akin to the psychoses than to the conditions ordinarily classified as neuroses.

On the whole, it may be said that Freud expressed a rather negative view of human nature. He felt that people are largely governed by rather primitive impulses of which they are unaware. At the same time he presented an equally negative view of human society, which seemed bound by its nature to produce discontent. Perhaps Freud's views were colored by the fact that he was a member of a cultural outgroup subject to varying amounts of discrimination within Austrian society. In any case, he saw all present-day societies as characterized by exploitation of one group by another. He perceived aggressive conflict at the very roots of society. In *Totem and Taboo,* originally published in 1913, he presented his notion of the primal horde, the original unit in which one male dominates and claims all the females as his own property until his sons succeed in killing him and one of them then claims the position of power.[10] In this primitive setting Freud discerned the origins of the Oedipus complex and of a host of societal customs.

In the Freudian view, it is in the nature of society that any individual or group in power will seek to prevent the free expression of impulses in those who are not in power. Thus, there is an inherent conflict between civilization and instinctual gratification and between the individual and the society in which he lives. In viewing society as a system that inhibits natural expression and pleasure, Freud was in agreement with the earlier Romantics, including Diderot and Rousseau, who felt that the benefits of civilization were gained at the cost of the natural happiness of the Natural Man. Freud obviously had some doubts as to whether civilization was worth the sacrifices that it entailed. He saw the great harm caused by the repression of sexuality, but he rejected an unbridled hedonism as a solution to the problem. Certainly, he would not have espoused the cause of anarchy, for he was not convinced that the "natural" condition, devoid of social regulations, was such a happy state. He saw a need for a social system that would regulate the expression of human aggression. If society was not needed primarily to regulate pleasure, it was needed to prevent unnecessary pain, but the two are inseparable since one person's pursuit of pleasure may lead to another's pain.

Freud saw society as necessary but also as fraught with inherent dangers. The dictates of the society tend to be incorporated by the individual, who then applies them himself through his own superego. Then his actions and his thoughts become an occasion for guilt. In Freud's view the guilt was not altogether undesirable, but he saw the development of civilization as bound up with an increase in guilt and wondered whether it would build to an intolerable point. He felt that a fairly strong superego was a good thing (he had one himself), as it is responsible for most of the actions that we perform for the benefit of others. By virtue of the formation of the superego, of course, the inherent conflict between the individual and society is mirrored in a basic inner conflict between egoistic and altruistic impulses.[11]

Under the best circumstances, a society would operate for the maximal benefit of all its members. Many people have envisioned such a society, based on love or mutual interest. Freud not only felt that societies did not originate in this way: he was skeptical of the possibility of creating such a society. Obviously he viewed love in its immature forms as fundamentally subversive, as one of the basic forces that societies were designed to inhibit. He had greater hope for the possibility of a society governed by the rational authority of the ego. He pursued this theme in his main work on religion, *The Future of an Illusion*.[12] In that book he spoke of religion as an illusion that serves to protect people both from the threats posed by nature and from the threats posed by society. He saw religious belief as analogous to an obsessional neurosis, perhaps necessary so long as we must control our instinctual impulses by repression. The desirable alternative for Freud would entail placing more faith in science, seeking greater understanding, and making greater use of the rational operation of the intellect. He expressed doubt about the capacity of people for moving quickly in this direction, however, and did not foresee a society based on reason as a likely prospect for mankind's near future.

FREUD'S VIEW OF THE OPTIMAL CONDITION

Psychoanalytic theory was basically designed to account for psychopathology, rather than conditions regarded as desirable or ideal. Hence, it lends itself readily to a conception of the optimal condition as an absence of pathology or of conditions associated with pathology. Yet Freud himself recognized that a given pathogenic situation might lead to neurosis in one individual and not in another, and he thereby had occasion to consider factors that afforded resistance to psychopathology. He really had no concepts, however, for dealing with the individual of superior accomplishment and sensitivity. Even in writing about Leonardo da Vinci, he produced pathography.[13] Though he did not consider Leonardo a neurotic, he accounted for his unusual qualities in terms of disturbances in development.

What qualities would Freud consider desirable? One of the most obvious is that represented by the notion of a strong ego. From this standpoint, the ideal person is intellectually competent, is highly rational, and acts on the basis of a realistic appraisal of himself and of his environment. In Freud's early work this basic idea is represented by an emphasis on consciousness. This remains a part of the picture in so far as the ego is an agent of consciousness and of self-awareness, but in later work primary importance is attached to reality contact and rationality, rather than to consciousness per se.

An emphasis on independence and originality is part of the same picture. An individual lacks autonomy as long as his ego and ego ideal remain closely identified with the parents or with the group of which the individual is a part. Through participation in many groups, we gradually develop egos and ego ideals that do not depend heavily on any one source, and we then have the capacity for acting independently of any particular group. While Freud rejected the concept of free will, it is evident that something on the order of self-determination or self-direction, however conceptualized, was very important to him. In stressing independence, realism, and rationality, Freud was following the tradition of the Enlightenment more than that of Romanticism. He admired poets and artists, but his system does not really provide adequate tools for conceptualizing aesthetic creativity and can treat it only in terms of a combination of the pleasure and reality principles, or a balanced operation of id and ego. In a similar vein, Ernst Kris spoke of "regression in the service of the ego." [14] In treating development in terms of a growing capacity for realistic thinking, rather than in terms of a capacity for creative functioning, Freud in effect advocated the detached scientific observer, or Scientific Man, as the model for an ideal person.

The emphasis on the ego is balanced in Freud's thinking by a second notion of the ideal condition, represented by the concept of genital character. This is a concept that is concerned more with a capacity for genuine love, for relatedness, for altruistic concern for the welfare of another person. Here he drew on another major theme in Western thought, but in a rather restricted way, for his concern was primarily with the capacity for one intimate relationship rather than a capacity for relating in a loving way to people in general.

Two other, less central themes in Freud's view of the ideal should be noted. One is the superego. Although the superego can be a source of problems, it is important from a Freudian standpoint to possess the moral qualities that depend on a well developed superego. The other theme is sublimation. Freud felt that primitive instinctual impulses that are denied expression may be expressed indirectly through many very constructive activities as well as through neurotic symptoms. Normally during the latency period we learn many of the means for sublimating our basic impulses and expressing them in a constructive and socially acceptable way. Freud felt that many of the great artistic and cultural accomplishments of mankind depended on the sublimation of sexuality and aggression. Thus, a capacity for sublimation could be considered one characteristic of a superior individual.

At one time, when asked what a normal or healthy person should be able to do, Freud replied simply: "Lieben und arbeiten"—to love and to work. This is a concise way of summarizing all the ideas contained in the concepts we have just examined, for they all involve either a capacity for relating or a capacity for functioning competently in the world. Most centrally they involve rationality and altruism, and in espousing these two elements Freud expressed two of the basic themes in Western thought. They correspond to the modes of fulfillment that I have called relatedness and efficiency.

SIX

CARL JUNG AND ANALYTICAL PSYCHOLOGY

In June 1961, a spiritual leader in Ceylon remarked to his disciples, "A great yogi has died." There was only one individual in the Western world whose death could have occasioned such a comment. Carl Jung was 85 years old when he died; by then he had come to be known by many people throughout the West as "the wise old man of Küsnacht." Although he was fundamentally a product of the Western world, he was widely regarded in the Orient as the one Western psychologist who had achieved the basic insights of Eastern culture.

Since Jung's analytical psychology is in part an offshoot of psychoanalysis, it shares many of the same roots and must be viewed as a product of the same period and setting in European thought. Henri Ellenberger says that analytical psychology, like psychoanalysis, is a late product of Romanticism and that it embodies the spirit of that movement in a more consistent way.[1] The scientism, positivism, and Darwinism that colored Freud's thinking seem to be absent from Jung's. Freud's early views were very much in line with the predominantly materialistic outlook in the natural sciences, but Jung, while intensely interested in science in his youth, saw that outlook as a barrier to intellectual progress. He was interested in mediums and spiritistic phenomena and wanted to study them without being hampered by any preconceptions regarding the reality of underlying processes.

Like Freud, Jung was trained in medicine but had wide-ranging interests that extended far beyond that field. Like Freud, he sought

133

early to understand psychopathology but hoped to provide a comprehensive account of human experience. In the work of Freud and Jung, we find the most comprehensive theoretical systems ever devised by individual psychologists. In many respects, Jung's system is the more comprehensive, and in all, Jung was probably the man of more massive erudition. To a greater extent than Freud he used as his data base the whole realm of human thought and expression, rather than just his immediate clinical observations. In his youth he read works of the leading European thinkers of the nineteenth century, including Schopenhauer, Goethe, and Nietzsche, and was influenced by them. He also read the works of mystics like Meister Eckhart and Emanuel Swedenborg. Later he studied many other realms of thought—the writings of the alchemists, the gnostics, mythology. He had abiding interests in ethnology and archaeology, and in the course of his life he managed to travel widely and study life in a variety of cultures. He spent some time among the Pueblo Indians of New Mexico, in tribal settings in Kenya and Uganda, in North Africa, and in India. He had a great interest in Oriental thought and had much contact with such men as Richard Wilhelm and Heinrich Zimmer, who devoted their careers to the study of it.

In seeking to understand Eastern thought and comparing it with Western outlooks, Jung may have achieved some insights that would not have been possible if he had confined his attention to just one part of the world. In a number of his writings he contrasted Eastern and Western views and apparently found both to be one-sided.[2] Each outlook is deficient and each has something to offer that the other lacks. He expressed doubts about the blessings of Western civilization and questioned the value of its adoption by the East, but he had similar misgivings about the adoption of Eastern spirituality by the West. He felt that the Westerner, when confronted with a discipline such as yoga, tends either to reject it altogether without due consideration or to fall into the trap of faith and simply swallow it uncritically. The Western person is not properly prepared by his own background to follow the Eastern path in the way that someone who has grown up in the Orient would. He felt the West needed to find its own paths of liberation instead of borrowing those of the East.

Jung described the difference between the East and the West in terms of introversion and extraversion. The Western individual is extraverted in the sense that he finds greatest certainty in the material realm, while the Easterner is more certain of the psychic realm. Another way of putting this is that the Westerner projects meaning outward and regards it as existing in objects; the Easterner finds meaning within himself. According to Jung, the meaning is both without and within.[3] He also suggested that the Eastern view is the more defensible one insofar as psychic existence is the only category of existence of which we have immediate knowledge or verifiability.

Another difference between East and West that concerned Jung was that having to do with the universality or individuality of mind. According to Jung, the basic position of Eastern thought is that the individual mind is merely a manifestation of the one universal mind, while the Western view is that individual minds are indeed separate. Jung contended that there is really no intellectual way of determining which position is correct, but he seemed personally to lean more heavily toward the Western view. He noted that the idea of a "world mind" is not really foreign to Western thought and that the idea of the separate individual mind is a modern conception. He saw the stress on individuality as tied to an emphasis on consciousness, for it is in the realm of consciousness that things become differentiated and experienced as discrete. In the unconscious, distinctions are lost, and every element is contaminated with the totality. It was in terms of this "all-contamination in the unconscious" that Jung accounted for the sense of oneness or mystical unity that we experience when we relax the discriminations of conscious thought.[4] For Jung the discriminative power of conscious thought was very important, and he felt that the East tends to underrate it, but he also felt that the Western world tends to underrate the much larger realm of the unconscious. There are additional aspects to this matter that we shall be in a better position to consider after we have reviewed the basic ingredients of Jung's theoretical system.

THE DEVELOPMENT OF JUNG'S IDEAS

Jung is often pictured as a disciple of Freud who departed from the fold in 1913 and proceeded from that time to deviate from a Freudian position. In two important respects this picture is inaccurate. For one thing, many of Jung's major ideas predate his exposure to Freudian theory. For another, some of Freud's most central theses were never accepted by Jung.

Both Freud and Jung grew up and lived in the German-speaking region of Europe, but in other respects their cultural backgrounds differed. While Freud was of Jewish ancestry and spent nearly all his life in Vienna, Jung was born in Switzerland and lived there throughout his life. His father was a Protestant minister, and others in the family had been prominent figures in the Church. While Jung had many complaints about the Church and about doctrinaire approaches to religion, there is no doubt that his weltanschauung was tempered by an early exposure to Christian theology.

During his school years Jung had strong interests in such fields as philosophy and archaeology that competed with his growing interest in science. Ultimately he decided upon a career in medicine, and before completing his medical studies he chose to specialize in psychiatry. Unlike Freud, he was never able to muster much enthusiasm for the details of anatomy and physiology. Shortly after completing his studies, he undertook a residency under the supervision of the eminent psychiatrist Eugen Bleuler at the Burghölzli Psychiatric Hospital in Zürich.

In his later years Jung worked mostly with neurotic patients who could afford analytic treatment, but at the Burghölzli he worked primarily with psychotic patients from the lower social strata. In this respect his early psychiatric experience was much different from Freud's, and it is quite possible that the universal symbols manifested in the symptoms of his psychotic patients had much to do with launching him on a course that could not quite merge with that of his Viennese colleague.

While at the Burghölzli Jung began a series of experiments with the word-association test at the request of Bleuler. In effect, he developed the first projective test in the course of this work, using word associations to detect and analyze complexes. Actually, neither the word-association test itself nor the concept of the complex was altogether new, but Jung's work served to enhance the general usefulness of this approach to diagnosis. It also provided an occasion for him to develop some of his ideas about the unconscious.

Two other features of this period in Jung's career may be noted. First, as a result of his work at the Burghölzli, he produced a volume entitled *The Psychology of Dementia Praecox*. Second, he became progressively interested and involved in the work of Freud. In 1907 he went to visit Freud in Vienna. The two men met early in the afternoon and continued conversing, almost without interruption, for thirteen hours. It was evidently a momentous occasion for both of them. Jung had known such prominent figures in psychiatry as Bleuler and Pierre Janet, but he regarded Freud as the "first man of real importance" he had encountered, a man of true genius. Freud recognized in the younger man an intellectual brilliance of an order that he had not found in his other associates.

Freud soon began to think of Jung as his "son and heir," his intellectual successor—the man who would carry the banners of psychoanalysis and lead the movement when he could no longer do so himself. He seemed intent on pushing Jung into a prominent role in the movement. Thus, when the International Psychoanalytical Association was founded in 1910, he regarded Jung as the one logical person to be its president. Jung, for his own part, naturally assumed the role of a son early in the relationship in the sense that he greatly admired Freud and saw him as a more mature man from whom he could learn a great deal, but the pressures exerted on him by Freud proved a source of embarrassment to him. He did not relish the role of organizational leadership. It seemed an unnecessary burden that did not suit his needs or his temperament. Still more disconcerting was the fact that Freud apparently expected him to champion doctrines that he had never been able personally to accept.

Jung clearly valued his own intellectual independence more than any prestige that might come from assuming a leading role in the psychoanalytic movement. He felt that Freud had made a major contribution to the intellectual world by developing a method for exploring the unconscious, but he harbored many doubts about the theories that Freud had devised to account for his findings. He had never been convinced of the importance of the infantile sexual traumata stressed in

Freud's early work, and he could not accept the doctrine of psycho-sexual development that succeeded it. For Jung, the first three or four years of life constituted a presexual period, and the Oedipus complex was at best a deviant condition rather than a universal pattern. He preferred to see neurosis as an expression of the current life situation rather than a product of events in early childhood, and he felt that Freud grossly over-emphasized sexual symbolism. Jung appreciated Freud's work on dreams as a contribution to methodology, but from the outset he had reservations about the dream theory—particularly Freud's idea that dream symbols serve to disguise the underlying content. Jung believed that the essential function of any natural symbol was to express content, not to conceal it.

The sexual theory of neurosis was perhaps the greatest obstacle to a continued friendship between Freud and Jung, for Freud saw it as the most essential thesis of psychoanalysis and told Jung that it was necessary to make a dogma of it. Jung persisted in pursuing his own thoughts, and his intellectual divergence became more and more evident. The high expectations that Freud had maintained for him made a break between them all the more inevitable, and in 1913 Jung resigned from the Psychoanalytic Association and had no further contact with Freud thereafter. Undoubtedly there were important elements in the personalities of both men that affected the course of their interaction, but we need not attempt to analyze them at length here.[5]

Jung had held a post at the university in Zürich since 1905. In 1914 he resigned from that position, and until 1919 he devoted himself to private practice and published very little. From his own accounts, however, this was a very important period, for he spent much of his time exploring his own unconscious. He analyzed his dreams and made extensive use of procedures that came to be known later as active imagination. It was during this period that he developed his basic understanding of the individuation process and of such basic structures as the anima, the shadow, and the self—the most basic concepts that run through his later writings. Ellenberger surmised that this was a period of "creative illness," comparable to one that Freud experienced in the 1890s—a period in which Jung underwent a major personality transformation and emerged with the insights and energy needed to found and lead a new school of thought.[6] The period was followed by many productive years in which Jung wrote voluminously. In 1921 he published *Psychological Types,* one of his best-known books and in many respects his most outstanding single work.[7] Jung preferred to regard himself as an independent thinker who never ceased to search for the truth, rather than as a founder of a school, and he was never one to build organizations. The founding of the C. G. Jung Institute in Zürich in 1948 required a good deal of effort and pressure on the part of such followers as Jolande Jacobi.

Some of the differences in theory between Freud and Jung can be understood in terms of differences between the personalities of the two men. Jung, who always viewed intellectual products as expressions of the individuals who produced them, suggested this himself. In *Psychological Types* he not only argued that one can trace extraverted and introverted streams in Western thought to Aristotle and Plato, he extended that reasoning to the psychological systems of Freud, Adler, and himself. He saw the Freudian outlook as extraverted because of its emphasis on environmental determinants of character. Adlerian theory he viewed as introverted because of its emphasis on the inner attitude, embodied in such concepts as the will to power and guiding fictions. His own system, with its more elaborate treatment of the inner world, is also introverted. The implication is that Freud was an extravert, whereas Adler and Jung were introverts. This analysis is bound to seem puzzling to anyone who is at all familiar with the lives of the three men. Only Jung's analysis of himself seems to fit. Adler was certainly the most extraverted of the three, at least if we judge from accounts of his later years, while Freud appeared to possess an extensive private world that he did not share with others.

Ira Progoff offers one possible solution to the puzzle: he says that Freud was basically an introvert who repressed his own introversion.[8] Thus, Freud regarded introversion as a precondition for psychopathology and stressed an extraverted ideal as the model of health—the individual attuned to objective reality (the well-developed ego) who invests his interests outside himself (the true object cathexis). He had difficulty perceiving and accepting his own introversion. In contrast, Jung seems to have been much more comfortable with his introversion. In his autobiography, he pictures himself throughout life as an individual with an elaborate inner world. Indeed, the autobiography is largely concerned with the development of that inner world, rather than with outer events. It is hardly the sort of account that an extraverted author would have written. Progoff suggests that Jung became more markedly introverted in the course of his life and that he underwent a shift from a thinking-function type in his youth to that of an intuitive type in his later years.

Progoff suggests that Alfred Adler was forced by severe illness in childhood to focus on his inner world and develop as an introvert but that as an adult he became progressively more extraverted. From the accounts of people who knew Adler, he appears to have been a rather aloof, seclusive young man who preferred to be alone much of the time. Ernest Jones, who knew him in the period of his association with Freud, describes him as "morose and cantankerous." He changed over the years, however, and was seen by most people in his later years as a very warm and sociable person, a man who relished almost constant social interaction during his waking hours. There are corresponding shifts in the focus of his theorizing, too, from an early emphasis on inferiority and compensation to a later emphasis on *Gemeinschaftsgefühl.* In his later work he certainly stressed an extraverted ideal of adjustment, and he seems to have come close to fulfilling the ideal himself.

Progoff's characterizations of Freud, Adler, and Jung with respect to the introvert-extravert polarity are based mainly on social behavior, which from a strictly Jungian standpoint would be a rather indirect indicator of the basic type, but they are probably essentially correct. Assuming a Jungian view of human temperament, perhaps we could summarize most of the personal data on this matter by saying that Jung remained true to his basic nature, while Freud constantly strove to be something that he was not and failed, and Adler, though forced in early life to be something that he was not, finally succeeded in fulfilling his own destiny. To this overall picture, I would add a couple of qualifications. For one thing, Jung's analysis oversimplifies the three theoretical systems. There is much concern with environmental influences in Adler's work, but this is more true of the work that came after

Jung wrote his analysis than it had been before. Freud on the other hand could not reasonably have been described in 1921 as an extreme environmentalist. As I have noted, the conflict between inner and outer forces is basic to his system. He may seem an extraverted theorist when compared with Jung, but compared with some varieties of behaviorism, his theoretical position is a highly introverted one.

The other point I would make is that if we want to do a very adequate job of relating theory to the temperament of the theorist, we shall need additional personality constructs. *Introversion* and *extraversion* encompass only part of the territory. Progoff acknowledges this point in effect in noting the shift from thinking to intuition in Jung's own personality, a shift accompanied by changes in his style of production as a theorist. It is useful to apply Jung's function concepts to Freud and Adler as well. Freud's emphasis on detached objectivity and rational analysis indicates a preference for thinking over feeling. Adler's work suggests more emphasis on feeling, and in the course of his life Adler seems to have changed from a feeling introvert to a feeling extravert. In terms of concepts that I have used elsewhere to characterize theoretical orientations, both Jung and Adler are fluid types, while Freud, in comparison, is a more restrictive type of theorist but, compared with psychological theorists in general, his position is a moderate one. (In general, fluid theorists are holistic and subjectivistic and tend to deal with human existence in all its complexity, while restrictive theorists stress order and control in both observation and theory.) [9]

Needless to say, many of the generalizations we might make about the personalities of these three theorists would apply as well to the people who are drawn most strongly to their respective camps. Granting the inevitable pitfalls in sweeping generalizations, I would suggest that Freudians on the whole are more likely than Jungians or Adlerians to delight in intellectual analysis, while Jung has somewhat greater appeal for introverts who like to sense the meaning in symbols. Extraverts who prefer to focus on the interpersonal realm rather than the inner world are likely to find the later works of Adler much more meaningful than those of Freud or Jung. To the extent that differences in theoretical orientations are rooted in differences in termperament, of course, there is little prospect of reconciling them. If that sounds pessimistic, think how much duller the world of psychology would be if the reconciliation were accomplished.

JUNG'S MAJOR CONCEPTS

We might best begin our consideration of Jung's concepts by examining in greater detail the typology that we have just applied. Jung's typological scheme is essentially a three-dimensional system of classification that allows for a total of sixteen fully developed types. The individual is characterized in terms of those qualities that predominate in his conscious adaptations. The most important dimension in the system is that of the two opposing attitudes, introversion and extraversion. Extraversion is understood in terms of an "outward turning of libido," or psychic energy. This means that the individual's interest is invested primarily in the objective realm (i.e., in people and objects in the world around him). As a consequence, his actions, thought, feelings, and decisions are determined primarily by objective conditions—by events occurring in the environment. Introversion on the other hand is understood in terms of an "inward turning of libido." Interest is invested mainly in the subjective realm—in the experiences and psychological processes of the individual himself. In this case, actions, decisions, thoughts, and feelings are governed more by the individual's own predispositions and are less likely to represent direct responses to the outer object.

In addition to the two attitudes, Jung distinguishes four psychic functions, thinking, feeling, sensation, and intuition. Thinking and feeling are said to be rational functions, in the sense that they are concerned with the formation of judgments. Sensation and intuition are considered irrational functions, since they are more concerned with the immediate perception or apprehension of things and events. Thinking is defined as a function concerned with judgments about truth; it deals with facts and ideas. Feeling is concerned with evaluative judgments. An individual who emphasizes feeling would be less interested in determining whether something is true than with deciding whether it is good, desirable, or beautiful. Sensation is the function that focuses on

142

the immediate contents of experience, whether these are conceived in terms of the objective reality that elicits the experience or in terms of the sensory effect. Intuition is concerned with something less immediately evident, with possibilities experienced as inherent in the experienced situation. To the individual who stresses intuition, the raw data of experience are viewed as relatively unimportant in themselves and are used as a symbolic ingress to a less obvious reality.

The specific mode of manifestation of each function would depend on whether it is combined with introversion or extraversion. Thus, the thinking extravert would seek truth in the realm of objective data or facts, while the thinking introvert would seek it in the realm of ideas. The feeling extravert is more likely than the introvert to find positive value in the outer realm, and his judgments are more likely to be governed by available traditions and standards. The sensation extravert tends to be oriented toward concrete reality, while the sensation introvert emphasizes the subjective side of perception—his own sensations and images. The intuition extravert seeks possibilities in the objective realm: in people, in the business world, in the physical environment, in mechanical devices, etc. The intuition introvert is more likely to be concerned with symbols that point to a deeper psychological reality.

Jung assumes that both attitudes and all four functions operate in every individual. In the course of ordinary living we shift from one attitude to the other and from one function to another. An individual can be said to approximate a certain type only to the extent that he characteristically favors certain of these elements in his conscious functioning. Jung's typological scheme assumes that to the extent that any of the elements is so favored, its opposite will tend to be suppressed and to operate with less conscious awareness and control. Sometimes the unconscious function manifests itself in a lapse in organized functioning, as seen, for example, in the individual of the thinking type who falls in love and experiences feelings with which he has not learned to cope.

In some individuals the characteristic balance may be evident even in infancy. Ordinarily in the course of development the dominant attitude first becomes apparent. The most preferred function, which is

143

called the superior function, emerges next. Its opposite (thinking in the case of feeling, feeling in the case of thinking, sensation in the case of intuition, and intuition in the case of sensation) will be the inferior function—the function least developed in consciousness. At this stage, there would be eight possible types (either attitude combined with a superior function). Still later the individual may display a preference for one of the functions of the remaining pair, which will then serve as an auxiliary function supporting the operation of the superior function in conscious adaptations. Since both attitudes and all four functions necessarily operate and are essential for certain purposes, all of these elements tend ultimately to be integrated to some extent into conscious functioning in the course of development.

Jung distinguishes three basic levels within the psyche: consciousness, the personal unconscious, and the collective unconscious. In Jungian theory, the term *ego* is nearly equivalent to *consciousness,* but the latter term simply implies awareness, whereas the former implies a certain organization. For Jung, the ego is the conscious complex—the system or constellation of contents and operations utilized in conscious functioning. Thus, the individual type designation indicates the attitude and functions that are integrated into the ego. The personal unconscious contains content that has been repressed or forgotten—content that accumulates in the course of the individual's lifetime but which can be made conscious.

Of greater interest to Jung is the collective unconscious. This consists of the archetypes. Unlike the contents of the personal unconscious, the archetypes are not a product of the present lifetime. They are inherited dispositions, representing tendencies that have developed over many generations and that are universal within the species. If we think of them as evolutionary products comparable to instincts and anatomical structures, they would presumably be subject to the same sort of individual and subspecies variation that those manifestations are, but Jung did not deal very directly with this issue in his writings and was apparently uninterested in developing a biological rationale for the formation of the archetypes. In any case, the notion of the archetype is closely akin to that of the instinct, with one essential difference. We usually think of the instinct as manifested in action, whereas the archetype is characteristically manifested in experience. The recurring experiences or images governed by an archetype may be distilled in the form of a symbol. The symbol is thus an expression of the archetype, and the recurrence of very similar symbolic patterns in dreams, art, mythology, and religion throughout the world constitutes the primary basis for postulating the existence of the archetypes. According to Jung, the archetypes as such can never be directly observed or experienced; we know of them only through symbols.

A question often raised is whether Jung assumed that the individual has immediate access to psychic contents arising outside his own mind and inaccessible through sense perception. Obviously through the collective unconscious the individual has access to contents that are transpersonal in the sense that they are common to the species and not individualized in form. Yet if the archetypes are construed as inherited tendencies, then the collective unconscious is still personal in the sense that each individual has his own separate collective unconscious. Even if my collective unconscious is identical with yours, I do not have direct access through the contents of mine to the contents of yours. Throughout his life, however, Jung was interested in paranormal phenomena of all kinds, and he was clearly convinced by his own experience of the existence of such things as telepathy. This is a realm that he never managed to handle successfully in theory, but it was one of the things that led him to introduce the principle of synchronicity.[10]

Evidently Jung continued to struggle with this problem throughout his life. Progoff tells us that in his later years Jung began to distinguish a fourth stratum of the psyche, below the collective unconscious, that he called the psychoid level. Apparently at this level we have a realm of mind not so clearly confined to the individual person. According to Progoff, "the psychoid level is open to influences of every possible kind. It is accessible to whatever forces and factors happen to be present at a given moment in the continuum of the Self, whether these are factors operating within one's own psyche, within the psyche of others, or whether they are forces of any other kind active in the universe."[11]

In addition to distinguishing three or four components of the psyche in terms of levels of awareness, Jung distinguished a number of components that may be viewed as subpersonalities. The most important of these are the persona, the shadow, the self, and the anima and animus. These are comparable to the ego in the sense that each one is a function complex that commands a certain amount of the total energy of the psyche and is thus capable of influencing experience and behavior. Each has an archetypal core that causes it to form and develop in every individual, but various contents, functions, feelings, and attitudes become associated with this core. These are subject to some individual variation because they depend on the life experiences of the individual, and they depend on what function and contents are integrated into the ego. Each of these subpersonalities may include both conscious and unconscious elements.

The persona contains the greatest proportion of conscious elements and is often regarded as an aspect of the ego. The persona embodies the roles, attitudes, and modes of interacting that we employ in relating to the social world around us. It is governed in part by the specific constitution of the individual and in part by the traditions and standards of the family, social group, and society, and it can usually be seen as a compromise between the two sets of demands—those from within and those from without. The shadow embodies instinctual forces, particularly those of a sexual or aggressive character, that are denied free expression by society and that have not been integrated into conscious functioning. The anima and animus embody the qualities of the sex opposite to that of the individual. Thus, the anima is that component of the man that embodies all his feminine qualities. The animus embodies the masculine qualities of the woman. The self is the core or center of the total personality. Since it embodies all opposing elements in the psyche, realization of the self amounts to achieving a balanced or integrated expression of one's total being.

We can consider these concepts further in the context of the developmental process, but perhaps we should note that while each of these terms has a core of constant meaning, it is also subject to some variation in usage in Jungian literature. Thus, at times the terms *persona, shadow, anima, animus,* and *self* are defined simply in terms of the underlying archetype or in terms of images or symbols in which the archetype is expressed. When used in the sense of subsystems or subpersonalities, the terms obviously encompass much more than this. In some writings, Jung virtually equates anima and animus with the unconscious. This makes sense from a Jungian standpoint, since Jung assumes that psychologically we are all inherently bisexual and that whatever qualities are not integrated into the ego operate compensatorily on an unconscious level. Hence, to the extent that the individual is consciously masculine, the unconscious as a whole has basically a feminine character, and vice versa. The variation in usage is perhaps only a minor problem, since in Jung's writings the specific meaning of these terms is usually clear from the context.

The development of the personality, or in Jung's terms *individuation,* involves both the differentiation of contents and functions from the unconscious mass and their integration into the ego. Ego development as such, however, is largely the work of the early stages of life. In the course of childhood and adolescence we develop our intellectual faculties and our awareness of ourselves and the world. We emerge in early adulthood as beings with much rational self-control and power of conscious decision, but we also tend to be rather lopsided beings. Just as we have simplified the whole problem of motor coordination and movement by becoming either right-handed or left-handed, we have selectively concentrated on certain psychological qualities—perhaps thinking, sensation, extraversion, and masculine qualities—and neglected those qualities that lead in an opposite direction. We have repressed impulses that interfere with a smooth relationship with the world around us. The developmental task for the adult years of life is to achieve an adjustment that permits appropriate expression of all parts of our nature. There is a tendency in the Western world to overemphasize the importance of conscious analysis and control and, hence, to emphasize the development of the ego as the all-important personal goal. Perhaps this is the reason our society tends to be so youth-oriented and why even psychological theorists, apart from Jung and Erikson, tend to neglect the later stages of development.

These later stages are marked to some extent by the development of the other subpersonalities. An obvious prerequisite for continued growth is a recognition that one cannot do everything by conscious manipulation, a recognition of the limitations of the ego. Without this

147

recognition we will tend to oppose and undermine any further development that might occur spontaneously. An awareness of the persona also seems rather essential. People who achieve positions of prominence in our society tend to have well-developed personas and often identify with them. As a consequence, life consists of playing a professional or business role: physician, business leader, professor, social worker, or whatever. For some people there is an over-identification with a narrowly defined sex role—the he-man, the glamour queen, the dedicated mother. Any of these roles may be valuable at a certain stage of adjustment, but it may prove a trap if we invest too much effort in fulfilling the role and ignoring other parts of ourselves. Often people experience intense emotional crises when life circumstances change and no longer support an accustomed role. If circumstances continue to support the role, the individual may continue to play it and fail to realize how much of life he is missing.

If the individual recognizes the limitations of the ego and can avoid identification with the persona, he can begin to achieve reconciliation with other parts of the psyche. Much of the content that must emerge first is that associated with the shadow. To the extent that shadow contents are unacceptable to the ego, they tend to be experienced as not belonging to oneself. We become aware of them only in negative projections, as the evil qualities of the scapegoat, the outsider, the enemy. The shadow may appear in dreams as a dark, sinister figure from whom we seek to escape. As we begin to resist the contents of the shadow less and to own them, we may experience its qualities as a needed complement to our own, and ultimately we recognize the qualities as a part of ourselves. In dreams, fairytales, and fiction, the shadow may be represented either as an adversary or as a helpful companion who supplies qualities lacking in the hero. In Tolkien's *Lord of the Rings* we see both possibilities, for the hero is accompanied both by a sturdy, practical-minded auxiliary (Sam Gamgee) and by a more sinister dark companion (Gollum), and he is at least dimly aware that he needs them both.[12]

The feminine side of the male and the masculine side of the female are also experienced primarily in projections. The anima and animus are both multifaceted, and they may be projected in a variety of forms. Indeed, we need to experience them in a variety of forms to recognize their total content. The form of manifestation will shift in the course of development. The anima and animus are first experienced in the relationship with the parent of the opposite sex. Later, the anima may be experienced in terms of female sexuality (and perhaps projected onto a Hollywood sex symbol). It may be experienced in terms of more romantic and aesthetic qualities (and be projected onto the girl or woman with whom one falls in love). It may also be experienced in terms of an object of spiritual devotion (such as the Virgin Mary) or in terms of the essence of feminine wisdom. The animus of the female may be experienced in terms of virility or physical masculinity (the athletic hero), in terms of the qualities of effective action (the conquering, romantic hero), in terms of the power and expression of the intellect (the intellectual or political champion), or in terms of the wisdom embodied in a spiritual leader or prophet.

To the extent that we are threatened by the contrasexual elements in ourselves, we will tend to project them in a negative form. Thus, the man may become preoccupied with mother-figures who threaten to overpower, smother, or destroy him. Many of the dragons of mythology represent negative maternal forces that the hero must overcome. If sexuality is emphasized, the negative anima figure may be a seductive siren or Circe who can destroy men by appealing to their appetites. For many women, the attractive but exploitative lecher is a comparable source of concern. In general, as we learn to relate better to the qualities embodied in the anima or animus, negative images tend to be superseded by positive images, and we experience the feminine and the masculine in all their possible forms. Presumably the anima and animus can never become fully conscious or fully integrated into the ego; they will continue to be experienced through relationships with people of the opposite sex. They embrace many qualities that we can integrate into conscious functioning, however, and hypermasculinity and hyperfemininity must be viewed as defensive reactions to a threat from unconscious forces. A fully functioning person may be predominantly masculine or feminine but will permit expression of both sides of his nature.

There are additional aspects of the psyche, beyond those most

149

clearly associated with the shadow, anima, and animus, that may emerge in later stages of development. These include the spirituality personified by such images as the old wise man and the materiality personified by images like the great earth mother (or magna mater). Jung at one time thought that the image of the old wise man typically appeared in the dreams and projections of men, while that of the great earth mother appeared in women, but later concluded that each was found in both sexes. Jung assumed that certain spiritual qualities tend to emerge in the later years, but presumably what needs to emerge then depends on the course that the individual's development has followed up to that time. Late in development, symbols representing the integrated totality of the self become more frequent. To realize the self means to permit all parts of one's nature to operate and find spontaneous expression, so that the self, rather than the ego, becomes the effective center of one's actions.

JUNG'S VIEW OF THE OPTIMAL CONDITION

The Western goal of conscious analytical understanding and control, which was evidently accepted as an ideal condition by Freud, was viewed by Jung as an appropriate goal for the first half of life. The more important, ultimate goal of development lies beyond. The realization of the self represents a relinquishing of the struggle for conscious mastery of everything in favor of a natural harmony and spontaneity of expression. In effect, Jung has moved toward an Eastern position without quite adopting one, for the ego continues to play an essential role in Jung's idea of the fully individuated person. As the agent of individual will and conscious decision, the ego must continue to assess the circumstances of the outer world and maintain an awareness of the needs of the person as a separate individual distinct from the rest of the world. Thus, the ego has the vital role of mediating between the self and the outer world. It must attempt to be attuned to both and to know both, though it can never fully know either, and to plan and direct action accordingly.

This essential role of the ego does not evaporate as the self comes closer to achieving full expression. The self possesses the greater wisdom in so far as it encompasses all sorts of contents that the ego has not integrated, but it can proceed only in the automatic way dictated by its natural unfolding. It lacks the ego's differentiated awareness and capacity for deliberation. There are two basic ways in which the ego can fail to assume or maintain its proper responsibility. It can simply relinquish all responsibility and let the self assume control. The result of this movement is not the integrated wholeness of the fully individuated person, but the undifferentiated wholeness of the infant. This is the loss of organized functioning that we see in some forms of profound psychotic regression, and it can be manifested to lesser degrees in other conditions. As a temporary condition, this movement may be beneficial, for it may provide the ego with resources for new organization, but it does not represent the most desirable end state.

An equally hazardous course would be one in which the ego attempts to assume control of everything. Instead of being absorbed by the self, the ego seeks to absorb the self. The individual identifies with the images of vast wisdom and power that reflect the archetypal contents of the unconscious. The result is an experience of megalomania or psychic inflation, which is seen in an extreme form in some paranoid psychoses. Broadly speaking, it corresponds to the sin of pride or hubris long recognized in Western traditions, and it is a pitfall to which trends in Western society often lead. By the same token, Jung seemed to suggest that Eastern paths may lead as easily to the other pitfall, the loss of the ego.

Perhaps we can better relate Jung to Western traditions if we note that the relationship he described between ego and self is analogous to that between the individual and God assumed by much Judaeo-Christian thought. In a sense, the ego is a part and a product of the self. Yet it has a responsibility to maintain its distinctness, while at the same time accepting the ultimate authority of the self. The part must neither attempt to become the whole nor deny its quasi-separateness as a discrete part: the proper relationship between part and whole must be achieved.

Obviously the crucial difference between Jung and Eastern thought has to do with the role of the ego in the optimal condition.

While Hindu and Buddhist traditions stress the ultimate recognition that the ego is an illusion or that its individual separateness is an illusion, Jung saw an abandonment of the ego as a loss of consciousness. Contrasting East and West, he said:

> To us, consciousness is inconceivable without an ego; it is equated with the relation of contents to an ego. If there is no ego there is nobody to be conscious of anything. The ego is therefore indispensable to the conscious process. The Eastern mind, however, has no difficulty in conceiving of a consciousness without an ego. Consciousness is deemed capable of transcending its ego condition; indeed, in its higher forms, the ego disappears altogether. Scuh an ego-less mental condition can only be unconscious to us, for the simple reason that there would be nobody to witness it. I do not doubt the existence of mental states transcending consciousness. But they lose consciousness to exactly the same degree that they transcend consciousness. I cannot imagine a conscious mental state that does not relate to a subject, that is, to an ego. The ego may be depotentiated—divested, for instance, of its awareness of the body—but so long as there is awareness of something, there must be somebody who is aware. [13]

Jung went on to suggest that the Eastern idea of enlightenment is equivalent to the concept of the collective unconscious. On a practical level, the difference between Jung and the East may be slight. Jung often points to the benefits of temporary regressive conditions in which the differentiated functioning of the ego is lost for a while and the individual experiences more directly the resources of the collective unconscious. Presumably he would regard deep meditative states as having this same value, as states in which the individual abandons ego control temporarily but after which he can return to the ordinary world and function with increased effectiveness. There are few people in the East who would regard the deep meditative state as a desirable permanent condition, but Easterners may differ from Jung in feeling that some sense of oneness experienced in that state can and should be carried out of it into the rest of one's experience of living.

Alan Watts felt that Jung came close to grasping the message of the Eastern world but failed because he was caught in a simple language trap. [14] Having learned to think in an Indo-European language, Jung could not imagine consciousness without an ego because syntac- .

152

tical conventions dictate that a verb must have a subject. Perhaps Watts had a point, but I am not sure that he quite understood the point that Jung was making. Jung could certainly imagine mind or raw awareness without a subject, whether that subject be the ego or some other organized center, but what is lacking when the ego is lost is a certain kind of organized awareness.

Undoubtedly the difference between Jung and Eastern thought is partly a matter of language, but I do not believe it is quite as simple as Watts suggested. Unfortunately, the word *ego* has a rather elastic meaning, both in Jung's writings and in the East. We may note three aspects of Jung's usage to which we might give primary attention in defining the word: (1) organized awareness and cognitive functioning, which are reflected in planned activity and the systematic meeting of needs over time; (2) the complex of contents utilized in consciousness, including ideas pertaining to a personal identity (or "self-concept"); and (3) an agent of will, consciousness, and action.

Perhaps the third of these notions most clearly represents a language convention. Much of our causal thinking, including that pertaining to our own behavior and awareness, is certainly rooted in the structure of our language. In arguing that the agent is necessary for consciousness, however, Jung apparently was saying that without it, the organization implied by the first aspect would be lacking. Implicitly he was defining *ego* in terms of the organization, rather than in terms of the agent, but his thinking does not seem to be altogether clear on this point. The Buddhist view that the ego is an illusion may apply either to the notion of the ego as an agent (which controls behavior whether or not we are aware of it) or the notion of a self-reflective sense of personal identity and separateness. Obviously a recognition of the illusion would not necessarily be accompanied by a loss of organization. I suspect that any enlightened Buddhist would continue to act as if he had an ego in the Jungian sense, even after he had come to realize that it did not exist. Perhaps he would also feel that this whole exercise in conceptual analysis was rather futile.

SEVEN

OTHER THEORIES RELATED TO PSYCHO-ANALYSIS

In this chapter we shall consider several additional theorists whose ideas either have their roots in Freudian theory, have been strongly influenced by Freudian theory, or bear clear parallels to Freudian theory. Perhaps it would be difficult to find a contemporary psychological theorist who has not been influenced in some way, directly or indirectly, by Freud. My immediate concern is with fairly direct relatives, and here I find it best to be quite selective. If my purpose were a more exhaustive historical treatise, I might attempt to cover the work of dozens of early associates of Freud, of people who joined the movement later, of all the neo-Freudians and ego psychologists, and of a host of people not formally a part of the psychoanalytic movement who have been clearly influenced by it. My purpose, however, is to elucidate major perspectives on the nature of the optimal personality. The theorists I shall consider now are not all of equal intellectual merit, but each represents a viewpoint that is both distinctive and influential. One of them, Eric Berne, has become influential just in the last few years, but he has achieved too much popularity to be ignored.

ALFRED ADLER AND INDIVIDUAL PSYCHOLOGY

Like Jung, Adler was an early associate of Freud. Like Jung, he is often pictured as a disciple of Freud who eventually rebelled against

154

the teachings of his master and then proceeded to develop his own ideas, but, as in the case of Jung, this picture is quite inaccurate. The seeds of Adler's later theories are evident in the writings that predate the period of his association with Freud. Adler regarded Freud's methods as the heart of psychoanalysis, but throughout the period in which he interacted closely with Freud he maintained theoretical views that differed from those of Freud. He never accepted Freud's concepts of libido and the Oedipus complex. In much of his work, he did stress the importance of early childhood events in the formation of adult character and neurosis, and he acknowledged an indebtedness to Freud for indicating the importance of early events, but his own treatment of these events differed considerably from Freud's.

In the preceding chapter we noted some basic differences between the personalities of the two men. There are additional differences in their motives and outlook on life that help to illuminate differences in theoretical views. Freud was interested in achieving scientific understanding and in being recognized for contributions to theory. Adler had a much more direct interest in human welfare, and it was this interest, rather than a primary interest in science, that led him in his youth to seek a career in medicine.

He also had a different view of man's relationship to society. Freud saw a basic conflict between the individual and society and saw no possibility of an ultimate remedy for this conflict. He saw guilt and neurosis as almost inevitable prices to be paid for the benefits of civilization. Adler saw the human being as a social animal. From an Adlerian standpoint, the individual fulfills his nature in society rather than sacrificing part of it to accommodate the group. While Adler saw many ills in contemporary society and felt drastic reforms were needed, he was optimistic about the possibility of building a society compatible with the basic needs of people.

Freud was inclined to remain aloof from political matters and certainly refrained from becoming involved in a political cause. Adler, on the other hand, became quite interested in socialism during his student years and attended political meetings. His thinking was undoubtedly influenced to some degree by Marx, though some writers have exaggerated this influence. Certainly Adler was not a doctrinaire Marxist. He was not particularly interested in Marx's economic theory, but he was interested in Marx's description of the social nature of the human being and the contemporary social condition of mankind. He shared much of Marx's social philosophy and sympathized with his views on the ideal state. He took a dim view of the Bolshevik revolution in Russia, because he felt it was led by men who were too interested in wielding power and because they employed violence, rather than democratic means, to achieve their ends. He was a member of the Austrian Social-Democratic Party until the 1920s. Nevertheless, political activities never became his primary interest. Although he held a minor political office in Vienna shortly after World War I, he was never particularly active in the political meetings that he attended. He was more a listener than a participant, and his interest in party affairs progressively declined after 1920. To the annoyance of some of his political associates, Adler had a greater interest in promoting the cause of his own movement, individual psychology.

Like Freud, Adler came from a Jewish family, but in his thirties he converted to Protestantism. While religious beliefs were evidently never of great importance to either man, the two were affected in different ways by the Judaeo-Christian tradition. Freud attacked religion on intellectual grounds, essentially equating religion with theological doctrine, which held little interest for Adler. Apparently he became a Protestant because he preferred the social perspective of the Protestant churches with which he was familiar and because he felt his children should have a religious education. The ethical side of religion was more important to him than theological doctrine, and his basic model for the ideal person is based on the Judaeo-Christian ethic of love.

Adler was born in Vienna in 1870 and lived there until 1932, when he foresaw some of the catastrophic events that were soon to erupt in Europe and emigrated to the United States. He died in Scotland in 1937 during a lecture tour. His early family life probably set the stage for some of his later clashes with Freudian theory. The second child in a family of six children, he admired his older brother and competed with him, and was envied in turn by a younger brother. He was the favorite son of his father, but his mother favored his younger brother. Perhaps this helps to explain the fact that Adler emphasized sibling rivalry as a factor in child development and rejected Freud's concept of the Oedipus complex. In contrast, Freud was the oldest and favorite child of a young, attractive mother, who was in fact closer in age to her son than to her husband, and for Freud the Oedipus complex was an obvious fact of life.

It is also undoubtedly significant that Adler suffered from much illness as a child. For a period of time he was incapacitated with rickets and could only sit idly by, watching the other children run and play instead of joining in their games. Organ inferiority was for him a fact of life. Like Freud and Jung, Adler chose a career in medicine, but he appears to have been relatively undistinguished as a student. In 1895 he received his medical degree and soon undertook a general medical practice. After several years, he began to specialize in the treatment of neurotic patients.

His early writings as a physician—those written before he became involved in psychological theory—show a great concern with the social conditions that lead to disease. One booklet dealt with the health problems of tailors that related these problems to economic and occupational circumstances. In the course of his work he became interested in the writings and ideas of Freud. He met Freud in 1902 and soon became an active participant in a discussion group that met on Wednesday evenings in Freud's home. He was an active participant in the psychoanalytic movement from 1902 to 1911, and during the last few months of that period he was president of the Viennese Psychoanalytic Society.

During that period he published his book *Study of Organ Inferiority.*[1] In this work he developed the thesis that certain diseases may be attributable to an inherent weakness in certain tissues. The inferiority leads to compensation, whereby the individual attempts to overcome the effects of the inferior organ by concentrating either on the organ itself or on some other organ. In organ inferiority and compensation Adler saw a basis for neurosis. During his psychoanalytic period he also introduced the concept of masculine protest, a form of compensation wherein the individual strives to realize an ideal of masculine strength and power. This concept reflects a subtle departure from the Freudian perspective. Freud apparently assumed that it was natural for both boys and girls to regard the male as biologically superior to the female. Adler recognized early that the idea of male superiority is a cultural imposition. While the concept of masculine protest is parallel to such Freudian concepts as penis envy, from an Adlerian standpoint it represents an unhealthy trend in the individual and in our society as a whole, not an inevitable feature of development.

In 1911 Adler left the Viennese Psychoanalytic Society. One can find several versions of the specific details of Adler's departure, but it is clear that certain differences in theory between Freud and Adler had become both glaring and irreconcilable. Adler soon formed a new group, which was initially called the Society for Free Psychoanalysis—to the annoyance of Freud and some of his loyal associates. Later the name was changed to the Society for Individual Psychology.

In the work that he published subsequently he moved progressively toward more general psychological theory. In 1912 *The Neurotic Constitution* was published.[2] In this book he still treated organ inferiorities as a precondition for neurosis, but he also recognized social factors, such as rivalry with siblings, as a source of inferiority feelings and broadened the concepts of compensation and masculine protest. He was less concerned with manifestations on a physical level and more concerned with self-assertion in the entire psychological and social life of the individual. The concept of fictions, which Adler borrowed from Hans Vaihinger, also entered into Adler's work at this point. This is a rather crucial innovation, for with this concept Adler's writings took on a flavor that is more distinctly teleological and phenomenological. Much of life is to be understood in terms of striving toward fictional goals, and much of our behavior and perceptions of the world can be seen in terms of fictions that we impose on the world. The masculine protest reflects an artificial structuring of the world into the masculine and the feminine and a striving toward a fictional goal.

The ideas presented in *The Neurotic Constitution* were developed further and modified to an extent in later writings. Through most of his post-Freudian writings, Adler stressed guiding fictions and goals as the keys to understanding behavior, where Freud would stress instincts. The individual is assumed to be largely unaware of his goals, but they are nonetheless something he has created rather than something imposed on him by biology, and they form the basis for his basic strategy for dealing with life and the world, for what Adler called the individual's style of life. This concept—style of life—better than any other epitomizes Adler's effort to deal with the human individual as a totality and as a being with considerable capacity for self-determination.

The idea of inferiority feelings continued to be important in Adler's work, but in later writings he came to view them not just as a consequence of organ inferiority or of the relationships within the family, but as a universal feature of human experience. Man's psychic evolution is seen as a response to his physical inferiority as a species, and the great achievements of civilization are viewed as products of our efforts to replace inferiority with superiority. At the same time, the striving for superiority, or will to power, is seen in later writings in a more favorable light. In earlier writings Adler had dealt with it primarily as an undesirable effect: strivings for superiority were seen in terms of an effort to achieve a position of dominance over other people, though Adler recognized many forms of expression. The strivings could be expressed fairly directly in aggressive efforts directed against others, or they could be expressed in a more indirect and devious form in neurosis, where the desire for superiority might be masked by a strategy of avoidance or weakness. In later writings Adler viewed the striving for superiority as a natural and universal part of the human condition, and not just a consequence of inferiority. Superiority or power was not equated with dominance of others or with aggression. It connoted a sense of adequacy, competence, mastery, or control, and its most natural forms of expression Adler considered socially constructive.

An equally important part of human nature, stressed in all of Adler's writings after World War I, is *Gemeinschaftsgefühl*. This word is usually rendered in English as "social feeling" or "social interest," but there seems to be no exact English equivalent. It implies a sense of intimate relatedness with other people. Adler regarded both the striving for superiority and *Gemeinschaftsgefühl* as facets of human nature that played a key role in evoluton, as traits that enabled the species to survive in spite of motor and sensory deficiencies. The full development of the individual was viewed by Adler primarily in terms of the development and expression of *Gemeinschaftsgefühl*. Since this represented to him a natural tendency of mankind, the most natural forms

159

of expression of the striving for superiority would be those that are consistent with it and socially constructive. Destructive and neurotic life-styles, on the other hand, are pathological expressions of the striving for superiority, for they entail a suppression of *Gemeinschaftsgefühl*. Adler viewed the competitive individualism of Western society as productive of pathology.

Thus, the ideal goal of development for Adler was one of altruism, which he considered an intrinsic part of human nature. In contrast, Freud perceived an inevitable conflict between the strivings of the individual and the pressures of society, viewing people as inherently egoistic and envisioning a goal that included altruism to a more limited degree and treated it as a transformation of egoism. From an Adlerian standpoint, it is in our nature to relate positively to other people, and we are frustrated only by a society that pushes us in an egoistic direction. An ideal society would not do this.

The concern for human welfare that led Adler into medicine in the first place thus became a central theme in his later writings and was embodied in his concept of the optimal personality. This concern also led him to become involved in areas of human activity that took him far beyond an ordinary private medical practice. It had stimulated an early interest in politics, and after World War I, when the Social Democrats came to power in Vienna and provided the opportunity, it led him to become involved in new professional developments. He became active in reforms in the educational system, in the founding and development of kindergartens and experimental schools, in adult education, in teacher training, and in the founding and operation of child-guidance clinics. These activities reflect not only his concern with human welfare but also the fact that he had a stronger direct interest in social relations of all kinds than did any of the other people associated with the early history of the psychoanalytic movement.

It has often been noted that in a variety of ways Adler anticipated later developments in the psychoanalytic movement for which he is not usually given credit. Freud's concern with the death instinct and aggression after World War I may be viewed as a tardy effort to deal with a realm of human behavior to which Adler had repeatedly pointed earlier. The neo-Freudians in the 1930s and 1940s began to

160

stress social and cultural determinants and expressions to which Freud had given little attention, but they were preceded by Adler. Still later the ego psychologists moved in a direction similar to that taken earlier by Adler.

Psychoanalysis on the whole has become more Adlerian than Freudian over the years, but psychoanalysts have generally tended to avoid describing themselves as descendents of Adler. Perhaps one reason is that they see him as a relatively unsophisticated theorist. Adler himself definitely tended to de-emphasize formal theory. He was more concerned with developing a very practical psychology. He was more interested in helping people understand themselves and others than in achieving an accurate intellectual analysis of them. Even in deemphasizing intellectual analysis and formal theory, however, he anticipated later theorists. It has been noted that Adler's thinking has much in common with the existential psychological movement that emerged later. Like Adler, existential psychologists object to the determinism, mechanism, and analytical understanding stressed by Freudian theory, and they find inspiration in some of the same traditions in philosophy that inspired Adler. Among the existentialists, Rollo May and Victor Frankl in particular appear to have been directly influenced by Adler.

OTTO RANK

There is one more theorist I want to consider who was associated with the early history of psychoanalysis. Like Jung and Adler, Otto Rank represents a movement away from the materialism, mechanism, and strict determinism of Freud and away from the Scientific Man model. As in Jung and Adler, we find an orientation that is more consistently in keeping with Romanticism and that reflects the spirit of the humanities more than that of the natural sciences. At one stage of his work, Rank espoused a psychology of consciousness that has much in common with the ideas of Adler. In later work, we find a depth psychology closer in basic outlook to Jung. Yet there are some distinctive features in Rank's work that make it worthy of separate consideration. It provides still a different view of the fully developed person that has stimulated much subsequent thinking.

Rank was born in 1884. He joined the discussion circle that had gathered around Freud in 1905 or 1906 and remained in close association with Freud until he moved to Paris in 1926. He moved again, in 1935, to New York, where he died in 1939, one month after the death of Sigmund Freud in London.

Rank's early family life appears to have been a bit more chaotic than that of the other men we have considered. His father was an alcoholic with a violent temper, and Rank found interaction with him very unpleasant; when he was sixteen, he and his brother resolved to discontinue all verbal communication with their father. Lacking a parent whom he could accept as an appropriate masculine model, as an adolescent Rank looked for heroes he could emulate in literature, philosophy, and the arts. He read widely and was particularly impressed with Schopenhauer and Nietzsche. Perhaps in some respects he had the temperament of an artist, for he had a lifelong interest in the artistic process and in the lives of artists, but faced with the necessity of earning a living he enrolled in a technical school with the intention of becoming a mechanic. Because of health problems, however, he was compelled to take an office job.

He encountered the work of Freud when he was twenty and experienced something tantamount to a religious conversion. Freud's ideas fascinated him and seemed to provide a needed source of inspiration. In 1905 Adler introduced him to Freud. Rank was barely twenty-one years old at the time, and he lacked the medical training of the other members of the Freudian circle, but Freud soon recognized in the young man a brilliance and creative capacity that exceeded that of his other Viennese colleagues. At Freud's urging, Rank attended the gymnasium and the university and eventually earned a doctorate. Freud took a warm, personal interest in him and often assisted him financially. If he regarded Jung as his intellectual heir, he regarded Rank as a son in a much more personal sense. And in Freud, Rank found the revered father figure that had theretofore been lacking in his life.

Rank served as secretary to the Vienna Psychoanalytic Society from 1905 to 1915 and kept faithful records of the meetings. At times, he served as Freud's personal secretary. Until the 1920s he was essentially a disciple of Sigmund Freud, but he brought to the psychoanalytic movement his own special talents and background. He had no medical training. Instead, he had extensive training in such fields as philosophy, psychology, history, and art. On the occasion when he first met Freud, he came armed with a book manuscript dealing with the artist. Perhaps he was better qualified than Freud himself to apply psychoanalytic theory to art, literature, and mythology. Among the members of the psychoanalytic society, only Rank could approach Carl Jung in his knowledge of mythology and culture. After the departure of Jung, Rank was the leading expert within the society in those fields. By virtue of his unique background, Rank was also the first practicing lay analyst in the psychoanalytic movement.

Perhaps it was inevitable that a man of Rank's intelligence, energy, and creative bent would eventually formulate ideas at variance with those of the master. Some dissenting views first become apparent in a book on therapeutic techniques that Sandor Ferenczi and Rank authored jointly and had published in 1923. The two men recommended several departures from orthodox procedures, such as experimenting with a more active role for the therapist and setting a time limit for the termination of therapy in order to shorten the length of treatment. A greater furor was aroused, however, by a book that Rank published the following year, *The Trauma of Birth.*[3]

In *The Trauma of Birth,* Rank argues that the experience of birth is the first and prototypical traumatic experience. It produces primal anxiety, but the experience is lost from conscious memory because the anxiety leads in turn to primal repression. Before birth, we enjoy a condition of uninterrupted bliss, our physical needs being constantly met while we remain in the womb. At birth, we are separated from the situation in which primal pleasure prevails. Later traumatic experiences, such as weaning, also entail separation and arouse our lifelong need to reestablish the security of our intrauterine existence. Whenever this need is aroused, we tend to reexperience anxiety. The need remains in any case, and we find indirect ways to satisfy it. According to Rank, in sleep and in dreams we return to the original blissful state, and dream interpretation provides abundant evidence for the continuance of the need. Religion also expresses the need, for it characteristically provides images of a protective being to whom the faithful can return in a future life. Creative acts provide a different kind of expression. In women, the biologically creative process of pregnancy and childbirth is of paramount importance. While the woman must relinquish any possibility of being reunited with the mother, she can do the next best thing by having the experience of becoming a mother herself. Such a possibility is not available to men, but the creation of artistic and other kinds of cultural products serves as a substitute for the productive process of childbearing.

The idea of the birth trauma had originally been suggested by Freud himself, but it had never been accorded the psychological significance Rank gave it. When Rank's book appeared, Freud initially viewed it favorably and was prepared for a time to regard it as a major contribution to psychoanalytic theory. He continued to hear critical comments about the book and about Rank from a number of his followers, however, and he eventually decided that the criticism was justified. He expressed rather sharp criticism of the hypothesis of the birth trauma in a paper published in 1926. Altogether, Rank's relations with Freud and other psychoanalysts became increasingly strained following publication of the book, and he had little contact with any of them after 1926.

The period from 1924 to 1926 was apparently an exceedingly painful one for Rank. He had not lost his great admiration for Freud and did not wish to end his relationship with him. He was upset by some of the harsh treatment he experienced from others of the psychoanalytic society and made some efforts to reconcile himself with them. Yet he had taken a very bold step that could not be retracted. In publishing *The Trauma of Birth,* he had done something unprecedented for a member of the close-knit Freudian circle—he had not discussed any of the material in the book with anyone else in the group before publication. He must have realized that the book would produce a big splash and that some of the attention it was destined to arouse would be unfavorable. Perhaps he naively expected to become a sudden recipient of untempered praise. Perhaps, wittingly or unwittingly, he was really preparing to launch himself on his own independent course whatever the cost. For a man of his sensitive nature, the cost included a good deal of agony. He wanted the security of his relationship with Freud, and he wanted the freedom to develop and express his own ideas. He suffered acutely from this conflict, and the pains of his own birth were protracted. Once the separation was complete, he was free to move with less restraint in new directions. In his later work, however, we can certainly see the imprint of his own personal experience.

In later publications the original birth trauma ceased to have the same importance that Rank had given it in the book of 1924. Apparently he decided that he had exaggerated the significance of that one experience, but the idea of a basic conflict between a need for dependent security and a need for independent, creative expression and the idea that individuality emerges through experiences of rebirth continue to play a prominent role in later writings. The next major period in Rank's work was marked by the appearance of such books as *Will Therapy* and *Truth and Reality*.[4] In this period, Rank's work essentially contains a psychology of consciousness. The unconscious is de-emphasized, and the central theme is the self-creative development of the individual. The basic outlook is similar to Adler's in its emphasis on conscious self-direction and, like Adler, Rank foreshadows some of the later developments in ego psychology.

The central concept of this period is the will. The will plays a role somewhat like that ascribed by Freud to the ego, for it can come into conflict with both instincts and society, but it is a more autonomous part of the personality than the Freudian ego. It is not a derivative of the id but has a prior existence of its own. It is a force that underlies and spurs development. It gives the individual the power of initiating and guiding action and selecting and organizing experience. It is an inherent part of the individual but is distinct from the instincts, which it can utilize for its own purposes or inhibit and control.

The will has an existence prior to consciousness, but it is responsible for the development of conscious awareness. Once the individual has achieved a conscious existence, the development of consciousness and the development of the will tend to go hand in hand. The ego, in the sense of an agent of consciousness, may function to support or to repress other inner forces. The ego is, in effect, a conscious will, but it does not represent the striving of the total psyche. Once it is formed, it sometimes functions in such a way as to block full expression of the individual and prevent further development. In this case, there is a conflict between differing wills within the individual, a failure to experience and express a total integrated will. The conscious intention of the individual is to maintain an established mode of adjustment, but there are underlying needs and strivings that call for further creative growth. The established mode of adjustment nearly always provides more security than any movement into unknown territory. In general, development means for Rank a movement toward full, creative affirmation and expression of the will. Otherwise stated, it involves a movement from established, dependent security toward greater freedom, independence, and individual creativity. This may require many successive experiences of separation and rebirth.

Development can also be described from a Rankian standpoint in terms of an alternation between negative and positive willing. The will is first experienced in a negative form—as a counterwill asserted in reaction to obstacles and restraints. The infant begins to experience a sense of his own independent existence as a willing agent by opposing external forces, such as the demands of his parents, and by opposing the compulsive force of his own instinctual drives. He acquires a capacity for truly saying *yes* by first saying *no*. Having experienced the force of his counterwilling, he learns to ally his intention with that of others. He desires what they desire. He merges his will with that of his parents or of the social group. To develop further requires taking responsibility for one's own individual willing, however this may differ from that of the group. Under some circumstances, our actions at this point may oppose the will of the group, but they now represent a position of autonomy rather than counterwill. In the early stages of development, the will of others provides a necessary frame of reference; it is first something to reject and then something to affirm. When we achieve true autonomy, however, we no longer measure ourselves against the standards of others. Our own individual wills become the source and the measure of our actions.

166

Rank distinguishes three adult types that correspond to three levels of development. The first is the normal or average person. From a Rankian standpoint, what is normal in a statistical sense is far from ideal, for Rank defines this type as the individual who accepts the majority will as his own. What he was compelled to do as a child, he now wills. He adjusts to the surrounding society. He experiences little conscious distress and he feels secure, but he is essentially unaware of his own individuality.

If the individual ventures out on his own and explores forbidden pathways, he experiences anxiety, for he is acting contrary to standards previously accepted and following a course that threatens to destroy his security. At the next stage, there is inevitably disunity and distress. The individual finds the majority will unacceptable. He rejects the standards of society, but he has nothing with which to replace them, for he had not yet experienced and accepted standards that represent his own will. According to Rank, this is the level of the second type, the neurotic.

The third level of development is that of the creative type. At this level, the individual is no longer torn by conflict. He experiences unity of purpose. He fully affirms and expresses his own will. He asserts his right to existence as a separate independent being, and he may to some extent choose or create a world that suits his own needs. The creative type thus represents Rank's concept of the ideal personality. The essential features of this view of the ideal are independence and creativity. This focus on creativity provides an interesting contrast to the Freudian emphasis on realism and points to a difference in underlying models. If Freud took as his model the objective scientist, Rank was equally inclined to find his ideal embodied in the innovative genius in the arts. Obviously, we could find good examples of the creative type among scientists and people in other walks of life, while many ordinary painters and sculptors would fail to fit the specifications of the type. Yet it is clear that Rank had a lifelong interest in artists and in the process of creation in the arts. The theoretical focus manifested in his definition of the ideal reflects this interest and highlights some important differences between the traditions that he represents and those represented by Freud.

167

Rank's efforts to unravel the puzzles of human development did not end with the formulation of these levels. He had depicted an ideal type characterized by creativity and by unity of purpose. He had also characterized this type as "self-conscious" and his descriptions seemed to imply an individual in whom conscious awareness was highly developed. In later work, particularly in his last book, *Beyond Psychology,* he moved from a psychology of consciousness to a depth psychology similar to that of Jung.[5] In this last period he saw a danger in an overemphasis on consciousness and rationality. He regarded this emphasis as an effort on the part of the modern individual to assert intellectual control over the irrational, prompted by a fear of the unconscious. As a result of this emphasis, the individual becomes imbalanced because he is separated from many of his own inner resources. In short, Rank recognized that total consciousness is an impossibility and that an emphasis on consciousness necessarily means an emphasis on a part to the neglect of other parts. The central propelling and organizing force, the will, he came to view as fundamentally unconscious. He conceived of it as something comparable to the Jungian self, representing the united, balanced force of the total personality. Creative expression of the will would necessarily require the abandonment of any effort at full conscious awareness and control.

In *Beyond Psychology,* Rank applied this line of thought to our society as a whole. He postulated a basic urge or will to immortality and distinguished four historical eras in terms of the ways in which people have expressed or sought to fulfill this basic striving. The first is the primal era, or "era of emamism," in which the individual does not recognize his individual existence as separate from that of the group. In the second, the era of the soul or animism, he copes with the fact of physical death by conceiving of a soul that is separate from the body and that can survive after the body is destroyed. In a third era, the sexual era, family ties become important and immortality is achieved through the survival of one's descendents. We have moved into a fourth era, the psychological era. This is an era of self-conscious preoccupation born of the conflict and demise of older ideologies. Psychoanalysis and other systems of psychology are products of this era. In the psychological era, we seek to alleviate our ideological conflicts by explaining away our beliefs, but the era furnishes no new belief system to satisfy our striving for immortality. Rank saw the heightened and tormented self-awareness of this era as a kind of neurosis that we must transcend. Psychology attempts to provide rational understanding of the irrational, but what we need is a deeper spiritual realization that cannot be provided by rational analysis. We need to move beyond our present experience of individual self-consciousness and give more direct expression to the irrational source within through creative living.

Rank provided only a general prescription for our future development, but the trend that is apparent in his views is interesting. Ira Progoff believes that Freud, Jung, Adler, and Rank all moved in a common direction in the course of their work and that they all recognized ultimately the importance of establishing "contact with a larger realm of reality in which man's psychological nature transcends itself." [6] He feels that we have virtually come to the end of the analytical period in psychology and that our task now is to develop a psychology that will help people reestablish contact with the creative and spiritual forces of life, instead of trying to reduce those forces to intellectual schemata. He feels that of all the theorists associated with the early stages of the psychoanalytic movement, Rank realized this most clearly and recognized the important transitional role that psychology can play in leading people to "an experience that is beyond psychology."

ERICH FROMM

Erich Fromm is one of several theorists who are commonly labeled neo-Freudians and who have in common a concern with the cultural factors affecting human personality and with cultural forms of expression. Like Rank, Fromm is a lay analyst, and as a student he devoted his attention primarily to the fields of psychology and sociology. Perhaps no other psychoanalyst has shown such a broad grasp of the contemporary social sciences, and certainly none has attracted so much attention from workers in different fields of social science.

Fromm was born in 1900 and grew up in Germany. He received

a doctorate from the University of Heidelberg in 1922 and then secured training at the Psychoanalytic Institute in Berlin. In 1933 he moved to the United States. In recent years he has divided his time between the United States and Mexico and has held positions at the National University in Mexico City, The William Alanson White Institute, and New York University.

Fromm's basic outlook has much in common with those of Rank and Adler, but he regards Freud and Marx as the men who have influenced his thinking most strongly. A few events in his life led to an early interest in both. In one work he systematically compared the views of these two theorists.[7] Of the two, he apparently considers Marx to be the more profound and historically significant thinker, but he feels that each theorist supplied some necessary insights lacking in the work of the other. Conversely each theoretical system is deficient in certain respects. Fromm considers it important to deal with psychological and societal (including political and economic) variables in combination for an adequate understanding of human problems. He thinks it is a mistake either to view history as just the result of psychological forces or to neglect the special dynamics of human nature in attempting to understand history. Freudians tend to do the former, while behaviorists and people in other social sciences often do the latter. Thus, throughout his work, Fromm stresses the fact that our adaptation is subject to a great deal of cultural patterning, but he rejects the idea that man is just a blank screen that passively reflects whatever cultural conditioning has been cast upon it.

Two features of Freudian thought that he specifically eschews are the assumption that one can safely generalize to all of mankind from observations made of a limited segment of Western society and the assumption that there is an inherent conflict between man's instinctual nature and society. People are an integral part of the society in which they live, and their nature must be understood in terms of the societal context.

According to Fromm, the basic problem that characterizes the human situation is a sense of isolation. We did not experience this so long as we remained an integral part of nature, but in the course of human history we have come more and more to see ourselves as separate entities. Throughout most of our history, the sense of individual separateness has been very dim, but it has gradually increased over the ages and it develops anew in each individual as he progresses through infancy and childhood. Societies of all kinds represent attempts to resolve the feeling of isolation that stems from our experienced separateness, and in the early life of the individual the bonds within the family provide a sense of security and belonging that serves to varying degrees to enable the individual to cope with the sense of isolation.

The sense of isolation is a relatively recent problem for our species. Since the Renaissance we have become increasingly aware of ourselves as separate individuals, and this awareness reached its peak at some time between the Reformation and the present. In recent times, both Protestantism and the rise of capitalism have promoted an ambiguous spirit of freedom in the people of Western democracies. We have enjoyed increased independence from external authority, whether political or ecclesiastical, but along with this we have experienced a growing feeling of personal isolation, individual insignificance, and powerlessness. Protestantism has contributed to this on a doctrinal level, while capitalism has generated increasing alienation in the individual worker as it has progressed from a system of small entrepreneurs to a modern industrial society. Fromm echoes Marx's treatment of this thesis and expands it.

In *The Sane Society* and *The Revolution of Hope* he pointed to some of the novel hazards that have developed in our society in the present century.[8] These include such diabolical technological achievements as nuclear weapons, of course, but most of the developments in the social system may be characterized in terms of bureaucratization, automation and cybernation. Some of the new developments in our society are potentially very beneficial, but there is good evidence that the nations that have progressed farthest with respect to abundance of material goods and abundance of leisure time are also the nations in which people display the greatest amount of psychological disturbance. In the process of achieving technological gains, we have moved toward greater dehumanization of the individual citizen. There is a serious danger that that there is now emerging in the Western world "a completely mechanized society, devoted to maximal material output and consumption, directed by computers; and in this social process, man himself is being transformed into a part of the total machine, well fed and entertained, yet passive, unalive, and with little feeling." [9] More and more the efficient industrial system seems to operate on principles that run directly counter to the needs of people. It operates for maximal efficiency and quantitative output, and work tends to be organized in such a way as to reduce experiences of relatedness and of creative participation in the individual worker.

Like Rank, Fromm sees the human being as drawn both toward the state of union that he has lost and toward a condition of increasing individuality and freedom. In experiencing his separateness, the individual has been faced with a set of existential dichotomies that he cannot resolve. He transcends nature, yet remains in some way a part of it. He longs for immortality, but is confronted with the fact of his individual mortality. He longs for unity with the world, but his self-awareness sets him apart from it. The special conditions of human existence result in a set of needs that assume a greater importance in our behavior and experience than the physiological needs that we share with other animals. These human needs include:

1. *relatedness*—a need to be united with other living beings, to be related to other people.
2. *transcendence*—a need to transcend the condition of being a passive creature and to be a creative agent.
3. *rootedness*—a need to feel that one is a part of a family or of the world, that one has a home and that one belongs.
4. *a sense of identity*—a need to be aware of oneself as a distinct, particular individual.
5. *a frame of orientation and devotion*—a need for a consistent way of perceiving the world and responding to it intellectually and emotionally.

Broadly speaking, the first and third of these needs involve experiencing oneself as part of a larger whole, while the second and fourth involve the enhancement of individuality. (Fromm's use of the word *transcendence*, it will be noted, is a bit different from mine.) Properly expressed, the fifth need can provide a sense of balance be-

172

tween the individual self and the totality of nature and society. Religion, ideology, and neurosis are all forms of expression of the need for a frame of orientation and devotion.

Under the conditions of modern society, people often experience the sense of isolation and powerlessness so acutely (not necessarily with full conscious awareness) that they find it intolerable and turn to various forms of escape to reduce the experience. Four basic forms of escape have been described by Fromm: *masochism,* accepting a passive, dependent status and submitting to the control of external forces; *sadism,* assuming the right to exert absolute power over others or to exploit them as one wishes; *destructiveness,* seeking to eradicate external forces so that they cease to constitute a threat to one's separate self; and *automaton conformity,* relinquishing individual uniqueness and accepting the patterns of the society as one's own.

Any one of these forms of escape may involve behaviors that are appropriate for a limited time in a particular situation, but people often cling desperately to their preferred modes of escape in an effort to overcome isolation. Fromm speaks of four social character types that correspond to these four kinds of escape—the receptive character, the exploitative character, the hoarding character, and the marketing character. Fromm says that this is not an exhaustive list of the possible forms of escape, but it encompasses the ones that most pervasively color the social life of the Western world. Sadism and masochism are the major forms of escape manifested in authoritarian systems. They receive particular attention in *Escape from Freedom,* a book in which Fromm attempted to show how the totalitarian governments of Fascist Italy and Nazi Germany provided escape for the people in those countries.[10] In *The Sane Society,* he dealt more focally with contemporary democracies, where people are more inclined to seek escape through automaton conformity.

In addition to the four forms of escape, Fromm speaks of a fifth possible orientation to the world, one in which we genuinely relate to others while respecting both our own individuality and theirs. He speaks of this as the orientation of love, and the corresponding character type is the productive personality. This represents Fromm's view of the optimal personality, or of mental health. He notes that in our society, where alienation prevails, people tend to conceive of mental health in terms of qualities that are a part of alienated character. Thus, they stress such things as adjustment to the society, aggressiveness, ambition, cooperativeness. They tend to value distorted ideals of love. They value happiness and think of it in terms of an unrestricted, passive consumption of pleasure. They stress security, though a sensitive and alive person who experiences his individuality cannot really experience a high level of security; rather he needs to experience the strength of relationships that will enable him to tolerate his insecurity.

Fromm has described his concept of the ideal condition at length in several books. It is one that involves meeting all five of the needs that he describes. Thus, it involves the full realization of individuality and the spontaneous expression of one's total self, and it also involves an experienced unity with others and the world. In *Escape from Freedom* Fromm indicated that he sees the former as a precondition for the latter. The characteristics that most often recur in Fromm's descriptions of the ideal condition are spontaneity, creativity, productiveness, love, and a sense of unity with nature and other people. One of his most comprehensive definitions of the ideal state is as follows:

> Mental health, in the humanistic sense, is characterized by the ability to love and to create, by the emergence from the incestuous ties to family and nature, by a sense of identity based on one's experience of self as the subject and agent of one's powers, by the grasp of reality inside and outside of ourselves, that is, by the development of objectivity and reason. The aim of life is to live it intensely, to be fully born, to be fully awake. To emerge from the ideas of infantile grandiosity into the conviction of one's real though limited strength; to be able to accept the paradox that every one of us is the most important thing there is in the universe—and at the same time not more important than a fly or a blade of grass. To be able to love life, and yet to accept death without terror; to tolerate uncertainty about the most important questions with which life confronts us—and yet to have faith in our thought and feeling, inasmuch as they are truly ours. To be able to be alone, and at the same time with a loved person, with every brother on this earth, with all that is alive; to follow the voice of our conscience, the voice that calls us to ourselves, yet not to indulge in self hate when the voice of conscience was not loud enough to be heard and followed. The mentally healthy person is the person who lives by love, reason and faith, who respects life, his own and that of his fellow man.[11]

174

How is this ideal to be achieved? Unlike many other psychoanalysts, Fromm insists that we must not just think of this in terms of changes within individuals. Unlike many other socialists, he also insists that a solution that focuses just on changes in the political or economic realm is inadequate. We must understand the interrelationship of individual and societal variables and seek changes simultaneously in cultural activities, in individual adjustment, in our philosophical outlook, and in industrial and political systems. In any case, a change in the society is needed, for we cannot make people sane by getting them to adjust to this society. We need instead a society that is adjusted to the needs of people. In short, we need a sane society. What is the nature of such a society?

> First of all, a society in which no man is a means toward another's ends, but always and without exception an end in himself; hence where nobody is used, nor uses himself, for purposes which are not those of the unfolding of his own human powers; where man is the center, and where all economic and political activities are subordinated to the aim of his growth. A sane society is one in which qualities like greed, exploitativeness, possessiveness, narcissism, have no chance to be used for greater material gain or for the enhancement of one's personal prestige. Where acting according to one's conscience is looked upon as a fundamental and necessary quality and where opportunism and lack of principles is deemed to be asocial; where the individual is concerned with social matters so that they become personal matters, where his relation to his fellow man is not separated from his relationship in the private sphere. A sane society, furthermore, is one which permits man to operate within manageable and observable dimensions, and to be an active and responsible participant in the life of society, as well as the master of his own life. It is one which furthers human solidarity and not only permits, but stimulates, its members to relate themselves to each other lovingly; a sane society furthers the productive activity of everybody in his work, stimulates the unfolding of reason and enables man to give expression to his inner needs in collective art and rituals.[12]

Fromm believes that the ingredients of such a society are clearly lacking both in the capitalistic democracies of today and in the Communist societies of China and the Soviet Union. They would be realized, however, in a democratic socialist society to which he applies the

175

term *humanistic communitarian socialism*. He describes the characteristics of that society in a general way and says that the essential requisites of such a society have been recognized by various kinds of socialists (not always most clearly by Marxist socialists, who tend to focus
too narrowly on the economic variables). The most important properties of such a society are those that concern social relationships and
the sharing of work and experience, rather than those that concern
such legal problems as the ownership of property and the sharing of
profits.

When we compare Fromm with others in the psychoanalytic tradition, he seems most clearly distinguished by his emphasis on the
total society. But he has a psychological message that is equally important in his view of full individual development. In many ways this view
is similar to that of Jung, though not so amply explicated, and like
Jung, Fromm makes an effort to find a ground that is common to Eastern and Western thought. Like Jung, he arrives at a position that
bridges the cultures to some extent but that is still basically Western.

Fromm sees his idea of relating to humanity as one that has ancient roots in both the East and the West—in Judaism, in Christianity,
and in Buddhism. It is possible to construe his emphasis on combining
individuality and relatedness, or universality, as a fusion of Eastern and
Western ideas or as an effort to blend the Western traditions that
emphasize individualism and love. In any case, at times he employs
terms that have been used to describe Eastern ideas. He says that
"man's task in life is precisely the paradoxical one of realizing his individuality and at the same time transcending it and arriving at the experience of universality. Only the fully developed individual self can drop
the ego." [13]

This view is probably compatible with much of Eastern thought,
though the stress on individuality reflects a Western orientation. The
idea of dropping the ego does not mean that to Fromm individuality is
an illusion. He does believe that our society tends to cultivate an
illusion of individuality, so that we feel we are acting freely and thinking for ourselves when in fact we are conforming. The experience of
true individuality and freedom is something that most of us have not
yet attained, but it is an attainable reality.

In a book that he coauthored with D. T. Suzuki and Richard De

176

Martino, Fromm addressed himself to the experiential goals of psycho-analysis and Zen Buddhism and argued that the two systems of thought are much closer to each other in their aims than is generally believed.[14] The basic aim of Zen, as he sees it, is the immediate, full grasp of the world. He says that this is essentially the condition that results when repression and defensively distorted views of the world are eliminated through psychoanalytic treatment. Freud himself did not clearly formulate his goal in the terms of Zen enlightenment, but in the course of his work he moved in the direction of such a position. At the beginning he had stressed intellectual understanding, believing that he could cure a patient by providing information, but later he stressed a nonintellectual kind of insight. While Western traditions in general place a heavy emphasis on the intellect, Fromm believes that both in methods and goals contemporary psychoanalysis (which would include Fromm himself) has much in common with Zen Buddhism.

ERIK ERIKSON

Erik Erikson is one of a number of psychoanalysts who are commonly called ego psychologists. Like the others to whom this label has been applied, he has focused much attention in his work on the develop-ment and functions of the ego and has been less concerned with what Freud called the id and superego. For him, it is the ego that merits the greatest attention. It does not follow that he neglects either biological or social variables in his work, for he stresses the idea that any psy-chological phenomenon must be understood in terms of the interplay of biological, behavioral, experiential, and social variables. If we use Freud as a point of reference, however, we could say that Erikson de-emphasizes the biological substrate and emphasizes cultural and phe-nomenological variables. Before proceeding to examine his ideas in greater depth, perhaps we could briefly summarize the other features that distinguish his work and his viewpoint.

1. His main contribution to theory is a doctrine of development that postulates eight stages covering the entire life cycle.
2. Although he is a practicing analyst, his emphasis both in theory and in

177

research observation has been on the "normal" or "healthy," rather than the pathological.

3. He attaches particular importance to the development and experience of a sense of identity.

4. He is interested in cultural determinants and cultural variations in development and has made observations in other cultures.

5. He has made significant contributions to the psychological treatment of biographical material. His published books include major works on Martin Luther and Mohandas Gandhi. [15]

An excellent biography of Erikson has been written by Robert Coles. [16] Erikson's parents were Danish, and both of them had grown up in Copenhagen. Before his birth, however, his parents separated, and his mother left Denmark. Erikson was born in 1902 near Frankfurt in Germany. When he was three years old, his mother married a Jewish pediatrician named Homburger. He grew up in the home of Dr. Homburger in Karlsruhe.

When he completed his studies at the gymnasium at eighteen, he spent a year wandering through Europe instead of going on to the university. He then enrolled in an art school in Karlsruhe. After another year, he left again and studied for a brief time at another art school in Munich. He then went to live in Florence, where he spent much of his time walking through the streets and hills of the surrounding countryside. At twenty-five he returned to Karlsruhe, where he resumed his study of art, preparing for a career as an art teacher. Before long, however, he received an invitation from an old friend, Peter Blos, that was to mark an important turning point in his life. Blos had been living in Vienna and had been asked by Anna Freud and an American named Dorothy Burlingham to form a school for the children of English and Americans living in Vienna. Peter Blos asked Erik Erikson to join him in this venture, and Erikson accepted. He moved to Vienna, where he lived from 1927 to 1933. He soon came into contact there with members of the Vienna Psychoanalytic Society, for the school had been founded essentially to meet the needs of children whose parents were undergoing analysis. In the course of time, he commenced his own analysis with Anna Freud and soon undertook psychoanalytic training.

For a man destined to assume an important place in the psychoanalytic movement, his background was unusual. He was provided early in life with an incentive to study medicine, for he was reared in the home of a pediatrician who would have liked to see his stepson pursue the same profession. Apparently the interest in working with children took firmer hold than the interest in medicine. Erikson was not a diligent student in his childhood or his youth. Whatever his interest in education, he resisted the formal regimen of the gymnasium in his early years, and he was not eager to proceed at the age of eighteen to the rigors of a university education. His subsequent formal training was primarily in the field of art, and he spent considerable time in his youth wandering, seeking his own personal identity and his own place in the world. When he entered analysis and analytic training, he brought with him a rich background of life experience and was recognized as a very promising prospective psychoanalyst.

It is interesting that he entered analytic training with no clear intention of making a career of clinical work. He was still concerned with being an artist. But in 1933 he completed his training and, like many other psychoanalysts threatened with extinction under Hitler's regime, moved to the United States, where he became the first child analyst in the city of Boston. Despite the fact that he lacked a university degree of any kind, he was shortly given a post at Harvard Medical School. While in Boston he also did a bit of work with Henry Murray at the Harvard Psychological Clinic. In 1936 he took a position at the Institute of Human Relations at Yale University. He was interested in the work of the anthropologists at Yale, and in 1938 he made a trip to Pine Ridge Reservation in South Dakota to study the Sioux Indians. The next year he moved to California to assume a practice in child analysis in San Francisco and became involved in work at the Institute of Child Welfare of the University of California. He also undertook a study of the Yurok Indians. In 1950 he accepted a position at the Austin Riggs Center in Stockbridge, Massachusetts, and in 1960 he became a Professor at Harvard University.

Erikson's best known work, *Childhood and Society,* was first published in 1950.[17] In that book he presented the essential features of his developmental theory. In later publications he elaborated on various facets of the total sequence of development. He speaks of human development in terms of an epigenetic sequence of eight stages that cover the entire life span. His theory also assumes eight corresponding basic areas of psychological functioning. The experiences, expressions, and interactions associated with each one of these areas assume critical importance at a particular stage of development. Each area exists throughout life, of course, and there may be important experiences that concern it at any point in life, but according to Erikson there is one period of life for which each area is "phase-specific." Thus, the problems of establishing a sense of identity assume particular importance in adolescence, though significant experiences relating to identity begin to occur in infancy and the sense of identity may be also affected by events that occur late in life. Similarly, the period of the early school years is of special, but not exclusive, importance for the experience of industry. The phase-specificity is assumed to be governed to a high degree by a natural readiness resulting from maturation, but societal pressures also affect it.

Erikson assumes that the eight stages are a universal feature of human development, though there is cultural variation in the way in which the individual deals with the problems of each stage and in the possible solutions to these problems. Some degree of cultural uniformity is dictated by biology. Thus, puberty rites vary from one culture to another, but we do not have to assume cultural diffusion to account for the fact that such rites exist in all cultures. Erikson speaks of each stage in terms of a "psychosocial crisis" associated with that stage. He characterizes each crisis in terms of a polarity—two alternative conditions, such as trust versus mistrust or intimacy versus isolation, that represent respectively a criterion of relative psychosocial health and a corresponding criterion of relative ill health. Both alternatives are a necessary part of the experience of every individual, but the most desirable or normal resolution of any psychosocial crisis is one in which the healthy experiences outweigh the unhealthy ones. With this favorable balance, the individual is better prepared to meet the problems of the next phase of development. The solution reached for the psychosocial crisis specific to each stage is not altogether final, but it is assumed to be a relatively durable solution that colors all subsequent experience.

Erikson's developmental schema may be viewed as an adaptation and expansion of the Freudian psychosexual theory of development, since he began with Freud's system. Erikson's first three stages obviously correspond to Freud's oral, anal, and phallic stages. Erikson attempts to deal with a complex interplay of variables at each stage, however, and does not emphasize the same content as Freud. His system of psychosocial stages is more concerned with ego functioning than with the expression of sexual instincts. Elaborating on Freudian theory, Erikson speaks of the first stage, that of infancy, as the oral-respiratory-sensory stage, and he says that this is a stage in which the incorporative mode of functioning dominates all activity and experience. The major psychosocial crisis of this period is that of basic trust versus basic mistrust. The extent to which the infant experiences basic trust is largely determined by the quality of maternal care. An absence of trust is most clearly seen in cases of infantile schizophrenia.

Erikson speaks of the second stage as the anal-urethral-muscular stage. While the infant was pretty much a passive recipient of stimuli in the first stage, the development of the musculature sets the stage for new modes of functioning and of interaction with the environment. The modes of holding on and letting go, of retention and elimination, now become important. As the child senses increasing possibilities for assuming control of his own body—with respect to prehension and locomotion as well as eliminative functions—he may display much stubborn persistence and resistance in his efforts to experience this control and to exercise choice. The psychosocial crisis of this stage is that of autonomy versus shame and doubt. For a lasting sense of autonomy and pride, the child must be permitted in this stage to experience self-control without a loss of self-esteem.

Erikson calls the next stage the locomotor-genital stage. At this stage the child has an established capacity for moving about the environment. He can walk and run without being preoccupied with the movement itself. He becomes more concerned with the activities and interactions that he can initiate. According to Erikson, the child at this stage is typically "on the make." This stage is characterized by the psychosocial crisis of initiative versus guilt, and the child may emerge from it with confidence that he can meet his needs in the world and a feeling that he is entitled to do so or he may emerge with a feeling of guilt and resignation.

The fourth stage corresponds in time to the latency period of Freudian theory. While Erikson assumes that the sexual instincts remain largely subdued during this period, he is more interested in what is present than in what is absent in this stage. He speaks here of a psychosocial crisis of industry versus inferiority. This is the period of life prior to puberty when it is customary in all cultures for the child to receive systematic instruction and to cultivate the skills he will ultimately need in order to function as an adult in the social world around him. He may develop a confidence in his capacity for mastering and exercising those skills or he may come to feel that he is inadequate to meet this demand. Much depends on the interactions that occur with teachers and with available adult role models.

The fifth stage, the period of puberty and adolescence, is marked by the psychosocial crisis of identity versus identity diffusion. The developmental task that the individual now faces is to arrive at an adult identity. The adult sexual role and career role are important aspects of this identity, and foundations for both of these have been laid in earlier stages. Identity, or "ego identity," has received much more attention in Erikson's writings than any other developmental goal.[18] As a result of his writings, the concept has acquired considerable currency and received much attention from other writers as well. Perhaps the concept has become popular because it resonates with something in contemporary America that causes the search for identity to assume unusual urgency for many groups in this country, including young people, ethnic minorities, and women.

Just what does Erikson mean by *ego identity?* It is more than merely the adoption of particular adult roles. Erikson uses the term in a very broad sense that is difficult to capture in a precise definition. We may note first of all that he speaks of a *sense* of ego identity, just as he speaks of a sense of basic trust or a sense of autonomy. In each case, the "sense" involves a conscious experience, but it is more than that, for it encompasses behavior and unconscious inner states as well. Thus, it is a pervasive quality of the individual's existence. In the case of identity, it is a sense that concerns one solidity and continuity as a unique individual being. The meaning of the term shifts a bit in the course of Erikson's writings, but in a fairly late work, he defines *ego identity* as "the awareness of the fact that there is a self-sameness and continuity to the ego's synthesizing methods, the style of one's individuality, and that this style coincides with the sameness and continuity of one's meaning for significant others in the immediate community." [19] Erikson apparently regards the need for identity as one of the most distinctive products of human evolution and the sense of identity as the crowning achievement of child and adolescent development.

In the search for identity, the relationship to the group assumes a special importance, for we derive much of our sense of identity from identification with the social group—which might consist of a tribe, a clan, a small clique, a class, an ethnic or religious group, or an entire nation. In some writings Erikson is concerned with the special problems of ethnic minorities with respect to the problem of identity. For some people, identification with a movement or with an ideology may be an important source of a sense of identity; conversely, disidentification with a group and the rejection of a set of values by which one is expected to abide may serve as a way of defining one's own self. Whatever choices the individual makes, he is likely to emerge from the adolescent period with a fresh and much more elaborate system of values. As Erikson's theory recognizes, this is an important period for moral development of a kind not encompassed by the Freudian superego concept.

The relationship between the individual and the group is a complex one. A well-organized group may support various ego functions and contribute much to a sense of identity. Erikson notes that men in highly mechanized military units often enjoy a high level of morale while they are in military service and then suffer a drastic loss of effective functioning after they are discharged. There is an obvious danger in depending too much on a group as source of identity. On the other hand, there is a serious danger in going to the other extreme and refusing to recognize oneself as a part of any possible group. Com-

183

monly adolescents depend heavily on peer groups and display considerable cliquishness, but this tends to lessen as they develop a clearer sense of individual identity.

Adolescence is essentially the period of life that extends from the time of biological maturity to the time at which one is expected to assume the full responsibility of adulthood. This period tends to be extended in more complex societies. In most, perhaps all, societies, special delays in the assumption of adult commitments are granted to certain segments of the youthful population. To these periods of delay Erikson applies the term *psychosocial moratorium.* The psychosocial moratorium may provide the individual with a period in which he can acquire special skills or just play, perhaps a period in which he can explore a number of different paths before deciding what he really wants to do with his life. At times, young people in large numbers have taken to wandering, exploring new relationships and territories and testing their powers away from home, before settling down in a community. This pattern has become rather common in the United States in recent years, and in Europe it was common at an earlier time. Erikson himself went through such a period in his youth. Sometimes juvenile delinquency serves as a way of creating a psychosocial moratorium.

Erikson deals with the problems of achieving a sense of identity in contemporary America from a number of standpoints. He notes a rather widespread alienation that has gained expression in a neohumanist revolt against a highly specialized and mechanized technological society, but he believes that alienation as such is not really just a modern phenomenon. If by *alienation* we mean a failure to combine one's identity development with the dominant techniques of production, Erikson would argue that this has probably occurred to some extent in all past historical periods, but perhaps it is taking new forms. He notes the rapid changes in our society and the breakdown of traditional sex-typing. These, combined with the great profusion of contrasts, polarities, and alternative life styles on the American scene complicate the developmental task of forming a clear sense of adult identity. Whatever the problems, Erikson sees a positive value in the variety of choices to be made. For the individual who can withstand

184

the inevitable conflicts and discontinuities, there is a possibility of achieving a more universal human identity than would be likely to emerge in a simpler society.

Identity diffusion, or a failure to form a clear sense of identity, is also a serious hazard in a complex society. It is most likely to occur when the individual is expected simultaneously to make a variety of choices and commitments for which he is not ready. The contributions to identity formation from earlier stages may make a big difference. Destructive and psychotic episodes are fairly common expressions of identity diffusion in adolescence, and Erikson says that these are particularly likely to occur in individuals who have had strong previous doubts about their sexual identity. He speaks of a variety of other possible expressions and effects of identity diffusion:

1. coalescence with a leader and relinquishment of the effort to establish a separate identity;
2. a disturbed time perspective;
3. a diffusion of industry;
4. the choice of a negative identity;
5. a painful self-consciousness or identity-consciousness;
6. using a group identity to reduce a sense of personal incompletness;
7. clannishness and intolerance of out-groups;
8. a confusion of values;
9. various symptoms of a failure to achieve an adult sexual identity: bisexual confusion, a concentration on early modes of genital activity without intimacy, or a pursuit of social, intellectual, or artistic aims to the exclusion of the genital element of life.

Some of these items are rather direct expressions of confusion. Others represent defensive attempts to cope with confusion, and some correspond to the modes of escape described by Fromm. The individual who passes through this stage of life most successfully emerges with a relatively clear sense of identity and a relatively clear system of values or ideological commitment.

It is the sixth stage, that of early adulthood, that corresponds most closely to the mature genital stage in Freudian theory. According to Erikson, this stage cannot coincide with biological maturity, for the individual must solve the problem of identity before he is ready for a

185

mature heterosexual relationship. Both love and sexual activity are prominent features of adolescence, of course, but Erikson feels that they are bound up in the search for identity at that time and serve more as ways of exploring and testing than as expressions of mature intimacy. The psychosocial crisis of the sixth stage is the crisis of intimacy versus isolation. The successful achievement of intimacy or mature genitality requires a capacity for a relationship that includes not only mutual sexual satisfaction, but a trust and mutuality with respect to various other aspects of living as well.

The seventh stage is one marked by the psychosocial crisis of generativity versus stagnation or self-absorption. For Erikson, the term *generativity* includes much that other writers might call productivity or creativity. It involves a genuine caring for whatever one generates. It may be expressed in a concern for one's children, but it may be expressed in many other creative ways and directed toward other creative products. It may be expressed in efforts directed toward the betterment of society. Sometimes it is lacking in young parents who are unable to care adequately for their children because they have not yet resolved the problems of intimacy.

The final stage of life, which is labeled maturity, is marked by the psychosocial crisis of ego integrity versus despair. Erikson's terms and description suggest that the issue of the overall meaningfulness of one's existence assumes paramount significance in the later years of life. Either one experiences this meaning or one despairs with the recognition that it is too late to create an entirely different life. The concept of ego integrity is subtle, however, and defies clear definition, and it is best to quote Erikson's own description of it:

> It is the ego's accrued assurance of its proclivity for order and meaning. It is a post-narcissistic love of the human ego—not of the self—as an experience which conveys some world order and spiritual sense, no matter how dearly paid for. It is the acceptance of one's one and only life cycle as something that had to be and that, by necessity, permitted of no substitutions: it thus means a new, a different love of one's parents. It is a comradeship with the ordering ways of distant times and different pursuits, as expressed in the simple products and sayings of such times and pursuits. Although aware of the relativity of all the various life styles which have given meaning to human striving, the possessor of integrity is ready

to defend the dignity of his own life style against all physical and economic threats. For he knows that an individual life is the accidental coincidence of but one life cycle with but one segment of history; and that for him all human integrity stands or falls with the one style of integrity of which he partakes. The style of integrity developed by his culture or civilization thus becomes the "patrimony of his soul," the seal of his moral paternity of himself. . . . . In such final consolidation, death loses its sting.[20]

It would be difficult to state in any simple way Erikson's view of the optimal personality or optimal state of being. In a sense, it is obviously something that varies with the developmental stage. At any point in life, it corresponds to a favorable balance with respect to the psychosocial crisis of that stage of development. Thus, at various points in life we could characterize it as basic trust, autonomy, initiative, industry, identity, intimacy, generativity, or ego integrity. The benefits of successful maturing are regarded as cumulative, however, and the individual who can most easily master the problems of any one stage is the individual who has passed through the preceding ones without difficulty—the individual who has the residual sense of basic trust and autonomy and initiative and so forth. Perhaps we should note that in characterizing the eight "basic virtues" that remain as a consequence of favorable balances in the eight successive stages, Erikson suggests the terms hope, will power, purpose, competence, fidelity, love, care, and wisdom. All of these qualities are important and their successful combination becomes increasingly evident as we consider people who are healthy (in Erikson's sense of the term) at later age levels. In a way, ego integrity, or wisdom, embraces all the other qualities, though it primarily implies a sense of meaning with respect to one's own life-style and an acceptance of life in general. Be that as it may, all eight qualities are important in Erikson's developmental theory. Together, they represent a more comprehensive description of the optimal condition than we have seen in the other theories we have considered. They cannot be reduced to a single extant model of the ideal person. They embrace a variety of qualities that have been stressed separately in other theories. The qualities pertaining to emerging individuality are seen as products of the first five stages, while those pertaining to love and relatedness are viewed as products of the sixth and seventh stages. There are obvious parallels to Jungian theory, since the early stages are concerned with the development of the ego (in Jung's sense), while the later ones are concerned with the relation of the ego to something more inclusive. There are many differences in detail, since Erikson is inclined to stress the individual's relationship with the outer world where Jung speaks of a relationship to the inner world. In sum, Erikson's view of optimal development is a complex and comprehensive one that allows for great individual variation.

ROBERTO ASSAGIOLI

Roberto Assagioli was born in Venice in 1888 and spent nearly his entire life in Italy, where he died in 1974. He received a medical degree from the University of Florence in 1910, specializing in neurology and psychiatry. At that time he wrote a doctoral thesis on psychoanalysis. To further his understanding of psychoanalytic techniques, he went to Zürich for a time to study with Eugen Bleuler. He then returned to Italy to practice psychoanalysis. In those early days, he had a bit of correspondence with Freud, who apparently hoped that Assagioli would promote the psychoanalytic movement in Italy. In his thesis, however, Assagioli had already noted what he regarded as some limitations of psychoanalysis, and he became increasingly convinced of its shortcomings in the course of his work and began to develop his own theories and methods. He had some direct contact with Jung, whose thinking appeared to be more compatible with his own. He regarded Jung as the major theorist whose views were closest to those of psychosynthesis, the term he came to apply to his own system of theory and psychotherapy. In 1926, Assagioli founded an Institute of Psychosynthesis in Rome. Since then, psychosynthesis has gradually come to the attention of people in distant cities and countries, and other institutes have been established. The publication of Assagioli's book entitled *Psychosynthesis* in 1965 has served to draw much greater attention to his work throughout the world.[21]

When we examine Assagioli's theoretical system, it is very easy to find a similarity to Jung. One easily gets the impression that he has borrowed a number of basic concepts from Jung and simply added to them to form his own system. Whether the additional ingredients improve the product is obviously a matter of opinion. Certain elements of Jung's basic outlook that Assagioli shares are readily apparent. He recognizes a spiritual dimension to the personality, and an unconscious depth that contains the seeds of virtue and wisdom, not just primitive impulses. In addition, he is generally concerned with the positive and constructive aspects of the personality, rather than focusing primarily on pathology. With Adler and Rank, Assagioli shares an emphasis on the will, conscious choice, and personal responsibility. Like Erikson, he is concerned with identity. There are other elements that have long been a part of his work that have recently become conspicuous in more recent brands of theory and psychotherapy—a concern with finding meaning in life, a recognition of experiences of joy and fulfillment, a stress on individual uniqueness.

Assagioli's system as a whole has evoked a mixture of reactions. Some see it as a comprehensive system of theory and procedures that may provide the core of an ecumenical movement in psychology, bringing together humanistic, transpersonal, and more traditional approaches. Others see it as an eclectic stew that does more to obscure than to enlighten. The single aspect that most often draws comment is the emphasis on conscious control and decision, which is seen in the use of exercises to develop the will and in the idea of a therapy based on a deliberately planned reconstruction of the personality. In an era dominated by psychoanalytic thought, such as emphasis would have seemed very naive. Currently, however, there is a growing tendency in therapy to employ procedures that involve goal-setting by the client and the formulation of plans for attaining these goals. Perhaps Assagioli will prove to be a man of great foresight.

Assagioli conceives of the total structure of the personality in terms of seven components:

1. the lower unconscious,
2. the middle unconscious,
3. the higher unconscious or superconscious,
4. the field of consciousness,

  5. the conscious self, personal self, or "I,"
  6. the higher or transpersonal self, and
  7. the collective unconscious.

The lower unconscious is comparable to Freud's unconscious and to the personal unconscious in the Jungian system. The middle unconscious is a realm of content that is similar to that in the field of consciousness and readily accessible to consciousness. This is essentially what Freud would call the preconscious. The higher unconscious is a source of "higher" impulses, feelings, and intuitions. Here lie the functions and the energy that provide the basis for altruistic love, for creative activity, and for religious experiences. In the Jungian system, this might be considered a part of the collective unconscious. Assagioli borrowed the term *collective unconscious* from Jung but used it to represent a domain that lies outside the individual psyche. He apparently thought of the individual psyche is being surrounded by a semipermeable membrane through which content from a more extensive psychic environment can seep.

The field of consciousness is the realm of sensations, images, thoughts and feelings of which we are directly aware. Within this lies the conscious self or "I." Assagioli speaks of this as the point of pure self-awareness and as the center of consciousness. By this he seems to mean a functional agent of consciousness, or the experiencer as such. The conscious self is clearly not equivalent to the total field of consciousness, and it is not equivalent to the "self-concept." It would correspond closely to the latter only in an individual who is highly self-aware. It is close in meaning to the *ego* in Jung's system and is sometimes designated by that term. The higher self, superconscious, or "true" self is akin to the self in Jungian theory. Assagioli thinks of this as the true center of the psyche, one which is constantly in operation—unlike the conscious self, it remains active in sleep. It is not directly available to conscious awareness, but it is actually the guiding force behind the conscious self. According to Assagioli, in a sense there is really only one self, but we experience a split. As we approach full integration, the conscious self moves closer to the higher self and becomes a more obvious and accurate reflection of its true source.

In this treatment of psychic functions, Assagioli accepted the four functions recognized by Jung—thinking, feeling, sensation, and intuition—and added three more categories. One is the function of imagination, fantasy, or imaging. The second category is that of the processes that impel us toward action—impulses, desires, drives. The final and most important function in the system is the will. This is regarded as the central and most fundamental function of the ego, or conscious self. While both psychoanalysis and behaviorism have tried to eliminate this concept and to account for behavior as simply the resultant of whatever drives are operating, Assagioli insists that the will cannot be reduced to the drives or to any other functions of the psyche. It is a separate component that stands above the multiplicity of the rest of the system and serves as a directing agent. Therefore, it is important to be aware of it and to develop it. Perhaps no other theorist has devoted so much attention to the expression and cultivation of the will. His last book is devoted to this subject.[22] He recognized six stages in the exercise of the will and devised procedures for strengthening its operation in all of these stages:

1. the recognition of motives, goals, purposes, intentions;
2. deliberation, consideration, weighing;
3. decision-making;
4. affirmation or commitment to the decision;
5. planning, organizing activity according to a clearly outlined program; and
6. execution or action and the maintenance of one's direction in the course of the act.

I must confess that I find this analysis a bit too labored for my tastes, and some of Assagioli's procedures, such as the performing of useless exercises, seem designed for people who have failed to enjoy the benefits of rigorous discipline in their early school years. Yet there is no doubt that many people—perhaps all of us in some ways—lack an adequate sense of control over their own actions and lives. Assagioli may have devised a very successful way of dealing with this problem, for he seeks to confront the individual very directly with the problem of self-control and responsibility in all its aspects—to confront the individual with the experience of his own will.

There is an obvious kinship between Assagioli and Rank, for Rank at one stage in his work saw the development of the will as the central goal of psychotherapy. His therapeutic strategy was designed to facilitate this. The methods that Assagioli employs for this purpose are a bit more concrete and perhaps more direct. On the other hand, Assagioli does not see the cultivation of the will as the primary aim of therapy. He considers it an important part of personal development, and it is an early aim of treatment, since the patient who can effectively use his will is better prepared to assume an active role in the rest of his treatment. The will, however, is still only one part of the personality, and the primary aim of treatment is the "harmonization and integration into one functioning whole of all the qualities and functions of the individual." [23] Arousing and using the will is one part of this. Gaining access to the contents, functions, and potentials that lie in the depth of both the lower unconscious and the higher unconscious is another. Closely related to this is the movement of the personal self toward the transpersonal self. Movement toward that true center, or movement toward more direct expression of that center, would be another way of stating the goal of full harmonization and integration.

Perhaps we can appreciate the ramifications of this therapeutic goal if we consider briefly the principal stages and techniques of therapy as conceived by Assagioli. He speaks of four basic stages in therapy. In the first stage the individual gains a more thorough knowledge of his own personality. This means gaining an understanding of the contents of the unconscious—the lower, middle, and higher unconscious realms. Assagioli believes that his treatment encompasses the basic goal of psychoanalysis at this stage, but goes beyond psychoanalysis in dealing with the higher unconscious.

The second stage is one in which the individual gains control of various elements of the personality. In part, this corresponds to what a psychoanalyst might call a "working-through" of material brought to light in the first stage. Assagioli speaks of two component phases, involving (a) the disintegration of the harmful images or complexes and (b) the control and utilization of the energies thus set free. He seems to feel that the ability to exercise something like the deliberate, decisive power of the will is important here, for we achieve mastery of the harmful images or complexes by critical analysis of them, by creating psychological distance between them and ourselves, by viewing them with detachment and objectivity. Assagioli speaks of a fundamental principle in connection with this stage: "We are dominated by everything with which our self becomes identified. We can dominate and control everything from which we dis-identify ourselves." [24]

All of the content with which we deal in the course of therapy may be part of us, but there is a danger in identifying too closely with any one part. As a result of such an identification, our existence becomes dominated by a single image of our being, by a single complex, by a particular emotional state, by a bodily function; we have to free ourselves from that identification in order to experience the totality of the personality.

The first two stages involve the actualization of many potentials, and they constitute what Assagioli calls a personal psychosynthesis. The later stages are increasingly concerned with what he calls spiritual psychosynthesis and their goal is the realization of the self. In the third stage, one aims to discover or create a unifying center—the higher self—and to expand personal consciousness in the direction of that center. In speaking of "discovery or creation," Assagioli recognizes that the process is partly one of recognizing one's actual potentials and partly one of creating images or ideals that can guide one's progress. While disidentification from limiting contents was important in the second stage, the cultivation of new constructive identifications may be important in the third stage.

Assagioli speaks of the fourth stage as one which involves the formation or reconstruction of the personality around the new center. This means that one moves toward fulfillment of the ideal at which one arrived in the preceding stage. Again the distinction between discovery and creation seems important, for it is possible to form a clear image of the ideal that one seeks to become or to operate without such a clearly envisioned goal and permit inner forces (whether conceived as the "spirit" within, the will of God, the Tao, or whatever) to guide one's course. The former course is more deliberate, the latter more spontaneous. Assagioli feels that both alternatives have their place and that some combination is usually best. There is a danger in being either too rigid and deliberate or too passive.

Movement toward the ideal involves three main parts or processes. One is the utilization of the available energies. These include energies associated with newly found potentials as well as those released by the analysis and disintegration of complexes. Assagioli assumes something akin to the mechanism of sublimation recognized by Freud. Behaviorally, the implication is a redirection of activity into more constructive and creative channels. The second part of the work of this stage entails the development of those aspects of the personality that are deficient or inadequate. The third part is one of achieving appropriate subordination and coordination of all energies and functions.

One feature of psychosynthesis that most clearly distinguishes it from other methods of psychotherapy is that it employs many different techniques to accomplish the tasks just described. It is difficult to provide a concise overview of these techniques because there are dozens of them, and Assagioli's writings consist largely of descriptions of techniques. He says that the treatment makes "systematic use of all available active psychological techniques," but contrary to the impressions of many people, he insists that he is not just an eclectic. Obviously he borrows a variety of procedures from a variety of sources, but each technique that he uses is designed to serve a very specific purpose in the therapy. Guided by the needs of personal development as he sees them, he employs many procedures that are not usually regarded as part of the repertoire of the psychotherapist.

Thus, there are a number of techniques for developing the will or for developing other functions that may be deficient—memory, intuition, various forms of imaging. There are techniques for working in fantasy with one's ideals, with the aim of disposing of inadequate models, developing better ones, and achieving identification with these. There is a basic procedure (essentially a modification of a yogic meditation formula) for effecting disidentification from the body, from feelings and emotions, from desires, and from the intellect, and for identifying instead with a center of pure consciousness. There are a number of procedures that make use of symbols. In principle, the therapist at any point in therapy would select an appropriate technique depending on what most needs to be done at that point, whether the immediate task is to strengthen a particular function, to awaken latent potentialities, to transform or redirect energies.

There appears to be a great deal in the way of conscious control and decision woven into the fabric of psychosynthesis. There is an emphasis on the cultivation of the will, at least as a preliminary goal. There is an assumption that very specific decisions can be made at each point in therapy about where the patient is to go and about the specific method needed to produce the desired effect. At first the therapist makes the decision, but the patient is expected to assume more and more active control. One can read into Assagioli's descriptions and into many of his techniques a systematic program for self-improvement, in the course of which the individual decides what he wants to be and deliberately moves toward his goal. This is the picture that many people have of psychosynthesis. To the extent that it is accurate, one could argue that Assagioli is really primarily concerned with developing what Jung would call the ego, rather than with the realization of the self. So long as one insists on maintaining firm conscious control over everything that happens, any movement toward an ideal amounts to a restructuring of the ego rather than a full expression of inner resources. Perhaps this kind of criticism does Assagioli an injustice, since he does employ techniques, such as inner dialogues, that permit the expression of inner forces not under conscious control. Furthermore, he allows for individual differences with respect to reliance on deliberate decision and construction as opposed to a reliance on a more spontaneous unfolding. Maybe it would be fair to say that on the whole Assagioli appears in practice to place somewhat more emphasis than Jung on the cultivation and use of conscious analysis and control. In theory, the two men may not be too far apart.

For Assagioli, the optimal state is obviously the condition that he views as the goal of psychosynthesis. As I have noted, he speaks of this in terms of the "harmonization and integration into one functioning whole of all the qualities and functions of the individual." He also speaks of it in terms of a reconstruction of the personality around the higher self and in terms of a synthesis between the personal self and the higher self. This much seems close to the Jungian position. There are a couple of additional ideas we can also glean from Assagioli's writings. For one thing, he recognizes some variation in the ideal models that people create in the later phases of therapy and distinguishes two principal types of models. One emphasizes "harmonious development, an all-round personal or spiritual perfection." The other emphasizes specialized efficiency, the development of effective self-expression along one particular line, such as art, teaching, or social action. Assagioli thinks that introverts tend to prefer the former type of model, while extraverts prefer the latter. The former type may provide a better fit to Assagioli's definition of the goal of psychosynthesis, but this is not altogether clear. It is clear that a fully developed person, in Assagioli's view, may follow any one of numerous paths once he has attained full development: He may be essentially a spiritual person, a creative artist, or one who works for social betterment.

We should also note that Assagioli speaks of two higher forms of psychosynthesis that go beyond the realm of individual development for which his methods were devised. One of these is interindividual psychosynthesis. This involves the relationships among individuals. While he does not elaborate on this or on methods for accomplishing it, he apparently sees great value in harmonious interaction among people. The ultimate goal of interindividual psychosynthesis would be for every individual to be aware of his relatedness to the whole of humanity and to express this relatedness in all interpersonal transactions. Assagioli speaks also of a cosmic psychosynthesis, which "consists of an ever increasing recognition and acceptance by the individual of the laws, the relationships and the rhythms governing life itself, in its widest sense." [25] In addition to speaking of this kind of personal recognition of universal order, Assagioli hints at a conception of a progressive unification of all living beings comparable to that described by Teilhard de Chardin, but he does not attempt to integrate such a notion into his theoretical system.

ERIC BERNE

Eric Berne, the originator of transactional analysis, received medical training at the McGill University Faculty of Medicine in Montreal before moving to the United States; subsequently he studied at the New York Psychoanalytic Institute. In the course of his career he practiced psychiatry and neurology in a variety of clinics and hospitals. At the time of his death, he was engaged in a psychiatric practice in Carmel, California.

Psychoanalysis provided the initial inspiration for Berne's system of theory and therapy, but he proceeded from a Freudian foundation to build a system in which the focus is shifted from individual dynamics and personality structure to the realm of interpersonal behavior. For some time Berne considered himself a psychoanalyst, but his efforts to gain recognition from psychoanalytic groups met with frustration. His ideas were first spelled out at length in the book *Transactional Analysis in Psychotherapy,* which received only limited attention from any quarter at the time of its publication. A later work, however, *Games People Play,* proved to be an international bestseller, and transactional analysis soon became a thriving, popular movement.[26]

Berne was accused of lacking originality and of presenting what is basically an over-simplified version of Freudian theory. Such a charge is not altogether just, although there is a Freudian base to his system that should be recognized. His basic structural concepts—the parent, adult, and child ego states—bear an obvious parallel to the superego, ego, and id of Freudian theory. To a fair extent they serve the same functions as the corresponding Freudian terms, but there is much in their application that is novel. For Berne's other concepts it is much more difficult to find Freudian equivalents. Like Freud, Berne attached importance to early childhood. He believed that "life positions" and "scripts" are formed early in life. In his actual treatment of early development, however, he was probably closer to Adler than to Freud. The early events that he considered important have little to do with the unfolding of the sexual instincts; they have more to do with power relationships and with the infant's validation as a person—whether he is treated as a being of worth and how he reacts to the treatment he receives. Berne's concept of scripts was also anticipated by Adler, who believed that everyone had a secret life plan underlying his style of life.

There is another respect in which Berne closely resembles Adler. Among all the theorists who have received attention in recent years, Berne was the leading populist. He strove for a theory language that everyone could use, a language that could be employed as readily by the patient as by the therapist. His system makes use of everyday language, though some common words are necessarily given rather specialized definitions. Although one must learn some new definitions, the language always has the ring of familiarity and it is easy to understand. Furthermore, in the case of the labels applied to "games," the terminology is catchy. For every intellectual sophisticate who is repelled by the terminology, a hundred nonpsychologists are hooked by it. Thus, transactional analysis has come to enjoy the status of a popular fad.

No doubt some people would disparage transactional anlysis because it is a popular psychology, assuming perhaps that any system with such a wide appeal must be lacking in subtlety. It is difficult to find any fault with popularity per se, however. Although I have moments in which I lapse into intellectual snobbery myself, I believe there is a great need for sound popular psychologies. We can better serve the needs of this society if we cease to regard "mental health" as the exclusive province of the expert professional and concentrate instead on augmenting the psychological understanding of people in general. We should give away as much of our knowledge to as many people as possible. If this is what we are to do, perhaps psychologists should devise more in the way of popular theory, or popular versions of nonpopular theory, to facilitate communication.

It is possible that popularity increases the chances of misuse of theory. On the other hand, perhaps the probability that a theory will be misused is simply proportional to the number of people, professional or otherwise, who pay any attention to it. In any case, a theory language that becomes popular is bound to be plugged into everyday conversation for various purposes. The language of transactional analysis lends itself readily to a game of "upmanship"—an "I've got your number" game. Of course, what is now true of transactional analysis may have been true of Freudian theory in the past. A few years ago, in the midst of ordinary discourse, people might suddenly accuse you of "projecting" or of displaying "reaction formation." Now they are more likely to say, "Aha! Your child ego state is showing," or "That remark came from your critical parent." Of course, a theory language must have a certain descriptive power before it can be used in this way, and this may be to the credit of transactional analysis.

198

Perhaps one can more legitimately charge Berne's theoretical system with being a bit simplistic. It employs a limited set of rather simple concepts to cover the complex realm of human interaction. I think we must grant that the system does a rather efficient job as far as it goes—otherwise it could not have attracted so many followers. Berne strove for comprehensiveness, however, and it is easy to note parts of the total territory of human interaction that he neglected. There are different levels of human interaction, for example, that we recognize when we speak of true intimacy or of the I-Thou orientation as opposed to more superficial or more object-oriented interactions. Transactional analysis is not designed to deal directly with such things, though it does not ignore them altogether. It does provide a varied language for describing conditions that would prevent intimacy, but not a language that is adequate for describing or conceptualizing this kind of interaction in itself. It is not the ultimate theory of human relationships. But then, nothing else is either.

Let us examine the actual constituents of Berne's theoretical system. One of his most basic concepts is ego states. These are "states of mind and their related patterns of behavior." [27] An ego state is a pattern of functioning that involves ways of feeling, thinking, perceiving, and acting. There are three fundamental ego states: the parent state, the adult state, and the child state. The first of these involves modes of functioning incorporated at any early age and borrowed from one's own parents or from the early parent figures in one's life. It is possible to distinguish subpatterns within the parent state. Those that are most often distinguished by transactional analysts are the natural or nurturing parent and the controlling or critical parent. In the adult state, we process information, seek facts, and make logical deductions. This state is characterized by objectivity and rationality, rather than borrowed attitudes. The child state involves attitudes and impulses that appear naturally in early childhood. Some of these are direct expressions of natural predispositions in childhood, while others represent an early reaction to external pressures. Again it is possible to distinguish subpatterns—Berne distinguished the natural child, the adapted child, and the rebellious child.

The parent, adult, and child are viewed as the main components of the total personality, and it is assumed that all three are present in everyone. These three concepts also constitute the principal tool for personality description, for it is assumed that the major differences among people can be described in terms of the ego states they characteristically exhibit and in terms of the ease or readiness with which they move from one state to another. The analysis of the patterns found in a given individual constitutes what Berne called "structural analysis." The term *transactional analysis* is used in a narrow sense to designate the analysis of interactions between people in terms of their ego states. (It is used in a broader sense, of course, to encompass the entire system of theory and therapy.) A complete transaction involves both a communication from one person to another and a response from the second person to the first. Berne distinguishes three or four basic kinds of transactions.

A complementary transaction is one in which a message coming from a given ego state in person A elicits a reply from B that expresses the ego state expected or anticipated by A. One example would be a straightforward exchange of information in which the adult states of two people are involved. A second example would be a situation in which one person assumes a dependent role and utters a plea for assistance and another person responds with help and sympathy—an expression of the child state followed by a solicited expression from a nurturing parent. Another type of transaction is the crossed transaction, in which the second person does not respond in the expected way, but instead responds from a noncomplementary ego state. This occurs, for example, if person A utters a plea for sympathy and B responds with straight factual information, or if A asks for information and receives critical comments in return.

In the case of ulterior transactions, communication operates on two levels at once. A superficial, ostensible message is accompanied by a more subtle message involving a different ego state. Berne notes two subtypes, the angular transaction and the duplex transaction. In the case of the angular transaction, person A directs an ostensible message to one ego state in B while implying a slightly different message directed to another part of B: on the surface he may simply be imparting information (directed to the adult of B), while at the same time conveying criticism, a seductive invitation, or a plea for support. B may respond either to the ostensible message or to the ulterior one. In the case of a duplex transaction, communication occurs on two different levels for both people involved. Thus, A and B may be verbally exchanging facts in adult-adult fashion, while a more playful interchange on a child to child level is reflected in their gestures, facial expressions, and tones of voice.

To describe human interactions over longer periods, Berne distinguished six modes of structuring time. One mode is withdrawal, an avoidance of communication. A second is rituals, stereotyped or stylized modes of interaction largely governed by social custom or tradition. A third is activities, or work, in which attention is largely directed toward producing some result in external reality. A fourth is pastimes, which resemble rituals but are not quite as stylized and predictable; much of the interchange at a formal gathering among people who do not know one another well consists of pastimes. The least stereotyped and most spontaneous form of interaction is intimacy. This tends to be the riskiest (though potentially the most rewarding) mode of interaction because its course is the least predictable.

A sixth kind of interaction is games. This mode of time-structuring receives much more extensive treatment in Berne's writings, and one of his books, *Games People Play,* is devoted almost entirely to this topic. The word *game* has a variety of meanings, of course, and it is important to understand the specialized way in which Berne used the word. As he defined it, a game is always an ulterior transaction that is calculated to produce a certain psychological effect. Berne spoke of the game as following a sequence that involves the following elements: a con, a gimmick, a switch, a crossup, and a payoff.[28] First, there is an ostensible message or invitation (the con) with an ulterior purpose from the person who wishes to play the game. For the game to proceed, this message must fit some need or inclination (the gimmick) on the part of the second person, who then responds in the way expected. The first person then delivers the switch, a response that takes advantage of the position of the other person and reveals the hidden purpose of the original message. This leads to a moment of confusion (the crossup) and ultimately leaves the second person with bad feelings (the payoff). Berne contended that games appear in all spheres of human interaction and that we very frequently resort to games of various kinds, instead of relating honestly and naturally to one another.

There are features that characterize the interactions of an individual over long segments of his life span, and Berne employed two additional concepts to deal with these: scripts and life positions. A script is a preconscious life plan that governs the way in which the individual relates to himself, to other people, and to the world over long periods of time. The foundation for the script is provided by parental injunctions very early in life. The nature of the script may depend on the birth position of the child, and it may have antecedents within the family that can be traced back over several generations. In addition to the early injunctions and actions that dictate the initial script, the parents may supply prescriptions and slogans that provide the basis for a counterscript, a life plan calling for an alternate course of action. The individual will revise the script a bit as he moves into the wider social world in childhood and adolescence, but he may end up applying the same basic plot to a more elaborate set of characters. Berne believes that most of the basic themes found in scripts have prototypes that one can find in myths and fairytales. Thus, a given individual may have a life script that contains the essential theme of Cinderella, Prometheus, or the Ugly Duckling.

A script usually implies a particular life position, and Berne distinguishes four possible positions:

1. I'm not OK—you're OK.
2. I'm not OK—you're not OK.
3. I'm OK—you're not OK.
4. I'm OK—you're OK.

The writer who presents the most extensive treatment of these positions is Thomas Harris, who says that the first one above appears first in the infant.[29] This idea accords with the Adlerian view of universal feelings of inferiority in childhood. The infant finds himself powerless in relation to the adults who must attend to his needs. According to Harris, by the end of the second or third year, the first position tends to be confirmed or to be replaced by either the second or third position. The second position is said to be characteristic of autistic children and arises in a situation in which there is minimal interaction between the child and parents. The third position may result from more overtly hostile or brutal treatment of the child and, in extreme cases, may provide the foundation for criminal psychopathy. The fourth position is the optimal one. According to Harris, it must come later, if it does develop, because it requires a more conscious decision on the part of the child.

It is fairly easy to identify both desirable and undesirable conditions with respect to any of the modes of description employed in transactional analysis. If we are to describe pathology in terms of ego states, it consists in an inability to shift flexibly from one state to another or in contamination of a given state with other states. Being unable to shift may mean that the individual is stuck in just one state. In this case, in all his interactions he may persist in playing the role of tyrant, nurturing mother, unfeeling computer, or playful child, regardless of the inappropriateness of the role to the immediate situation or the desirability of meeting needs that cannot be expressed through that role. Sometimes the inflexibility is better described as the exclusion of a particular state, so that the individual operates without a parent state, a child state, or an adult state. In the first case (absence of the parent state), the individual functions without an effective conscience. In the second case, he is likely to appear drab and boring, since he lacks the spontaneous feeling and expression of the child. The third case is found in the psychotic, who displays a severe loss of reality contact.

Contamination might be considered a lesser degree of exclusion. We would speak of contamination when an individual is unable to function in a given ego state without manifesting the elements of another state at the same time. The usual examples involve an inability to function in the adult state without contamination from either the parent state or the child state. Thus the individual cannot operate very objectively, because his information processing is contaminated by prejudicial attitudes or by compliant or rebellious responses to authority. According to Berne and his fellow transactional analysts, we need

203

all three ego states to live fully, and the ideal condition is to have access to all three, to be able to utilize each fully, and to be able to shift from one state to another as our needs and the situation require.

With respect to transactions, the optimal condition is again one of flexibility, since different ego states call for different kinds of transactions. The more we communicate honestly and directly with people, however, the more we will tend to minimize ulterior transactions and games (which utilize ulterior transactions for a destructive purpose). Under ideal circumstances, our time-structuring may take many forms, but intimacy will be among the available options. With respect to the longer segments of life, the ideal condition is one in which one is fully aware of the scripts dictated by early parent-child transactions and is able freely to abandon them and become fully the author of his own life. It is also a condition in which he is prepared fully to accept both himself and others, the "I'm OK—you're OK" life position.

In comparison with other methods of therapy or paths of liberation, transactional analysis places a heavy emphasis on intellectual insight. To benefit from it, the individual learns the language and applies it to his states of functioning, to his interactions with other people, and to the structure of his life as a whole. It is assumed that with the insights that he gains in this way he will recognize a need to explore paths that he has avoided, that he will seek ways to get unstuck from certain modes of interacting, that he will be able to abandon his games, and that he will be liberated from his script because he will know what he is doing. If intellectual insight is not viewed as the ultimate goal, it is certainly viewed in transactional analysis as the primary means to the goal.

Perhaps the word that best captures what Berne saw as the goal is *autonomy*. He assumed that the individual who has insight will be able to act and choose more freely. He will not be caught in patterns of feeling, thinking, and acting that were set in motion by interactions very early in life, but will be able to redirect his course altogether if it suits his needs. Berne says that autonomy is manifested in the recovery of three basic capacities—awareness, spontaneity, and intimacy.[30] In this context, awareness is not so much a matter of intellectual insight as a matter of being able to tune in fully to the present moment, to be able really to experience whatever exists here and now. Spontaneity implies flexibility of choice and freedom from the compulsion to play destructive games. Intimacy, of course, requires a readiness to relate to another person with spontaneity and full present awareness.

The emphasis on intellectual insight in transactional analysis is consistent with its psychoanalytic roots, but this movement appears to depend much more heavily on it than do other current derivatives of psychoanalysis. The optimal condition was not described in great detail by Berne, but the essential ingredients may be summarized by the terms *autonomy, immediate awareness, spontaneity,* and *intimacy.* These concepts together constitute a view of the ideal that overlaps in various ways with those depicted by Adler, Rank, Fromm, and contemporary humanistic psychologists.

EIGHT

EXISTENTIAL PHILOSOPHY AND PSYCHOLOGY

Existentialism, as a movement within philosophy and more recently within psychology, is essentially a development of the twentieth century, but the seeds of the movement were unquestionably sown in the nineteenth century. The movement represents a continuation of a mode of thought evident in such philosophers of the last century as Søren Kierkegaard and Friedrich Nietzsche, and the former is generally recognized as the seminal ancestor of existentialism. A more immediate ancestor of modern existentialism was Edmund Husserl, whose major works were published early in this century. Husserl cannot be viewed as an existentialist himself, but in his approach to phenomenology he developed a method of analysis that existentialists have borrowed. Martin Heidegger and Jean-Paul Sartre were both students of Husserl and were influenced by him.

The modern movement may be said to have begun in philosophy with Karl Jaspers and Martin Heidegger. Actually, both of these men rejected the existentialist label, but on both historical and substantive grounds they clearly fit within the tradition to which the term is usually applied. Among the many other philosophers who may be regarded as advocates of an existential viewpoint, perhaps the best known are Gabriel Marcel and Jean-Paul Sartre. In an earlier chapter, we examined the ideas of Martin Buber and Paul Tillich, whose thinking also reflects a definite existentialist influence.

It is difficult to draw a line between existentialist philosophy and

206

existentialist psychology, since all the philosophers we have noted are concerned with psychological issues as well as issues that pertain more strictly to philosophical method. On the whole, the people most often classified as existential psychologists manifest relatively little direct concern with issues in metaphysics or epistemology, and they tend to be interested in the application of existential thought to such domains as psychopathology and psychotherapy. Among the clearest representatives of the movement within psychology are Ludwig Binswanger, Medard Boss, Victor Frankl, Rollo May, and R. D. Laing. It is possible to find many points of similarity between the views of these men and those of other contemporary psychologists who are less clearly a part of the movement. Among the latter are such psychologists as Gordon Allport, Carl Rogers, and Abraham Maslow. There are traditions in American psychology that share many common elements with existentialism. Within the past twenty years, however, existentialism itself has gained recognition among American psychologists and has become an important influence in this country. The publication of the book *Existence,* edited by Rollo May and others, was particularly instrumental in calling the attention of American psychologists to the movement.[1]

Naturally there is much variation and some sharp disagreement among the various people I have just noted, but it is possible to note some central threads that run through the tradition and movement to which the term *existentialist* is broadly applied. Existentialism, as originally expressed in the writings of Kierkegaard and Nietzsche, began as a reaction against the dominant rationalistic and idealistic trends in philosophy. Hegel in particular was singled out for attack. Kierkegaard and Neitzsche, independently of each other, felt that their fellow philosophers tended to lose touch with the immediate reality of human experience in their efforts to grasp it through intellectual abstractions—that they tended to focus on essences and lose sight of the actuality of human existence. In science, too, they saw the same tendency to move away from the reality of human experience and existence in an effort to arrive at a truth embodied in abstract general laws.

Existentialists also seek to eliminate the "subject-object dichotomy," a conceptual division between the consciously experiencing human subject and the objective external world that he seeks to know.

This dichotomy has pervaded Western thought in recent centuries, and it underlies the idea of the detached observer in science. Heidegger attacked Descartes' distinction between *res cogitans* and *res extensa* as one influential expression of the dichotomy and insisted that the human being is a "being-in-the-world." [2] The world is an integral part of our experience from the outset, and it cannot be known apart from our experience of it and involvement in it.

What, then, is existentialism? Perhaps we could encompass most of its concerns by saying that it is a movement that stresses our immediate experience of ourselves and of our relationship to the world, but there is no generally accepted definition of the word *existentialism* itself. Perhaps it is most commonly defined as the philosophy that holds that existence precedes essence, but this is a bit vague and subject to various interpretations. In a very broad sense existentialism implies that our direct experience of ourselves and the world is more fundamental than any concepts that we formulate and that these concepts do not capture any "essence" that has a historical priority over the unabstracted realm that we know directly through our experience. A somewhat narrower interpretation has to do with freedom and choice. In this sense, existentialism would be a philosophy that stresses the fundamental importance of the human individual's freedom to choose and that holds that he has no individual essence, identity, or personality beyond that which he creates as a product of his choices. Freedom is a rather pervasive theme in existentialist literature, but this interpretation would probably fit the ideas of some existentialists much better than it would fit others.

It is doubtful whether we could devise a clearer definition that would satisfactorily embrace all the major themes of the existentialist movement. We can gain a rough overview of those themes simply by noting some of the terms that appear frequently in the literature of existentialism. Among these terms are *freedom, responsibility, commitment, value, meaning, encounter, presence, relatedness,* and *authenticity.* We can best examine the use of these terms in the context of individual philosophers and psychologists within the movement.

One final general comment is that, in its emphasis on immediate experience and its efforts to dispose of the subject-object dichotomy, existentialism resembles some Eastern modes of thought, such as Zen Buddhism. But, though it runs counter to some rather pervasive features of Western thought and yields some prescriptions that closely resemble those of Eastern disciplines, it certainly cannot be equated with any of the latter. It arose as a reaction to developments in the West, not through borrowing from the East. Furthermore, in their treatment of individual experience, existentialist writers generally focus on features that are characteristic of people who have grown up in Western society. As a result, their work deals with a variety of themes that are alien to the literature of the Orient.

SØREN KIERKEGAARD

Kierkegaard, a Danish philosopher and theologian, lived from 1813 to 1855. He was a solitary, introverted man who experienced great inner torment, and his writings clearly reflect his own personal experience. Most of the attention he received from other philosophers during his lifetime was adverse, and he was viewed as rather eccentric by his townsmen. He was occasionally treated as an object of ridicule in the public press. It was not until the present century that his works began to be seen as a valuable contribution to Western thought.

During his years as a student Kierkegaard rejected Christianity and devoted himself to the study of Hegel's philosophy, but he later became disillusioned with Hegel and with the traditions that Hegel represented. He found new meaning in Christianity but became a bitter critic of the established Church, in which he saw a worldliness that ran counter to a true religious spirit. In rejecting the abstractions of speculative philosophy, Kierkegaard espoused a doctrine of truth as subjectivity and relationship. He felt that the most important kind of knowledge could not be derived through analysis or rational manipulation but required direct involvement. He saw science, like speculative philosophy, as an escape from the full awareness of reality, and viewed the scientist as a man with a brilliant mind who lacked self-awareness and self-understanding.

With respect to ethical and religious matters, Kierkegaard's writings emphasize commitment and faith, which entail full personal involvement. Christianity must be lived, not reduced to the repetition of verbal formulae. True faith is difficult to achieve; one cannot arrive at it by a strictly rational, intellectual route since it is fundamentally absurd. One can cope with the basic Christian paradox—that God both is and is not absolutely other than man—by a route that requires increasing self-awareness and movement toward a personal relationship with God.

This route is one that we are free to choose or to avoid. In this freedom lies the greatness and uniqueness of mankind, but this freedom is also the source of our deepest agonies. In Kierkegaard's philosophy, the ideas of freedom, self-awareness, full selfhood, and relationship with God are all closely linked. The individual's task in life is to be fully himself. This requires being fully self-aware, which is only possible if one opens oneself to experiential possibilities and does not simply follow a path that is laid down by convention or one that is designed to yield easy satisfaction. The closer one comes to being fully open and conscious, the more he becomes aware of his possibilities. The possibilities include the experience of the divine ground of one's being. To be aware of possibilities is to experience freedom to choose. In the Kierkegaardian view, to the extent that the individual is aware of his possibilities and follows a course in accord with all of them, he is fully himself and stands in a personal relationship with God.

The route to this goal is a very difficult one to follow because it is inevitably marked by anxiety, guilt, and inner conflict. Anxiety (or "dread," in some translations of Kierkegaard's writings) is the state of the individual who experiences his freedom—who becomes aware of the possibilities available to him for being and creating.[3] The greater his creative capacity, the greater his possibilities and the greater his potential for experiencing anxiety. The greater the possibilities, the greater the potential for guilt as well, for guilt (or "sin") consists of a failure to actualize one's possibilities. We are all guilty to the extent that we have failed to actualize possibilities, or failed to be wholly ourselves, whether or not we are aware of our guilt.

Kierkegaard describes a number of courses that people pursue in an effort to eliminate anxiety and reduce awareness of guilt. They are essentially ways of reducing awareness of possibilities or awareness of the uncertainty occasioned by one's possibilities, and they could be translated readily into Freudian defense mechanisms or into Fromm's modes of escape. One such course is a belief in fate, which is tantamount to a denial that one has any effective independent choice. Another is "shutupness," an extreme form of withdrawal or encapsulation. A third course is denial of uncertainty through adoption of rigid, dogmatic attitudes and beliefs. Each of these courses amounts to an attempt to attain bliss through the achievement of ignorance, and such strategies can be only partially effective. The only way in which one truly overcomes anxiety and the experience of guilt is to accept these as the price of personal growth, to confront them and pursue a course that leads to full awareness, full selfhood, and faith.

In several works Kierkegaard spoke of three stages or modes of existence, and it is possible to construe his stages both as a conception of the course of personal development and as a commentary on the respective merits of various philosophical positions (including his own).[4] The first stage is the aesthetic. At this level, there is an openness to many forms of experience but a denial of the reality of personal decision. The individual skims the surface of the realm of possibilities but fails to assume the responsibility for choosing them and thus maintains only a limited form of existence. At this level, the individual wants to experience many things but will not bind himself with commitments. He seeks entertainment, pleasure, and excitement, but his limited existence tends to lead to boredom, melancholy, and despair. Kierkegaard distinguished two primary forms of expression of the aesthetic stage. One is romantic hedonism, exemplified by such figures as Don Juan. The other expression is abstract intellectualism, which is exemplified by Faust and, of course, by Kierkegaard's philosophical opponents, the Hegelians. In the former case, the individual is too preoccupied with the immediate experience of sensuality to deal seriously with the future toward which he is heading. In the latter case, the individual avoids full involvement with life and the responsibility for concrete personal decisions by retreating to the realm of abstract thought, where he plays the role of a detached observer and deliberates on universals.

211

The second stage of development is the ethical. At this level, the individual accepts the responsibility for making ethical choices. He lives for the sake of duty, rather than pleasure (in psychoanalytic terms, substituting superego-control for id-control). He is at a higher level of consciousness than the aesthetic individual, but he is still limited because the choices he makes are bound by established ethical laws. Having reached this level, however, the individual can transcend it and attain the third level, the religious stage. This is the level of the individual who accepts a personal relationship with God. At this stage he is open to a wider range of possibilities—indeed, an unlimited range that includes possibilities that defy convention or tradition, for, like Abraham, he may receive directives from God that run counter to the generally accepted moral laws. The optimal condition, the goal of personal development, is thus contained in Kierkegaard's notion of the religious stage. Kierkegaard's concept of the optimal condition emphasized self-awareness and acceptance of the responsibility of individual choice. It also emphasized a dependent relationship to God, but implicit in Kierkegaard's treatment of this is a concomitant independence from the established mores of the society.

FRIEDRICH NIETZSCHE

Kierkegaard produced most of his important works in the 1840s, and Nietzsche was born during this period. He lived from 1844 to 1900. He was born and died in Germany, but was a professor in Basel from 1869 to 1879. He apparently knew little of the work of Kierkegaard and was not directly influenced by him, yet there are many striking parallels between the two men. There are also some fundamental differences that foreshadow the alternative paths taken by existentialists in the twentieth century.

Like Kierkegaard, Nietzsche was a rather solitary, eccentric man who tended to alienate his contemporaries both with his ideas and his personal manner. He achieved more general recognition during his lifetime than had Kierkegaard, though his views were also bound to arouse much antagonism from some quarters. Like his precedessor, he experienced much inner turmoil and found in it a foundation for his own creative work. Freud once remarked that Nietzsche probably knew himself better than any other man who had ever lived or was likely to live. Perhaps the burden of self-awareness that Nietzsche assumed for himself was a bit too heavy for any individual; it may have contributed to the psychosis (a direct product of syphilitic infection) from which he suffered during his last few years.

In their philosophical views, Kierkegaard and Nietzsche have much in common. Both rejected much of the society around them, including the established Church, and opposed prevailing trends in philosophy and science. Both rejected the idealism of Hegel. Both advocated a greater reliance on direct personal experience, in opposition to the detachment of science and to the emphasis on intellectual analysis and abstraction which they found in philosophy and science generally. For Kierkegaard, however, the path of personal experience and increasing self-awareness led to a relationship with God. For Nietzsche, the path was one of pure self-reliance, for God did not exist.

Influential as Nietzsche has been, his writings do not contain a systematic philosophy. In many respects, they are more literary creations than philosophical treatises. If Nietzsche was not interested in developing a logically articulated system, however, he was intent on pressing a moral position. The position is one that shifts a bit in the course of his writings. In an early period, his work reflects the influence of Schopenhauer. He sees the will to exist as the source of suffering and advocates a negation of life as the way to achieve a release from suffering. In a second period, his position is more life-affirming and expresses something like the spirit of the Enlightenment. His best-known works, *Thus Spake Zarathustra* and *Beyond Good and Evil,* are products of a third period, where we find the views most often attributed to Nietzsche.[5]

In *Thus Spake Zarathustra* we find an attack on Christian belief and morality. The ideas of God and afterlife are regarded as delusions, and religious worship is considered a reversion to childhood. In the Christian moral code Nietzsche saw an ascetic relinquishment of the natural powers of the human individual; he spoke of Christianity as a "slave morality." His opposition to Christianity, however, was neither that of a hedonist nor that of a scientific materialist. He favored the creation of new moral standards, and these were not to be found in science. Unlike many of his contemporaries he did not see in science an awakening from the decadence of Christianity but a continuation of the same decadence in a new form. For him, Christianity, science, and democracy represented various forms of asceticism, and to achieve a sounder morality the individual must fully affirm his powers instead of practicing self-denial.

The creative force in human nature that will lead to new standards is the will to power, the urge to achieve mastery over oneself and one's fate. Nietzsche felt that the will to power may prove to be more fundamental than the need for self-preservation. Unlike the need for self-preservation, it is expressed not in a tendency to maintain a present status, but in a tendency to expand, to seek new experiences, to realize all one's *potentia,* to be a complete individual. Nietzsche believed that people devise many ways of avoiding full expression of the will to power and escaping from the responsibility for a full experience of life. They may use sleep to escape, and conventional morality provides many avenues of escape, such as renunciation of the body and the ideal of chastity. By virtue of the will to power, however, human nature demands the constant creation of new ethical standards. The will to power is itself essentially a creative force, and to express it fully we must be prepared to abandon old moral standards and go "beyond good and evil."

Nietzsche's ideal is embodied in the image of the *Übermensch,* or Superman, representing a level that mankind has not yet achieved. He spoke of man as a "rope stretched between the animal and the Superman." But the Superman is intended as an image that we should emulate, rather than a notion of our evolutionary destiny. The Superman is the individual who stands above the conforming, conventional masses of mankind because he gives full expression to his will to power and lives creatively. Independence and creativity are among the essential ingredients of Nietzsche's concept of the optimal condition. It is a heroic ideal found in early Greek thought, combined with an explicit rejection of any additional elements provided by the Judaeo-Christian tradition.

214

MODERN EXISTENTIALIST PHILOSOPHY

Martin Heidegger Heidegger, a German philosopher born in 1889, is often viewed as the originator of the modern existentialist movement, though he does not regard himself as an existentialist. His work appears to have been influenced greatly by Kierkegaard; and his thinking was undoubtedly shaped considerably through his direct contact with Husserl, though he rejects Husserl's phenomenology. However Heidegger chooses to identify himself, his ideas are a major source of inspiration for other existentialist philosophers, such as Sartre, and for existentialist psychologists and psychiatrists, such as Binswanger.

As I have noted, Heidegger rejects the subject-object dichotomy of Cartesian tradition and expounds a philosophy that stresses the existence of the human individual and the world as directly experienced.[6] According to Heidegger, the human being experiences himself in relation to his world and he experiences the world only as a realm of his human concern, never independently of that concern. The human being is a being-in-the-world. While Heidegger rejects the Cartesian dichotomy, however, he recognizes divisions within the world as experienced, and he distinguishes such regions as the *Umwelt* and the *Mitwelt*. The former is the world viewed as a realm of physical objects. The *Mitwelt* is the world as a communal region, a realm in which we experience a sharing or a commonness with others, a realm in which we are concerned with communication. This kind of classification differs from classical metaphysical classifications in that it represents a way of distinguishing different modes of experience, rather than different kinds of entities or substances.

Heidegger attempts in his writings to delineate the basic features of human existence, or *Dasein*. The most fundamental feature is something he calls care or concern (*Sorge*). Another feature is factuality or "thrownness"—the realization that we are already here, that we have been cast forth into the world in circumstances not of our choosing, that in part our destiny or lot in life has already been assigned to us. A third feature is existentiality, our recognition of ourselves as being (or existence) with possibilities, as being moving into the future and becoming, as being with freedom of choice and responsibility for choos-

215

ing. A fourth feature is fallenness, an everpresent tendency for us to become absorbed in the pursuits of the present and to lose sight of our possibilities for becoming.

Another feature to which Heidegger devotes considerable attention is anxiety, or dread (*Angst*). Anxiety is the mood that we experience when confronted with the fact that we are finite beings, the fact that implicit in our being is the possibility of not-being, or nothingness. Because of anxiety, we tend to retreat from a full awareness of ourselves and our possibilities. The result is an inauthentic existence, and it takes many forms. It may emphasize the established or conventional ways of the organized society. It may entail a preoccupation with present activities and a tendency to avoid thinking about the future and the past. It tends to involve depersonalization and objectification. The inauthentic individual relinquishes full experience of his individual being-in-the-world through a kind of "anonymous" existence.

Guilt plays a vital role in Heidegger's thinking as it does in Kierkegaard's. To the extent that we live inauthentically we are existentially guilty, and this is more or less true for all of us. Heidegger further assumes that each of us has a conscience that tends to make us aware of our guilt. Conscience calls our attention to our possibilities and presses us toward assuming greater responsibility. Of course, we are inevitably guilty to some degree, since in choosing any possibility we close off other possibilities (and are guilty for failing to actualize them). But we can at least minimize our guilt by trying to live authentically.

The optimal condition, for Heidegger, is an authentic existence. The individual who lives an authentic existence is an individual who affirms his being in the face of the reality of his guilt and his inevitable death. This is a concept that stresses self-awareness, particularly awareness of one's own finitude. It also stresses responsibility for choosing one's course of action with full recognition of the unique setting of one's life (one's past, thrownness, or factuality), of the available possibilities, and of the future toward which the chosen course is leading.

Karl Jaspers Jaspers, the other major figure in German existentialism of the twentieth century, lived from 1883 to 1969. He began his career as a psychiatrist before devoting himself to philosophy, and some of his early work was devoted to the development of a new classification system of mental illness. As a psychiatrist, he studied Kierkegaard and Nietzsche and was interested in the relationship of their personalities to their philosophies. In his subsequent work in philosophy, he acknowledged a debt to both these men, who he felt had revolutionized philosophy and forced philosophers to deal with the actuality of the human condition and human experience.

Like Heidegger, Jaspers rejected the existentialist label. Although he was certainly allied with other existentialists in his basic concern, he also differed from them in accepting some elements of idealistic philosophy and in not sharply rejecting the subject-object dichotomy. In his analysis of the nature of being, he shared some of the metaphysical presuppositions of Kant. While most contemporary existentialists can be identified as either Christian (like Kierkegaard) or atheistic (like Nietzsche), Jaspers falls into neither group. Some of his later writings have a religious flavor, and he saw value in both Christianity and Judaism, but he opposed any claim to absolute truth on the part of established religions. He rejected both religion and atheism as dogmatic positions and saw in both a danger of mistaking a one-sided view of the human condition for the totality.

Jaspers presented a more elaborate ontological system, or doctrine of the nature of being, than other existentialists.[7] His basic concept is the encompassing (*Umgreifende,* which has also been translated as the embracing and as the comprehensive). This is a notion of being that implies something that is quite pervasive and that includes much more than we can directly experience or know. He distinguished several different modes or forms of the encompassing or of being. One mode is empirical being, or being-there (*Dasein*), which is oneself as a known, physical, objective entity, a part of the world of stable objects that can be studied by science. A second mode is consciousness as such (*Bewusstsein überhaupt*), through which we can participate in a realm that extends beyond the limits of our individual lives in a given period in history. A third mode is spirit, and this term implies a striving toward universality, totality, or wholeness. Together, being-there, consciousness, and spirit are modes of the encompassing as being-which-

217

we-are. There is still another form of the encompassing—the encompassing as being-in-itself.[8]

These different modes of being are discontinuous. They must be explored by different methods, for the means by which we know one will not serve to provide knowledge of another. It is a common error to mistake one realm of being for the totality and deal with it exclusively. Thus, the positivist may preoccupy himself with one form of being and the mystic with another. In a sense, the forms of being constitute a hierarchy of transcendence. Through consciousness as such, we can transcend the realm of being-there, or empirical being, and come into contact with a broader spatial-temporal expanse. The encompassing as being-in-itself is essentially the world in its transcendence of our individual being, a level of being that we can never know directly but can only approach through the encompassing as being-which-we-are.

Two fundamental qualities that Jaspers emphasizes in discussing the nature of being are *Existenz* and reason. There is no satisfactory English equivalent for *Existenz* as Jaspers uses the term. In stressing this as a basic aspect of being, he underscores the point that being can never be understood as a static condition, for *Existenz* is to be understood as an everchanging process, as becoming, as the unfolding of possibilities. *Existenz* underlies being in all its forms. Insofar as it underlies those aspects of being that lie within our experience, we experience freedom and possibility. Reason is also a basic aspect of being, but the term is not to be understood just in the narrow sense of orderly, objective thought, but rather in terms of a basic tendency in our experience toward unity, order, and universality. Thus, a process of continuous transformation and a tendency toward unification are both part of the nature of being, and there is in our nature both an urge to become, to transcend our experienced nature, and a striving for unity and totality.

What is the optimal condition from Jaspers' viewpoint? For one thing, it would include an awareness of and participation in all forms of being. Thus, it is important for us to recognize our objective nature and the limitations of our empirical existence, which include suffering, various imperfections, and the prospect of death, but we must not deny other modes of being. It is important to recognize all modes, including the realm of being-in-itself, which we cannot directly know. The optimal condition would also include an acceptance and realization of our freedom. This acceptance requires a kind of courage and faith, for our unfolding possibilities arise from a level of being that we cannot directly know. We must make choices and decisions, seeking to transcend ourselves, without full knowledge of what we are becoming.

Gabriel Marcel The French philosopher Gabriel Marcel was perhaps the leading Christian existentialist. Born in 1889, he was baptised into the Roman Catholic Church in 1929 at the age of thirty-nine. Though he did not hesitate to reject religious dogmas that did not agree with his own personal experience, his work is characterized by a hopeful, optimistic quality that rests on his own theistic position.

Marcel was less concerned than Heidegger and Sartre with building a philosophical system, and in treating the nature of being he avoids the kind of metaphysical analysis that we find in the work of Jaspers. His emphasis was on existence as concretely experienced.[9] Its nature is process, action, participation, and we lose sight of its totality when we attempt to deal with it through analysis and abstraction. This is not merely an academic issue, for Marcel felt that there are many trends in modern life—not just in our modes of thinking about people but in the increasing bureaucratization of organized society—that tend to distort our experience of ourselves. We are in great danger of depersonalization, of loss of humanity, of loss of our creative individuality as we come to experience ourselves as things and as anonymous units in a system. We must try to remain in touch with the immediacy of our lived experience in order to combat this danger.

Perhaps the theme that most clearly distinguishes Marcel's brand of existentialism is the idea that our individual existence has a communal foundation. It is obvious that the experience of relatedness or community is an important part of our existence, but Marcel went beyond this point to contend that our existence is largely realized and disclosed through "living communication" with other selves. From the outset there is a communal aspect to the existence that we experience, and we fail to exist to the extent that we lock ourselves into the "prison of ego-centrism." Like Martin Buber, Marcel observed that in relating to

219

another, we may experience the other as either *it* or *thou,* as an object or as a person. We may relate to the "thinghood" or the selfhood of the other. In a true personal encounter, we relate to the selfhood of the other person, accepting the other as a personal center of subjectivity.

There is another quality, additional to this predisposition to relate to the other as a subjective center, that is required for communion. It is what Marcel called *disponibilité.* As he used it, this term implies a willingness to be available or accessible to the other person, a readiness to relate on a subjective level. The individual who has this quality is ready to respond sympathetically to the other and ready to reveal his own subjectivity. For Marcel, full selfhood and creative living depend on person-to-person dialogue, on experienced intersubjectivity.

The concept of freedom played a role in Marcel's thinking, as it does in that of other existentialists, but it was given a less central role and was treated mainly in the interpersonal context. We experience freedom, according to Marcel, when we recognize the possibility of relating either constructively and creatively or destructively, of committing ourselves to the relationship or betraying the other. The creative choice is one of commitment, and Marcel spoke of this in terms of faith or fidelity. Fidelity involves a willingness to respond genuinely to the other and to undertake certain responsibilities in the relationship. It involves a belief in the existence of the other person and readiness to act on that belief. At the same time, it entails an affirmation of one's own continuing existence and a willingness to be self-consistent. This implies a de-emphasis of "becoming" in the sense of being open to unpredictable movements from one state of consciousness or being to another, for to make commitments that involve the future is to foreclose capricious change. The person who manifests fidelity may still be open to change of some kind, but in a sense he has redefined the process of change by accepting responsibility for it, by acknowledging that by willing he can assume some control over the course of change.

For Marcel as for Buber, the terms applied to relationships to fellow beings are applied as well to the relationship to God. God is the absolute thou, the transcendent thou, and religious faith requires an openness to intersubjective communion and commitment. Marcel be-

220

lieved that we have a need for transcendence, a need for participation in an eternal reality that extends beyond the limits of our individual lives. Such a need can only be fulfilled through relationship with a transcendent thou.

Jean-Paul Sartre In some respects, the other leading French existentialist, Jean-Paul Sartre, represents a view that is just of the opposite of Marcel's. His position is strictly atheistic, and he does not idealize any condition of being-with-others. Indeed, his writings raise some questions as to whether close harmony between people is even possible. Some minor shifts are evident in the course of his work, and the viewpoint I shall attempt to summarize is essentially that presented in *Being and Nothingness*.[10] Born in 1905, Sartre has become widely known both as a philosopher and as a novelist and playwright. While his ideas have inspired much controversy, he is widely acknowledged as one of the foremost intellectuals on the European continent.

According to Sartre, being is coextensive with phenomena. He rejects all metaphysical categories—such as Kant's *Ding an sich*—that refer to realms of being that lie outside the range of our experience. Being has a transphenomenal character, however, because we can never grasp it all at once in its totality, and it overflows any categories that we superimpose on it when we attempt to describe it. Within the total realm of being, there is a fundamental split into two forms of being: being-in-itself (*être-en-soi*) and being-for-itself (*être-pour-soi*). The former is the being of objects or things, a being characterized by completeness, fullness, and stability. There is no becoming in this form of being, for everything is already wholly given, and there is no potential to be realized. The latter form of being is that of human consciousness, and it is characterized by incompleteness, lack of fullness, and unrealized potentiality.

Consciousness comes into being by negation, by separating itself from what it declares itself not to be. Consciousness requires an object for its own being, for it is always a consciousness of something, of some object other than itself. To put the matter in other terms, being-for-itself arises from being-in-itself and requires being-in-itself for its continued existence. Consciousness always entails both facticity and possibility. Its facticity is the given situation in which it finds itself. My facticity as a conscious being is the life setting in which I find myself thrown, the setting that has been given to me or in which I experience myself abandoned. It is a ground for my existence which I have not myself chosen. The possibility of being-for-itself is the not-yetness of existence, the prospective reality that may lie ahead, the reality to which consciousness strives.

The facticity of our existence is the being-in-itself from which we constantly separate ourselves. This is a never-ceasing process, for to be conscious is to separate oneself from what one has been and from that to which one is present. In a broad sense, this process of separation constitutes choice, and we may say that consciousness is choice. Furthermore, we may also say that choosing constitutes freedom, and hence the nature of man or the nature of human consciousness is freedom. According to Sartre, freedom is an intrinsic, inescapable part of our nature, whether we are aware of it or not. We are condemned to be free. To be aware of this freedom and of the responsibility for choosing, however, is to experience anxiety. We tend to seek an escape from our freedom through what Sartre calls "bad faith." There is no way of actually obliterating our freedom. To be in bad faith is simply to deny the reality of freedom and to act as if one lacks freedom. This is a matter of self-deception and is thus comparable to what Freudians would call a defense mechanism.

One feature of human existence that imposes a limit on our freedom is the presence of other people. Since others are a part of our world from the outset, being-for-itself always entails at the same time being-for-others. This poses a special problem, for it is in the nature of consciousness to distinguish between the conscious subject and the object of consciousness. There is no complication so long as the object is the world of inert things, but the other person is also a conscious being. For him, I am an object of consciousness, just as for me he is an object of consciousness. From an early point in our conscious existence, we experience in the interpersonal realm the threat of being reduced to an object and of losing freedom. Shame is an early expression of the awareness of the threatening other, for it is something we can only experience in relation to another conscious being. Sartre speaks also of "the look" as another example of the effect of the presence of the other. This is the experience of being seen by another and of being viewed by the other as an object. Through the look, the other threatens my freedom, and my basic defense against being reduced to an object is to attempt to render him an object through *my* look. I thereby initiate a repetitive cycle of mutual objectivization. For Sartre, this is not just one possible pattern of social interaction—it is the basic pattern.

Perhaps we might view the ideal relationship as one in which two consciousnesses merge in some kind of mutual affirmation, but Sartre seems to feel that close harmony is an impossibility. He discusses four interpersonal attitudes—love, masochism, hatred, and sadism—and finds that all entail a loss of freedom. Obviously in hatred and sadism, we seek to reduce the other to an object and destroy his freedom, while in masochism we seek to relinquish our own freedom, but even in love we cannot achieve harmony according to Sartre's analysis. The interaction is simply more complicated. To love is to seek to be the object of the other's love. While I may not wish to destroy the freedom of the other, that freedom threatens me, and I want to possess it so as to insure that the other will choose me as an object of love. In the resulting interaction, there is a tendency to revert either to masochism or to sadism, reducing either oneself or the other to an object. In principle, the enterprise of love is doomed to frustration.

Another basic feature of human consciousness is an inherent striving toward an impossible ideal. It is in our nature to seek to unite being-for-itself and being-in-itself in a totality that preserves the virtues of both, so that we will be complete as well as free. We want as conscious beings at the same time to be being-in-itself, but not the being-in-itself from which we have separated ourselves in consciousness. Rather, we want to be our own source, our own ground, our own facticity. This union of being-for-itself and being-in-itself, wherein consciousness becomes the founder of its own being—a self-creating pure consciousness—is essentially a definition of God. Thus, we have an inherent striving to be gods, but the striving is doomed to failure. If we project the ideal outward and make it an object of worship, we are simply trying to relate to an illusion. According to Sartre, there is no

God and there can be no God, for the concept is a contradiction in terms.

In Sartre's view, human existence by its nature is a rather unhappy state of affairs. Our efforts to relate closely to other people are bound to culminate in frustration, and it is in our nature to strive toward an ideal that is utterly impossible. Under the circumstances, we could hardly expect Sartre to endorse as appropriate goals those conditions that Marcel sees as the ingredients of the optimal condition, for Marcel's ideals would have to seem a bit chimerical to Sartre. The one condition that does seem fundamentally important to him is freedom from illusion. This would mean most basically accepting our freedom as an unavoidable feature of our existence and acting in good faith, with an awareness of our choices. It would also mean recognizing our striving for godhood as a part of our existence, while at the same time recognizing the impossibility of the aim. To follow this course of full awareness would entail accepting a bit of pain and frustration as a part of life, but at least it provides a basis for more intelligent choices.

EXISTENTIAL PSYCHOLOGY AND PSYCHIATRY

The existential movement in psychology is a more recent development than that in philosophy, and it is an outgrowth of the philosophical movement insofar as its basic themes are borrowed from the philosophers. At the same time, however, it represents a reaction to trends within society with which psychologists and psychiatrists are particularly concerned, and it represents a reaction to certain trends in psychological theory and psychotherapy.

Existential psychologists have been particularly concerned about the modern societal developments that I noted in Chapter 3. They have pointed to the dire effects of a bureaucratic society dominated by technological reason upon the life of the individual member. Rollo May argues that the most prevalent neurotic process in our time is a repression of the ontological sense.[11] The typical neurotic is an organization man who lacks a clear sense of himself as a responsible agent, who cannot effectively exert an independent will or make decisions, and who seeks to relieve his uncertainty by submerging his individuality in a social system.

Existential psychologists see many developments in the realm of psychotherapy as a direct expression of the societal trends that tend to depersonalize us and undermine the ontological sense, rather than efforts that can lead to a solution of the basic problem of the present day. Thus, the psychotherapist typically seeks to understand his patient by viewing him analytically from a distance and then applies techniques designed to remedy the diagnosed condition of the patient. The detached observation, the abstract and analytical approach to understanding, and the therapeutic method dominated by technical procedures are themselves all symptomatic of the conditions in our society that underlie the ontological neurosis. Psychoanalysis has been the primary target of existentialist criticism because it has dominated the world of psychotherapy in this century. More recent approaches have come under even sharper attack by existentialists. Thus, Laing sees the techniques of behavior therapy as much more depersonalizing than those of traditional psychoanalysis:

> Behavior therapy is the most extreme example of such schizoid theory and practice that proposes to think and act purely in terms of the other without reference to the self of the therapist or the patient, in terms of behavior without experience, in terms of objects rather than persons. It is inevitably a technique of nonmeeting, of manipulation and control.[12]

One could argue, of course, that there are much more dehumanizing procedures than those commonly employed by the behavior therapists. If a therapist has no interest whatsoever in the experience of his patient and considers it his technical task to produce a behavioral change, he may avoid verbal interaction altogether and prescribe electric shock, surgery, or drugs. These fashions of the medical profession have also been criticized by existentialists.

The themes of existential psychology are essentially those we have already observed in the philosophical movement, but with more focus on the psychotherapeutic situation. Existential psychologists consider it very important to attempt to understand the individual, patient or otherwise, as a unique being-in-the-world. From their perspective, the individual cannot be adequately understood through the methods of the natural sciences or through the forms of analysis employed by behaviorists or psychoanalysts. One must try to enter into his world of experience and see him and his world as he sees them. His world cannot be grasped by a detached observer, since it cannot be reduced to purely objective data. It is bound together with meanings that he brings into all his relationships as he participates in it.

In one way or another, all existential psychologists make use of a concept of freedom. They view the individual as a being who is inevitably free (as Sartre would have it) or who has potential freedom that he either affirms or denies. They see existence in terms of continuous process. The individual is not fully formed or fixed at any time but is always becoming. His orientation toward time and in particular toward the future are important. The concepts of anxiety and guilt also appear often in the work of existential psychologists, and they are usually used in the sense in which philosophers like Kierkegaard use them rather than in a psychoanalytic sense. Thus, anxiety (perhaps qualified as existential or ontological anxiety) is the experience of the threat of non-being, while guilt (existential or ontological guilt) is the denial of one's potentialities or a failure to fulfill one's nature.

The existentialist viewpoint has a number of implications for psychotherapy, and May has attempted to spell some of these out. He discusses six basic implications: [13]

1. Existential therapists will make flexible use of various techniques, for the primary concern is the present existence of the patient, not the technique itself.
2. All psychological dynamisms will be understood in terms of their meaning within the patient's own immediate life situation.
3. The therapist will view the encounter between therapist and patient as a real relationship between two people in which the therapist is fully present as a person, not just as a remote professional role-player.
4. The therapist will attempt to "analyze out" his own ways of behaving that destroy his full presence in the relationship.
5. The aim of the therapy will be viewed as enabling the patient to experience his existence as real and to become aware of his potentialities and to act on the basis of them.
6. There will be an emphasis on commitment, on the patient's decisions and decisive actions.

In addition to the common elements I have just noted, there is some variation in viewpoint from one proponent of existential psychology to another. To gain a broader picture of the contributions of this movement to an understanding of the human condition, we shall consider briefly a few of the more salient theorists in the movement.

Ludwig Binswanger A Swiss psychiatrist who lived from 1881 to 1966, Binswanger was one of the early pioneers in existential psychiatry. Early in his career he became interested in psychoanalysis and became a follower of Freud. In the 1920s he turned to psychiatric phenomenology, seeking a broader understanding of the experience of his patients. Ultimately he came under the influence of Heidegger's work and developed what he called *Daseinsanalyse,* or existential analysis. He borrowed many of Heidegger's concepts, and his approach is in many respects a blend of existentialism and psychoanalysis.[14]

Binswanger maintained contact with Freud over a period of many years, and it is interesting that, unlike many other rebels in the psychoanalytic movement, he managed to remain on very friendly terms with the great master after he had proceeded to chart his own separate course. He acknowledged a great debt to Freud, and a psychoanalytic influence is apparent in some features of his work, such as his efforts in his case studies to reconstruct a developmental picture of the lives of his patients. His basic outlook is markedly different from that of Freud in other respects. Binswanger felt that Freud's work represented the one monumental attempt to deal with human personality within a natural-scientific framework. Unfortunately, that framework itself is limited, and psychoanalysis, like any other natural-science approach, cannot really cope with the distinctly human part of man. It can only deal with that part of man that is shared with the rest of the animal kingdom, and it must ignore or destroy man's experiential knowledge of himself. It does not follow that the natural-science approach to man is worthless. What can be done by natural science has been done well by psychoanalysis, as Binswanger saw it, and his aim in existential analysis was not to construct an alternative depth psychology, but to provide a complementary perspective by examining human existence from a point outside the framework of natural science.

227

According to Binswanger, natural science is well designed to provide systematic *explanations* of psychological phenomena, but by seeking a comprehensive picture of the individual's experience existential analysis can come closer to a full *understanding* of the individual's world. A natural-science account is not likely to do full justice to the actual existence of the individual. Thus Freud, with a footing in biology, felt it essential to regard the human being as a being driven by instincts, and in the explanation of any psychological effects instinctual strivings took precedence over any other factors that might be reported or directly observed. For Binswanger it was more important to achieve an adequate picture of human existence than to achieve a biological explanation. He contended that being-human includes such varying existential forms as being-able-to-be, being-allowed-to-be, and having-to-be, and that psychoanalysis focuses too narrowly on the last of these—man's having-to-be, his facticity or thrownness—in its emphasis on our instinctual driveness. He suggested that this one-sidedness may have been in part a consequence of Freud's endeavors to account for neurosis (a condition in which a sense of having-to-be is prevalent).

While some of his insights undoubtedly came from psychoanalysis, the language employed by Binswanger is closer to that of Heidegger. He spoke of the human individual as a being-in-the-world, and he distinguished three modes of world: the *Umwelt* (the realm of objects or things), the *Mitwelt* (the realm of fellow beings of one's own kind), and the *Eigenwelt* (the realm of the self, the "own-world"). In later writings, influenced by Buber's treatment of the I-thou relationship, he used a more elaborate classification of existential modes, distinguishing the dual, plural, singular, and anonymous modes.

The relationships among such modes play a prominent role in Binswanger's descriptions of individual cases. He apparently felt that in the ideal case, the Umwelt, Mitwelt, and Eigenwelt would form a coordinated unity, such that the individual could be open to the contents of each, take each fully into account, and be guided and nourished by each. Sometimes there is conflict or opposition between different modes—the Eigenwelt may be set in opposition to the Mitwelt or the Umwelt. The individual may seek to avoid relationships with or influences from other people and be totally self-contained. In his absorption in the singular mode (or Eigenwelt) and compulsive opposition to the Mitwelt, however, he displays an inauthentic autonomy, for he is actually dominated by the Mitwelt in a negative form (his need to continue relating to others in an oppositional way).

These modes constitute only one kind of division with respect to which splitting and exclusion may occur. Binswanger saw as a common element in psychopathology an inability of the individual to accept his fate, his thrownness. He is at odds with the basic uncontrollable conditions of his life—his own body and the world in which he finds himself. In opposing these unavoidable conditions, he loses freedom, for he is dominated by his thrownness. The alternative course is that of freedom. The individual who is free, according to Binswanger, recognizes and accepts his thrownness, his unfreedom. Instead of resisting his unavoidable lot in life, he is committed to it and is able to act and to assume responsibility for his future.

Binswanger spoke of the individual's overall pattern of being-in-the-world as a world-design. From what has just been said, it is apparent that one characteristic that distinguishes the free or "healthy" individual from the mentally ill is that he is generally open to the conditions and possibilities of his existence. The individual who is not open and who seeks to oppose many of these conditions and possibilities may have a world-design dominated by just one or a few themes or categories, and most of his experience will be colored by those few themes. Such an individual is not only less free than the healthy individual, but he is also more prone to anxiety. One experiences anxiety, according to Binswanger, when the world becomes shaky or threatens to vanish, and the simpler and emptier the world-design, the more the world seems subject to disintegration. The healthy individual experiences a world of many themes and categories, a world of greater variety, and if a threat arises in one part of it, he can find security in other regions.

Medard Boss There are many parallels between Binswanger and Boss. Like Binswanger, Boss is a Swiss psychiatrist. He was born in 1903 and received a medical degree from the University of Zürich in

1928. Subsequently he was analyzed by Sigmund Freud, and later received psychoanalytic training in both London and Germany. For a time he and several other therapists held monthly meetings in the home of Carl Jung, but it was the influence of Heidegger, whom he met in 1946, that finally led him to shift to a position far from psychoanalytic orthodoxy.

He proceeded to develop his own approach to psychotherapy. Like Binswanger he calls his approach *Daseinsanalyse.* To distinguish Boss's approach, his translator, Ludwig Lefebre, has rendered this in English as "daseinsanalysis," since in translations of Binswanger's work the term "existential analysis" has been used.[15] Like Binswanger, Boss relies heavily on the ideas and concepts of Heidegger. He evidently feels that he has remained closer to Heidegger and interpreted his work more accurately, seeing in Binswanger's work a subjectivistic revision of Heidegger. Binswanger himself admitted that in his early writings he misinterpreted Heidegger and offered the hope that he had achieved a creative misunderstanding. Be that as it may, Binswanger was not alone in his misunderstanding. Boss notes a variety of common misconceptions of Heidegger and contends that even distinguished philosophers like Sartre, because of their own initial biases, have misrepresented him.

Boss considers daseinsanalysis to be quite compatible with psychoanalytic therapy, but he is critical of Freud's basic concepts, seeing them as more a hindrance than a help to effective therapy. He feels that Freud's importance lies in the brilliance of his observations and insights but that these are obscured by the theoretical scaffolding that he felt compelled to erect. He contends that there is a tremendous discrepancy between Freud's immediate observations and his theoretical insights, noting that the basic presuppositions underlying Freud's theorizing—those regarding the exclusive reality of the external world with its predictable causal connections and physical dimensions of space and time—are those that underlie the natural sciences. In his choice of concepts and modes of explanation, too, Freud proceeded in the manner of the natural sciences, whether he spoke of neurological processes or constructs analogous to physical energy systems.

Boss contends that for an adequate understanding of man Hei-

230

degger's analysis of *Dasein* is more appropriate than the concepts of the natural sciences, which rest on presuppositions that preclude an adequate understanding. Free of these preconceptions, in the approach of daseinsanalysis one seeks "to remain as open as possible and to listen and see how man appears in his full immediacy." [16] The basic nature of man is *Dasein,* or being-in-the-world. One's being-in-the-world is "always a concrete occurrence." It "occurs and fulfills itself only in and as the manifold particular modes of human behavior and of man's different ways of relating toward things and fellow beings." [17] Boss also speaks of being-in-itself in terms of "meaning-disclosing encounters," as "an original awareness or understanding of . . . 'Beingness as such.' " In short, the central feature of human nature is a direct and immediate understanding and elucidating of whatever is present in our world (even if sometimes this understanding includes a misunderstanding of some particular content).

Boss discusses various aspects or dimensions of *Dasein,* such as spatiality and temporality. These are not to be understood in their physical sense. The spatiality of *Dasein* is a function of the existential significance of the particular things or beings in our world. It varies with the intimacy of our concern for these things or beings, rather than with physical distance. Similarly, temporality is not a matter of clock time, but of the presence and unfolding of those features of the world that are meaningful to us.

The optimal condition, for Boss as for other existentialists, involves an acceptance of one's freedom and an openness to one's possibilities. Boss speaks of the goal of daseinsanalysis in the context of a discussion of guilt. According to him each of us is existentially guilty. At birth we begin to accumulate an indebtedness to our *Dasein,* for existential guilt consists of failing to carry out the mandate to fulfill all of our possibilities. We can never fulfill them all, but we can either avoid them excessively or we can heed the voice of conscience and attempt to fulfill them. The goal of daseinsanalysis, hence the ideal condition from Boss's standpoint, is for the individual freely to accept his debt to his existence (to acknowledge his guilt) and to accept the burden of that debt, to become aware of his possibilities for living and relating to the world, and to allow these possibilities to emerge and be used. If

231

the individual does this, he will no longer suffer from a bad conscience. He will live responsibly and experience freedom. At the same time, according to Boss, he will attain the goal of full capacity for work and enjoyment that Freud considered the aim of psychoanalysis.

Victor Frankl Born in Vienna in 1905 Frankl completed his university education there. He published his first article in 1924 in the *International Journal of Psychoanalysis* and was well on his way toward establishing his career and developing his own system of psychotherapy before World War II broke out. During the war he was interned by the Nazi government and spent some time in the concentration camps at both Auschwitz and Dachau. Of his immediate family only he and his sister survived the camps. All the rest—his parents, his wife, and his brother—either died in the camps or in the gas ovens built by the government. His long-term efforts to survive the camps, where one was robbed of virtually everything that normally makes life seem worth living and where one was faced with a constant threat of unpredictable annihilation, provided an additional foundation for his ideas on the nature of man and psychotherapy, and he has written an illuminating account of that period in his life.[18] Since the war he has taught both in the United States and at the University of Vienna. He calls his own existential approach to therapy *logotherapy,* and it has been called the third Viennese school of psychotherapy—the first and second being those of Freud and Adler.

Frankl sees merit in the theories of Freud and Adler. He feels that they both contain valid insights but that they are one-sided. While Freud stressed the will to pleasure and Adler the will to power as the primary human motivations, logotherapy stresses the will to meaning as the basic force in humans. The will to meaning implies a search for values or goals, for meanings to be fulfilled in the future. Thus it implies a force that pulls the individual. Psychoanalysis in contrast is more concerned with the past and with drives or instincts which are already there and which push the individual. Frankl does not deny the existence of instincts, but he denies that we are totally determined by them. With respect to goals and values, we have choice.

According to Frankl, life does not have a meaning that can be defined in a general way for all people, but he disagrees with Sartre's view that life is inherently meaningless and that we can only invent meanings. Meanings are to be *discovered* outside the individual himself, in his relationship to the world. He describes three main ways in which the individual can realize meanings or values. One is through creative action. A second is through experiencing; the object of experience may be nature or a work of art or some other facet of culture, or one may experience value in another person through love. The third way is through suffering or confrontation with a fate that severely restricts one's potentialities. People often realize values when brought close to death through near-fatal accidents or illnesses.

Since the realization of values requires the discovery of something beyond the limits of the individual himself, it is not a matter of mere self-expression. Since it does not strictly involve a realization of something within oneself, it is a matter of self-transcendence, rather than self-actualization. At best, something that might be called self-actualization will come as a by-product of self-transcendence.

There is a religious core to Frankl's system, for he believes, in contrast to Sartre, that life has an ultimate meaning, or suprameaning, which for Frankl evidently corresponds to God. He does not believe that this ultimate meaning can be grasped in rational terms, however, and there is no one verbal formula by which one can offer it as a prescription to everyone. The particular belief system through which one rationalizes this meaning does not appear to be of special significance, yet the experience of such a meaning does seem to be of paramount psychotherapeutic importance. Frankl recognizes the personal experience of God as the ultimate Thou—in the sense stressed by Buber and Marcel—as one form, but presumably not the only form, that this experience of ultimate meaning might assume.

The concepts of freedom and responsibility also play a central role in Frankl's view of human existence. Frankl believes that the will to meaning implies a choice that instincts do not. One can either accept or reject a given meaning potentiality. Of course, there are drives and instincts as well. More broadly, there are genetic and environmental influences that govern our behavior and experience to a degree. From Frankl's standpoint, however, we are not *just* products of heredity and environment, because given both these sets of influences, man still untimately decides for himself. He is not fully determined by forces beyond his control. Even in the confined, regimented situation of the concentration camp, the individual still possesses one final freedom—to choose the attitude he will adopt within and toward his circumstances.

There is obviously a part of everyone's lot in life, his destiny, that he cannot possibly control. It is simply given to him and he cannot be responsible for it. As we have seen, all existentialists recognize this and refer to it variously in terms of thrownness, facticity, and factuality. This given part includes the very finiteness of human existence, our mortality, and it is futile to quarrel with it. We must accept it. Beyond this, however, we have freedom to choose. Moreover, we have a responsibility to choose—to take an active role in shaping our destiny and in seeking meaning. Frankl speaks of a responsibility to one's conscience, which would imply that the individual is guilty to the extent that he does not assume responsibility. If one can extract from Frankl's writings his prescription for the optimal condition, it would consist of acknowledging one's freedom and assuming responsibility for living and for finding meaning in life. In such a condition, one is forever moving toward the realization of values, constantly striving toward worthy goals. Frankl rejects the idea that the ideal state is one of homeostatic quiescence.

The will to meaning assumes an urgent importance in our time that it has not had in the past, because its frustration, which Frankl calls existential frustration, is now the major source of neurosis. The neurosis that stems from existential frustration—i.e., from a frustration of our need for values—is called an existential, or noögenic, neurosis. the more generally recognized *psychogenic* neurosis involves a frustration or conflict of drives or instincts. Frankl notes that this is sometimes called the age of anxiety, but he believes there is no reason to assume that anxiety, or anxiety neurosis, is more prevalent than it was in past centuries. The disturbance that does distinguish our time from all periods in the past is a collective noögenic neurosis, which Frankl characterizes as an existential vacuum—the experience of the total and utter meaninglessness of our lives. In *The Doctor and the Soul* he describes four symptoms that characterize this neurosis: a planless, day-to-day attitude toward life; a fatalist attitude toward life; collective thinking; and fanaticism. All of these entail an evasion of responsibility and an escape from freedom. In the first two, the individual in effect denies that he has any freedom or power of choice. He denies the possibility of planning or insists that no matter what he does, his best efforts will be undone by an inevitable nuclear holocaust. In the third, he relinquishes his independence and submerges himself in the mass. In the fourth, he dogmatically asserts an opinion or value that he has not truly realized. Rather than truly possessing it, he is possessed by it. This represents an effort to escape the sense of meaninglessness by inauthentically claiming a meaning. In *Man's Search for Meaning*, Frankl notes that the existential vacuum may also be masked by the will to power or the will to pleasure. In this case, the individual engages in a compulsive quest for money, for political control, for sexual satisfaction, and the like.

Frankl believes that contemporary psychology and psychiatry cannot cope effectively with this collective neurosis so long as they reflect a nihilistic philosophy or espouse the idea that man is just a biological organism or just a product of biological and social influences. He is particularly critical of the pandeterminism of Freud. There is a need for a psychotherapy that recognizes man's essential freedom. A psychotherapy that denies this freedom cannot provide a cure for our existential neurosis. It is itself an expression of that neurosis.

R. D. Laing The Scottish psychiatrist Ronald D. Laing was born in Glasgow in 1927. He grew up in that city and obtained a medical degree from Glasgow University in 1951. Through his early writings he became known for innovative ideas on the nature and treatment of schizophrenia. In later writings he increasingly pictured the family as the proper target of treatment, seeing the "disease" not so much as a condition within an individual but as a disordered network of relationships and communication within the family. In his work there also appeared increasingly a criticism of the larger society that produces and is maintained by disturbed and destructive families. As a critic both of the society as a whole and of the mental health professions,

235

Laing has drawn much criticism. Some writers have described him as rude and inconsiderate, as demonic, and as given to occasional psychotic episodes himself. Such vilifications seem to have been amply refuted by people who know Laing well. Perhaps some of the fire he has drawn can be attributed to journalistic excess and some to professional jealousy—it is always easier, of course, to attack someone who is creative than to be genuinely creative yourself. Perhaps some of it is an expression of understandable wrath on the part of people on whose professional toes Laing has stepped, but some of Laing's opponents have certainly been much more pointedly personal in their criticism than has Laing himself.

Laing refers to his position as one of existential phenomenology. From frequency of reference, one might suspect he has been influenced as much by Sartre as by any other existentialist, but Laing's primary interest is not in embracing or formulating a general existentialist doctrine, but rather in finding a basis for understanding human beings as persons. He utilizes insights of existentialists, psychoanalysts, and others as they appear to be helpful. As a therapist he tries to proceed with a minimum of theory, believing that most of the diagnostic procedures, therapeutic techniques, and intellectual baggage that we carry with us into our work with patients serve primarily to make the therapist feel secure by enabling him to view the patient as an object. Thus, our professional training provides us with a host of devices for maintaining a comfortable distance between ourselves and the patient and avoiding the human contact that is necessary for real understanding. He believes that some of the views of human nature that underlie current therapeutic practices are more likely to produce depersonalization than to cure it. He notes that we tend to regard an individual as crazy if he thinks of himself as a robot or automaton and wonders why a theory that views people in this way is not considered crazy.

Laing stresses the importance of dealing with experience and behavior jointly in theory. He is particularly critical of behaviorists who seek to ignore the individual's experience altogether and focus only on behavioral expression. The folly of this is probably evident to anyone who has made an effort to understand individual schizophrenics. As

236

Laing notes, the schizophrenic often plays at being psychotic, doing and saying crazy things to avoid the possibility of being held responsible for a single coherent idea or intention. Recognizing the difference between what is considered crazy and what is considered normal by the surrounding society, the schizophrenic may also play at being sane and thus appear to be cured. Only a therapist who is genuinely interested in understanding what the patient is actually experiencing is likely to be very helpful. A therapist who simply identifies psychosis with behavioral symptoms and sees his task as that of shaping behavior and replacing symptoms with normal actions is naive at best and may be quite harmful. No one has made this point more ably than Laing.

He deals most extensively with individual experience in *The Divided Self,* where he treats disturbances in the experience of identity in terms of ontological insecurity, the unembodied self, and the false-self system.[19] The person who is ontologically secure has a clear sense of identity, autonomy, inner consistency, and worth. He feels real, alive, whole, and clearly differentiated from the rest of the world. The individual who suffers from ontological insecurity may feel dead or unreal. He lacks a clear sense of coherence or continuity and does not feel clearly differentiated from the rest of the world. Laing notes three forms of anxiety found in the ontologically insecure person, which he calls engulfment, implosion, and petrification.

The person who is ontologically secure has an embodied self—he feels inextricably bound up with his body. The person with an unembodied self, on the other hand, feels himself split into a mind and a body. He feels more closely identified with his mind and views his body as one object among the many objects of the world. The body is thus viewed as a kind of false front, a facade, inhabited by the more real being, the mind. According to Laing, this split is characteristic of schizoid individuals, who begin to manifest it in the early months of life. It is one form and aspect of a common split experienced between a false self and a true self. In such a split, the false self is essentially a mask, a facade, that the individual displays in his interactions with other people, and the body tends to be felt as the core of this false self. The true self, the part with which the individual actually identifies, what he considers his real nature, lies concealed—a system of thoughts, attitudes, and feelings that are clearly experienced but that may not be revealed to others.

This split occurs to some degree in everyone, but the "normal" individual can shift fairly readily from mechanical, polite behavior to spontaneous expression. In the hysteric individual, the split is more pronounced, while the schizoid, according to Laing, may regard his entire outward existence as the expression of a false self. If all commerce with the rest of the social world is conducted through the false self and the true self is cut off from all direct contact, there is a strong possibility that the schizoid will advance to a frankly psychotic condition. To maintain a stable sense of identity, the individual must be known by others. There must be some felt correspondence between how one sees oneself and what others recognize. With the true self thoroughly and consistently concealed, it may undergo the various drastic transformations seen in psychosis. It may become "fantasized," unreal, improverished, empty, or dead, or it may become charged with hatred, fear, and envy. Various schizophrenic adjustment strategies may follow.

In speaking of a split between a false self and a true self, Laing focuses primarily on the experience of the individual, but the overwhelming importance of the interpersonal realm is implicit in this distinction between a self that interacts with others and one that is concealed from them. In *Self and Others,* Laing addresses himself more directly and broadly to the interpersonal aspect of self-experience, dealing both with our awareness of the self-being of others and the dependence of our own experience of self on the actions of others.[20] He discusses our modes of pretense, the ways in which we deceive ourselves and others, the ways in which we confirm and disconfirm the identity of others, and the false and untenable positions that we assume either through our own efforts or through pressures from others. He shows, indeed, that the interpersonal aspect of self-experience is quite complex. In a more recent work, *Knots,* he further underscores this complexity by presenting in a more abstract, schematic form some of the tortuous patterns of interpersonal perception and behavior—

patterns for which he suggests such varied names as knots, tangles, fankles, impasses, disjunctions, whirligogs, and binds.[21]

As I noted, Laing's observations of the interpersonal realm led to a shift in his focus from individual experience to interactions within the family.[22] It led as well to increasing criticism of the whole society and its institutions. In his early works he criticized the society's treatment of the psychotic. He believes that our society represses not only our instincts but all forms of transcendence as well. Thus, we tend to be intolerant of any experience or behavior that we cannot understand, any experience or behavior that surpasses the bounds of what we generally accept as "normal." We cannot allow the psychotic to be as he is because he makes us uncomfortable, and we try to force him to act "normal." In later writings, Laing has pressed the view that what we call "normal" is itself a form of alienation, "a product of repression, denial, splitting, projection, introjection and other forms of destructive action on experience." [23] We learn, as we grow up in this society, to tune out much of our experience, particularly our feelings and the stream of fantasy that accompanies nearly everything we do. To assist us in this endeavor, we build up a false consciousness, consisting of the ideas and feelings that are deemed appropriate and acceptable by the society. Laing believes that many of our common child-rearing practices and many of the practices in our public schools are well designed to accomplish this falsification, or "mystification," of our experience.

Laing has given us graphic descriptions of departures from the ideal condition of living, but the ideal state itself is not described so much as it is implied in his writings. His critics have said that he glorifies madness as the optimal condition, but this is certainly not true. He does believe that schizophrenia may constitute a stage in a natural healing process and that we should try to assist the patient on his inner voyage by trying to understand him and helping him understand himself, instead of interfering with the process by drugs, shock, surgery, or depersonalizing regimentation. He believes that at his worst the mad patient is less to be feared than some of our political leaders who are sane by society's standards but who have formulated policies that have resulted in the massive destruction of human life. The psychotic suffers because he is unable to adjust to a society that is itself mad, and he is on a voyage that can lead to a higher level of sanity than that enjoyed by most of us.

Ideally, from Laing's standpoint, the individual should be fully in touch with his own experience—his feelings, his thoughts, his fantasies—and in touch with the natural forces operating within himself, and he should experience himself as a whole, embodied being. The "normal" individual in our society has developed a system of controls and filters—an ego—that enables him to adjust to the society but keeps him alienated from his own experience. The psychotic has suffered a loss of his ego, and this loss, though it may be terrifying, may prove a blessing. According to Laing, "true sanity entails in one way or another the dissolution of the normal ego, that false self competently adjusted to our alienated social reality; the emergence of the 'inner' archetypal mediators of divine power, and through this death a rebirth, and the eventual reestablishment of a new kind of ego-functioning, the ego now being the servant of the divine, no longer its betrayer." [24]

AN OVERVIEW OF EXISTENTIAL THOUGHT

We have now examined some of the common threads that run through the developments in philosophy and psychology that have been dubbed existentialist. We have also seen some of the variation among individual philosophers and psychological theorists associated with this tradition. Perhaps there is something novel in the overall pattern of ideas underlying this movement, but certainly the most conspicuous elements taken individually can be traced to earlier traditions. In its reaction against intellectual abstraction and analysis and its stress on the uniqueness and the totality of the individual human being, and in its emphasis on experience per se, it echoes the sentiments of the Romantic movement. In its prescription of fidelity to one's own nature and experience, it voices an idea that can be traced to classical Greece, but an idea that appears with some variation through the ages. For some, but not all, existentialists, fidelity to self is viewed as inevitably linked to one's relatedness to others.

> This above all—to thine own self be true;
> And it must follow, as the night the day,
> Thou canst not then be false to any man.[25]

This basic message of existentialism may be cast in an optimistic form or in a pessimistic one, but either way it is characteristically devoid of the hubris of early Greek thought. The existential man recognizes his mortality and does not try to deny or overcome it. Indeed, a recurrent theme is that one must accept one's unavoidable limitations as well as the unchosen conditions into which one has been cast in this lifetime. Given these circumstances, however, one should be aware that for the rest of one's destiny there is freedom, the possibility of choice. It is important to recognize this freedom, to become aware of all the active and emerging parts of one's being and of the possibilities that they present, and to assume the responsibility for choosing and for shaping oneself and one's world. Even this is not a novel idea nor one confined to the existentialist movement. It is the essential message of a well known prayer:

> O God, give us serenity to accept what cannot be changed,
> courage to change what should be changed,
> and wisdom to distinguish the one from the other.[26]

The fact that we are mortal beings and that life is finite is a recurrent theme in existentialist literature. It is a fact that we all recognize in the abstract, but we avoid a full emotional realization of it. We certainly refrain most of the time from contemplating our own demise and act as if we had the whole of eternity before us. So long as we do this, we can excuse any action with the thought that we will do better the next time. Thus, we need not care how we abuse others and we can ignore our own unfulfilled potentialities, for there will alway be time to set things right. Urgently and repeatedly, the existentialists tell us that we cannot afford to continue in this self-deceitful way, for life is very short indeed and time is running out. A full realization of our finiteness will deeply affect our attitudes toward ourselves, toward other people, and toward the whole of life.

> I shall pass through this world but once.
> If, therefore, there be any kindness I can show,
> or any good thing I can do,
> let me do it now;
> let me not defer it or neglect it,
> for I shall not pass this way again.[27]

NINE

OTHER CONTEMPORARY PERSPECTIVES

THE BEHAVIORIST TRADITION AND B. F. SKINNER

It would be difficult to ignore a movement that has played such an influential role in Anglo-American psychology in this century as behaviorism has. Yet I am not convinced that behaviorists in general have contributed much of substance to our thinking about the optimal personality or the optimal mode of living. Their basic stance prevents most of them from dealing very directly with such an issue and leads some of them to dismiss it as a pseudo issue.

I realize I am making a rather sweeping generalization and may be overlooking some important exceptions, for the term *behaviorism* has come to embrace a variety of viewpoints since it was first introduced over a half-century ago by John B. Watson. Perhaps we could distinguish three basic positions to which the term has been applied. One is a form of materialism, the view that only material things exist and that, unless they can be construed as physical processes, such things as consciousness and feeling states do not exist. A second is that of methodological behaviorism, the view that in research psychologists should focus exclusively on "objective" behavioral and stimulus data and that theories should be based on such data. A third is that of formal behaviorism, the view that theories should be cast in terms of physical (behavioral, physical-stimulus, and physiological) variables, not psychological variables.

These three positions have been combined in various ways. On

243

the whole, those who have adopted the behaviorist label have emphasized the second and third positions more than the first. They have not denied the existence of consciousness, but they have viewed it as their scientific task to account for behavior. To the extent that conscious events are regarded as lying outside this domain, of course, behaviorism has not been a movement within psychology (in the traditional sense of that term) so much as a movement away from it.

Few psychologists have ever adopted the behaviorist outlook in its most extreme form. Even a modified behaviorism would probably be rejected by most psychologists today, though it appears to be rather pervasive among those in academic positions. In any case, most of the viewpoints that are broadly labeled behavioristic at present represent some deviation from the Watsonian extreme. Behaviorism has been blended with other orientations. Edward Tolman's brand of behaviorism contained a strong admixture of Gestalt psychology and Lewinian field theory. In the work of Neil Miller and John Dollard we find a blend of behaviorism and Freudian theory. While early behaviorists tended to focus on very specific response variables, from Tolman on there have been holistic behaviorists. Some have made use of psychological or quasi-psychological concepts in their work. Thus, both Tolman and some of the more recent social-learning theorists have used such concepts as expectancy, which—however explicitly defined—carries an unavoidable psychological connotation. In the applied realm, behavior therapists often deal currently with such covert processes as fantasy and imagery.

With all the modifications evident in neobehaviorism and social-learning theories, the fact remains that psychologists in the behaviorist tradition have maintained a rather narrow focus on behavior. They have usually tended to avoid dealing with the broader aspects of personality trait structure and have focused on variables that are relatively specific in terms of either action pattern or situational context. They have tended to avoid dealing with forms of behavior, such as those of a creative character, that do not submit readily to laboratory study. Still more seriously, they have avoided dealing with broad realms of human experience that lack simple behavioral concomitants. Thus, feelings and emotions tend to be considered only in terms of behav-

244

ioral expressions, and the complex, fundamental phenomena of love are either ignored or reduced to such absurd fragments as positive reinforcement. In the motivational realm, behaviorists tend to deal mainly with strivings closely bound to physiological needs. In this respect, behaviorists have become progressively less restricted over the years, but there is still little room in their thinking for anything as behaviorally nonspecific as a will to meaning or a need for self-actualization.

When the behaviorist does see fit to admit the existence of a process that he cannot directly observe in another person, he usually regards it as mediating between events that he can observe. Thus, it has to be closely tied either to a preceding stimulus or to a subsequent effect. Yet most of the stuff that actually makes up the flow of our inner lives is only remotely connected to our immediate actions or the immediate physical environment. It is in the nature of dreams and fantasies, and the behaviorist is not likely to deal with these.

It is generally felt that one of the most distinctive features of the human being is his self-awareness, and many of the theorists we have considered have been centrally concerned with the way in which the individual views his own being. They have been concerned with his self-concept or self-image, with his sense of identity. They have been concerned with the many basic variations that can occur in this self-experience—whether one experiences himself as whole or fragmented, consistent or inconsistent, stable and continuous or subject to unpredictable change, worthy or unworthy, powerful or powerless. They have recognized important variations in our attitudes toward self-experience and have dealt with them in terms of openness, acceptance, or commitment. A behaviorist may devote a few paragraphs to a discussion of whether *self* is or is not a meaningful concept, but he is not likely to address himself very effectively to these very fundamental variations in human experience.

It follows that in the main behaviorists have not really addressed themselves to the issues of personality theory, for their work has dealt largely with behaviors rather than with total persons. As a result, in the literature of the behaviorist movement we can find few attempts to define an optimal personality. The issue is not likely to be treated in

245

such global terms. Where it is treated, it is more in terms of good versus bad habits. The behaviorist may avoid such ethically laden words, but he will note that some behaviors are desirable and some are not. The bad habits may be recognized as those that are viewed psychiatrically as symptoms, those that are generally offensive to our society, those that are obviously harmful to other people, or those that interfere with the individual's own satisfactions. Conversely, the good habits may be viewed as those that benefit others or those that tend to maximize the individual's own satisfactions. On the basis of such an analysis, the optimal person might be defined either as one with a repertoire of good habits or as an efficient learner—one who can readily acquire good habits and discard bad ones. Often the behaviorist is more interested in defining the good environment than in defining the optimal person within it, assuming that whatever special features the individual may display are a function of present and past environmental inputs: child-rearing practices, educational practices, societal practices, and so on.

Perhaps I oversimplify a bit, but this is what I see as the central trend of the behaviorist movement. If I seem biased, perhaps it is because I see the movement as one that has neglected and resisted the issues that interest me most as a psychologist. At the same time, however, I believe that behaviorists have made major contributions to our understanding of the learning process, and I believe that in such fields as education they have important practical contributions to make.[1] In any case, the behaviorist viewpoint is one of the major perspectives on the nature of man yielded by modern Western culture, and we need to examine it. It seem particularly profitable to consider the ideas of the leading contemporary behaviorist, B. F. Skinner, for they contrast rather sharply with those of many other writers we have discussed.

Skinner was born in Pennsylvania in 1904. As a young man he aspired to be a writer, and he majored in literature during his undergraduate years at Hamilton College. After some effort to pursue a career as a writer, however, he turned to experimental psychology and received a Ph.D. degree from Harvard in 1931. He has since held academic positions at the University of Minnesota, Indiana University, and

Harvard University. He is widely known for his behavioral research, his contributions to research equipment and techniques, and his controversial views on theoretical issues. His published writings include a novel, *Walden Two,* that contains his blueprint for an ideal society.[2]

Skinner's position emphasizes methodological behaviorism. He believes that psychological data should consist of events on which independent observers can agree and that the task of psychology is to elucidate the interactions that occur between the organism and its environment. He differs from some other behaviorists, notably Clark Hull and his followers, in objecting to theoretical speculation and the elaboration of formal theory unsupported by observations, maintaining instead that theory should be build inductively on the basis of experimental findings. His antiabstractionist outlook is perhaps the one and only bit of ground that he shares with the existentialists. He also differs from some of his experimental colleagues in decrying speculation about unobserved physiological processes. While he believes that physiological processes should be studied and related to organism-environment interactions, he feels that psychological theory as such does not require biological interpretations.

Skinner is not a strict materialist. He does not deny the existence of consciousness or of self-awareness. Indeed, he believes that a science of behavior must recognize such things and deal with them.[3] Skinner himself does not do much with such things, however, for he seems to regard them as having only minor importance. He espouses what amounts to a form of epiphenomenalism, denying that conscious events can operate as causes and insisting instead that our behavior is under the control of environmental events. Rather than being a source of actions, our awareness is something imposed on us by verbal exchange. We become aware of what we are doing, according to Skinner, when we are asked to talk about it. We come to think of ourselves as conscious entities with certain traits and needs when others demand that we explain our actions. Thus, self-awareness appears to be dependent on language.

This idea strikes me as a simple extension of a common view among psychological theorists that language is the indispensable tool of thought. Within the behaviorist tradition, this idea can be traced

247

back to Watson's view that thinking is nothing more than subvocal speech, but the basic idea is older than that and is not confined to behaviorists. I have often suspected that psychologists lean toward this view because they happen usually to be such highly verbal people that they cannot imagine a flow of experience that is not thoroughly laced and punctuated with words. I will grant that language adds a certain structure to consciousness that would otherwise be lacking, but the sort of equation suggested by the Watsons and Skinners of psychology has always struck me as very peculiar. Throughout my life I have been acutely aware of feeling states and perceptual effects for which I can find no appropriate verbal labels. I recognize some of these as qualities of my own being and some as qualities that arise in my interaction with the world around me. The mystery of the vast incommunicable realms of conscious experience is one of the great puzzles that led me into psychology. To say that these realms are subvocal speech, or that language generated these realms, or that I came to view some of them as a part of me because years ago somebody once asked, "Why are you doing that?" strikes me as utterly preposterous.[4]

Skinner distinguishes two kinds of behavior: respondent and operant. The former is distinguished by the fact that it depends on an eliciting stimulus, but the latter is distinguished more by the effects that it produces in the environment. Skinner considers operant behavior more important and has focused almost exclusively on it in his theory and research. He believes that most behavior is emitted by the organism, rather than elicited by stimuli. The performance of a given action, however, is dependent on the consequences that ensued when that action or similar ones were performed in the past. The most basic idea running through Skinner's theoretical work is that our actions produce effects in the environment and that these effects in turn determine future behavior. If the action yields a "reinforcing" consequence, it is more likely to be repeated. Skinner emphasizes reinforcement to a greater extent than most other learning theorists, and for him it appears to be the all-important determiner of behavior.

If behavior is strictly determined by effects that occur in the environment, this means, according to Skinner's logic, that behavior is externally controlled. Adopting an extreme environmental determinism, he elaborates on what he sees as the logical consequences of this position. One is that much that we speak of in terms of stable character traits and personal identity is illusory. An individual does not continue to act in his characteristic way because he is a certain kind of person or because he possesses certain traits; he continues acting that way because the reinforcement contingencies in his environment are relatively stable. Change the contingencies, and his behavior will change. Skinner does not deny genetic variability, of course, but he does appear to regard the human organism as a rather plastic block of wax, with individual differences governed pretty much by reinforcement histories. There is not too much room in his thinking for individual temperament or unique individual potentials.

Another consequence for Skinner is that freedom is an illusion. There is no such thing as an autonomous human being. We may think that we make conscious choices and decisions and then act accordingly, but in fact our actions—and our conscious processing, too—are strictly determined by the effects produced by our past actions. Our behavior is controlled by events in the environment. Naturally, this view has evoked a great deal of criticism. Most of Skinner's critics would probably agree that our behavior is at least partly determined by external events, but many would contend that Skinner presses determinism itself too far, and most would argue that he does not do justice to the role of cognitive processes in human behavior.

There will never be a generally accepted, final solution to the question as to whether we really can exercise a totally free choice and act independently of all environmental and biological determinants, but our experience of freedom or lack of freedom does appear to be very important facet of our existence, and it may itself have important behavioral consequences. This is something that Skinner is not prepared to grant, for he sees "freedom" as an outmoded concept that people should discard. Many other behavior theorists would take issue with Skinner on this. Of course, his position is still further removed from the existentialists, whose view of the basic human condition and of the optimal condition must seem essentially meaningless to him.

Since for Skinner the key to understanding behavior lies in reinforcement contingencies, rather than in person properties, he has shown much more interest in defining the ideal society than in defining the ideal person. His definition is presented most graphically in *Walden Two,* in which he described a community created by a behavioral engineer named Frazier that operates smoothly and efficiently through maximal use of positive reinforcement and minimal use of threats, punishments, or other forms of aversive control. To most readers, a society in which so much of our behavior—our work habits, eating habits, speech habits, modes of social interaction—is so efficiently controlled by a benevolent despot is rather abhorrent. Both the idea of being controlled and the presumptuousness of a behavioral scientist who decides what strings to pull are repellent. Skinner contends, however, that we are inevitably controlled by the environment. His society merely maximizes the satisfactions and minimizes the strains and pains in the process. For some reason, though, most of us still like to feel that we are exercising some choice and personal control as we act. If we are as malleable as Skinner believes, perhaps his behavioral scientocracy will be able to rid us of this perversity—but personally, I doubt it.

It is possible to piece together a Skinnerian view of the optimal personality by simply noting the kinds of behavior that are selectively reinforced in the community of *Walden Two.* The overall picture is one consisting of such old-fashioned virtues as altruistic behavior, productive work habits, and minimal self-indulgence. The component traits are cultivated by manipulation of their environmental consequences, and they are traits that are essentially definable in terms of effects deemed desirable by the community. They would be only indirectly describable in terms of self-experience. The application of Skinnerian methodology in the realm of therapy tends also to be accompanied by an emphasis on well-defined behaviors and their environmental effects. Thus, the psychologist who employs operant conditioning in a clinical setting usually does so simply to replace a symptomatic behavior with one more socially sanctioned. This is not altogether inevitable, since it is perfectly possible for a psychologist of phenomenological bent to recognize that the easiest way to effect a change in the self-experience of a given patient is to precipitate a change in some specific bit of behavior, and he might well employ a

250

standard behavioral technique for that purpose. On the whole, however, the procedures generally known as techniques of behavioral modification tend to be accompanied by a behavioristic rationale and often one tempered by the views of B. F. Skinner.

GORDON W. ALLPORT

For many years, following the publication of his first major work on personality theory in 1937, Gordon Allport embodied for American psychologists the clearest alternative to both behaviorism and psychoanalysis.[5] Born in Indiana in 1897 and reared in Cleveland, Ohio, he described his home life as one of "plain Protestant piety and hard work." His father was a physician, and his mother had worked as a school teacher. He was one of four sons. In his undergraduate work at Harvard Allport majored in economics and philosophy. After teaching sociology and English for a year in Istanbul, he returned to Harvard and secured a doctorate in psychology in 1922. He spent the next two years abroad, studying in Berlin, Hamburg, and Cambridge, England, then returned to Harvard as an instructor. Later he taught for a while at Dartmouth College, but he returned to the Harvard faculty in 1930 and remained there until his death in 1967. He was a popular teacher and was known to his students as a warm human being who encouraged their individuality, instead of trying to convert them to his own position. It is noteworthy that in 1963, fifty-five of his former Ph.D. students gave him a testimonial dinner, at which they presented him a bound volume of their own varied writings.

Allport was influenced early by the writings of William James, and he represents a tradition common to William James and William McDougall on the one hand and to contemporary humanistic psychologists on the other. In many respects, his work may be viewed as a historical bridge between the two. His grasp of the field of psychology was comprehensive, however, and he was more aware of European trends than were most of his countrymen. During his travels he had come into direct contact with the Gestalt psychologists and with William Stern and Eduard Spranger, and he was influenced by them.

251

Favoring a kind of "systematic eclecticism," Allport borrowed ideas from many sources, blending them into his own distinctive outlook. Although his basic area of concern was personality theory, he addressed himself to a variety of important social issues—prejudice, religion, rumor, and attitudes, among others—and tried to grapple with them in all their complexity. As a consequence, his writings display a constant effort to achieve a balanced, comprehensive outlook that does justice to the many facets of the problem at hand. He often appeared to other American psychologists to be an extremist because he held a minority view in theory, and yet his own position was usually better balanced than those of his opponents. He did not deny the value of the things they stressed but felt a need to stress the things they were neglecting. It is for this reason that he became identified with an emphasis on conscious intention, on an idiographic study of the individual, on the whole person, and on the functional autonomy of "higher" motives—ideas that were not very fashionable in American psychology when he began to endorse them.

Allport is sometimes called a trait theorist because he spoke of traits as the units of personality structure. In his early writings he distinguished between common traits, variables that can be used for describing all individuals, and individual traits, variables found only in single individuals.[6] While he argued that no two individuals have exactly the same trait, he felt that common traits are useful for descriptive and theoretical purposes. In a later work he used the term trait to refer to common traits and suggested personal disposition and morphogenic trait as possible replacements for the term individual trait.[7] His emphasis remained on the category that is uniquely descriptive of the single individual, and he distinguished three subcategories—cardinal, central, and secondary—in terms of the pervasiveness of their influence on an individual's actions. A cardinal disposition is one that is evident in almost every action or attitude of the individual. A central disposition is one that would be called into play frequently and that would thus be highly characteristic of the individual. A secondary disposition would be more incidental, a feature infrequently manifested and perhaps confined to limited situations.

Allport's approach to the problem of motivation also allows for

252

more variety and individuality than do those of most other traditions, but psychoanalysts have accused him of superficiality. Freudian theory stresses the perpetual operation of a limited number of instinctual forces, which continue when unrecognized to exert their influence from the depths of the unconscious. Our behavior thus expresses sexual and aggressive motives even when we consciously attribute our actions to something entirely different. Allport rejected this extreme irrationalist position and contended that we are usually aware of the motives for our actions. He did not deny the existence of repression or of unconscious motives but believed that they are more characteristic of the neurotic than of the normal individual, who is usually aware of the reasons for his acts and aware of his conflicting motives as well. In stressing conscious intentions as the primary source of behavior, Allport's thinking runs counter to that of both psychoanalysts and behaviorists, but it is difficult to challenge his basic argument: if we want to predict an individual's behavior, we will not achieve maximal efficiency either by analyzing a comprehensive record of past reinforcement contingencies or by probing his unconscious through dreams and projective tests; we will have better success if we simply ask the individual what he is trying to do.

With his emphasis on conscious intention, Allport opposed the rigid determinism found in the writings of both Freud and Skinner. He did not pretend to have an ultimate solution to the issue of free will, but since he saw behavior as consciously directed toward future goals, he thought that we have more freedom in some sense than most behaviorists would admit.[8] In this respect he is much closer to the existentialists. He also believed that it is important for the individual to develop a sense of responsibility for his actions, even though they are partly determined by biological and social influences that he cannot control.

Another distinctive feature of Allport's view of motivation is the concept of functional autonomy, the tendency for any mode of behavior or striving, once established, to become independent of the drive or motive that originally prompted it. By virtue of the principle of functional autonomy, any course of action that we pursue habitually tends to acquire its own motive power. To the extent that this is true, even if

253

we all start life with one common set of drives, in the course of development we will all become motivationally individualized. Allport distinguished two types of functional autonomy: a perseverative, or reactive, type and a propriate, or proactive, type. The former is a rather automatic process that is dependent on properties of the nervous system and evident in lower organisms. It underlies the development of addictions and routine habits. The latter depends more on the self-awareness of the human being and underlies the development of our interests, values, and most of our personal dispositions.

In Allport's view, the nature of our dominant motives is subject to developmental change. In the early years of life the most powerful forces may be ones that are common to the species and that fit a tension-reduction model—strivings that arise as we develop a deficiency in a certain bodily need and then subside when the deficiency is overcome. Later in development our strivings are subject to greater conscious direction and more concerned with personal growth. Allport saw the individual as becoming increasingly concerned with realizing all his possibilities and with cultivating a self-aware, self-critical, and self-enhancing style of life.[9] His view of development is obviously far from the psychoanalytic view, for he perceived the individual as becoming more and more independent of his original roots. As he becomes more conscious and rational, he develops motives that cease to be closely related to those that operated in early development. Allport admitted that disordered relationships in infancy and early childhood often leave lasting scars and result in the arrested development that we see in neurotics and psychotics, but he believed that in normal development the early relationships leave the individual free to become, to develop in an unhampered way. The character that is ultimately formed in this case is not greatly determined by events in the first few years of life.

Allport's view of development is one that stresses the growth of self-awareness, and its most important products are encompassed by his concept of the *proprium*. This term subsumes most of the qualities attributed by other theorists to the self or the ego, but Allport insisted that he was not postulating a homunculus that directs the organism from within. The term is meant simply to embrace certain psychological functions that must be recognized in any adequate theory of per-

254

sonality. The functions include the bodily sense, the sense of self-identity, the striving for self-enhancement, ego-extension (a sense of possession or identity with one's property, with a group, or with ideals), rationality, the self-image, propriate striving (self-aware, growth-oriented striving), and awareness or knowing as such.

In formulating a picture of the optimally developed, or mature, personality, Allport inevitably stressed qualities that were bound up in his concepts of the proprium and propriate striving, but he endeavored to develop a picture that reflects a consensus of informed people in our culture, rather than one that merely expressed his own theoretical biases. His description of the mature personality includes the following characteristics:

1. an extension of the sense of self—authentic participation in significant spheres of human endeavor, having interests that extend beyond one's immediate needs and duties;
2. warm relating of self to others—a capacity for both intimacy and compassion;
3. emotional security—which includes such qualities as self-acceptance and frustration tolerance;
4. realistic perception, skills, and assignments—realistic orientation to the world, the development of skills that can be applied to meaningful projects, and an involvement in such projects;
5. self-objectification—a realistic appraisal of oneself and an accompanying sense of humor; and
6. a unifying philosophy of life—values, sentiments, and directions that provide an overall meaning or purpose to one's life.[10]

This is indeed a rather comprehensive picture of maturity, but it is also an eclectic one. We may note that each of its components can be found in some form in either the psychoanalytic tradition or the existentialist tradition.

CARL R. ROGERS

Carl Rogers occupies a position in American psychology somewhat similar to that of Gordon Allport, for he is also a major representative of the tradition that has come to be called humanistic. While Allport is the leading personality theorist of that tradition, however, Rogers' main contribution is an approach to psychotherapy, one that he originally called nondirective and later called client-centered.[11] Client-centered therapy is probably the most significant American innovation in the realm of psychotherapy, as well as the therapeutic method that has been most extensively tested and validated by research. But Rogers is not known simply as a theorist and methodological innovator—he is known as a skilled and sensitive therapist, the one person who has often been regarded as a "therapist's therapist." Perhaps the basic reason for this reputation is that he seems to embody in his own personality the qualities most clearly required in a client-centered therapist. He is a warm, sensitive man, with a deep concern for the feelings of other people. Most people who have known him seem to be impressed by a basic honesty, genuineness, and lack of pretension. These are always refreshing qualities to discover in a person of Roger's eminence. Unfortunately, as genuineness and honesty have come to be stressed in the humanistic movement, one often finds them cultivated as part of a professional mask. If Rogers wears a professional mask, it is much more transparent than most.

Born in Illinois in 1902, he was the fourth of six children in the family. His parents were fairly well educated but nonintellectual people who clung to a very conservative system of Protestant values and beliefs. After completing high school, Rogers enrolled in the University of Wisconsin to study scientific agriculture. In his second year there, however, he decided to pursue a career in religious education. He graduated with a bachelor's degree in history and then enrolled in Union Theological Seminary, where he was exposed to a much more liberal philosophical and religious outlook than that which his family environment had provided. While studying at the seminary he cultivated a taste for psychology by taking a few courses at Columbia University; he soon transferred to the Teachers College of Columbia to study clinical and educational psychology, and there he received a doctorate in 1931. For several years thereafter Rogers worked in a guidance clinic in Rochester. He moved from there to assume a professorship at Ohio State University in 1940 and later held academic positions at the University of Chicago and at the University of Wisconsin. In 1967 he moved to La Jolla, California, where he is currently a resident fellow of the Center for Studies of the Person.

Rogers' work in psychology reflects a varied set of influences. Early in his clinical work he came into contact with colleagues with a psychoanalytic bias, and in his approach to therapy one can discern clear traces of the outlook of Otto Rank. As a theorist he was influenced by the phenomenological psychology of Donald Snygg and Arthur W. Combs and by the holistic and organismic views of Kurt Goldstein, Abraham Maslow, and Andras Angyal. In recent years, he has acknowledged a kinship with the existentialist movement. Kierkegaard in particular seems to have made a deep impression on him. While it is possible to trace most of Rogers' ideas to various sources, the resulting blend certainly bears his own imprint, and his own clinical experience has always been the ultimate testing ground for every idea that he accepts, rejects, or formulates.

The basic structural concepts in Rogers' view of personality are the organism, the phenomenal field, and the self.[12] Roger's theoretical system is one that stresses conscious experience, but in his use of the concept of the organism, he underlines the total organization and the biological foundation of all our experience and behavior. The organism is the locus of experience, and it is the organism that behaves. Behavior is not to be understood just as an expression of biological needs or in terms of a simple interaction with a physical and social environment, however, for like Snygg and Combs, Rogers holds that the organism reacts to the world as it is experienced and perceived. Just as Allport stressed the individual's conscious intentions as the best basis for understanding and predicting behavior, Rogers stresses an "internal frame of reference"—the individual's way of experiencing himself and the world.

The totality of experience at any time constitutes the phenomenal field. This includes both conscious (symbolized) experiences and unconscious (or unsymbolized) experiences. The self is one portion of the phenomenal field that becomes gradually differentiated from the totality and includes those perceptions that we regard as "I" or "me." Rogers also speaks of the ideal self, a system of ideas about what the individual would like to be.

257

Another basic concept employed by Rogers is congruence, the extent to which the self faithfully reflects the experiences of the organism. Incongruence, or a lack of congruence, would imply a defensive adjustment in which certain experiences are selectively repressed or denied. Rogers views psychotherapy as tending to promote congruence between self and organism, helping the person to be more truly what he organismically is. Congruence between self and organism is a difficult thing to assess directly, but much of the research on psychotherapy inspired by Rogers has made use of consistency measures of some kind—e.g., measures of agreement between self-description and description by others. Such measures provide interesting information about the individual's self-perception, but not information that is necessarily related to congruence between the self and the organism. Congruence requires the conscious acceptance and symbolization of experiences so that they can be related to the self. It implies something closely akin to self-insight, with perhaps the additional implication that behavior will express the totality of experience.

Like others in the humanistic tradition, Rogers stresses growth motives rather than strivings prompted by organic deficiencies. He holds that the one basic tendency and striving of the organism is "to actualize, maintain, and enhance the experiencing organism." The same essential idea appears in the work of Snygg and Combs, Goldstein, Angyal, and Maslow. Rogers notes, however, that both the organism as a whole and the self exhibit this tendency. The actualizing tendency of the self may conflict with that of the organism if self and organism are incongruent. If the two are congruent, however, there will be no conflict. Thus congruence is a prerequisite for the maximal expression and actualization of the individual's growth potentials. Rogers regards the actualizing tendency as a primary source of creativity and as the curative force that operates in effective psychotherapy. This means that basically the individual in therapy cures himself; the function of the therapist is to provide a situation in which this can happen.

Rogers also speaks of two needs that are learned in the course of development, the need for positive regard (to be viewed favorably by other people) and the need for self-regard (to think well of oneself). These needs can be powerful determiners of behavior and they often conflict with the actualizing tendency. We may then suppress many of our creative potentials in an effort to make a favorable impression or to live up to an ideal that we have introjected. From Roger's standpoint, it is clearly undesirable to be dominated by the needs for positive regard and self-regard to the detriment of one's own personal growth.

We tend to cling to sterile patterns of adjustment out of fear of losing self-esteem and of losing the acceptance of other people. To free the individual for growth, the therapist must provide a situation in which this threat is reduced. According to Rogers, a therapist must be open to the patient's experiences and try to tune in to them, and he must accept the patient. Ideally he provides both full empathic understanding and unconditional positive regard. Finding his feelings and impulses accepted by the therapist as they emerge, the patient can accept them himself and can grow in a positive, constructive direction. Rogers stresses congruence, genuineness, and transparency on the part of the therapist—to function in the way required for effective therapy, he must be open to his own feelings and must be fairly congruent himself. He must relate to the patient as a real person and not make a pretense of a warmth and acceptance that he does not actually feel. To protect himself from psychic bruises, of course, the psychotherapist is often tempted to treat his therapeutic function as a standard role he can don for the occasion and slip off at the end of the hour. During the hour, he makes all the appropriate textbook responses but insulates himself from real involvement with the patient. By withholding a large part of himself, he does not really encounter the patient but treats him, with detachment, as an object. If the therapist is too concerned with maintaining his own comfort and status, there is a great danger that the person-to-person exchange needed for constructive growth will be lost.

As I have indicated, Rogers views self-organism congruence as the fundamental goal of therapy. In a number of his writings he deals in a more elaborate and specific way with the qualities that he sees emerging in his therapeutic clients.[13] These specific qualities may be viewed as manifestations and consequences of congruence, or of the individual's becoming more fully what he organismically is. For Rogers, these therapeutic effects constitute the ingredients of the optimal personality, and we may note that client-centered therapy may be regarded as a research strategy for determining what the optimal personality is. To regard it in this way, we must make two basic assumptions: (1) that the optimal personality is that which emerges as a result of unhampered natural growth, and (2) that client-centered therapy permits natural growth to occur. Essentially the same logic underlies other clinically based views of the optimal personality, such as that of Jung, but Rogers and his students have made a more systematic effort that have any other group of therapists to identify and measure the effects of psychotherapy.

The effects of therapy have been listed in various ways by Rogers, but the following list seems to encompass all the qualities to which he has devoted much attention:

1. trust, openness, and acceptance of self—trust in one's organism, openness to all one's experience, owning all one's feelings, experiencing feelings with immediacy and richness.
2. acceptance of process and complexity—willingness to be a process, experiencing self less as a perceived object and more as a process, loosening of the static and simple categories in terms of which experience has been structured.
3. independence, self-direction—movement away from "oughts" and from meeting expectations, movement away from facades, less emphasis on pleasing others, an internal locus of evaluation.
4. acceptance of others.
5. full functioning, richer living.
6. creativity.
7. the experience of freedom of choice.

This is a fairly comprehensive picture, but it centers on qualities such as self-awareness, self-acceptance, independence, and relatedness, which we have met in the work of other people. On the whole, Rogers' view of the ideal condition is one that is particularly compatible with the existentialist tradition.

ABRAHAM H. MASLOW

Abraham Maslow is also a representative of the humanistic tradition in the United States, and during the past ten or fifteen years his theories have probably been the most influential in that tradition. Some of the facts of his life and of his development as a psychologist have been provided by Richard Lowry and Colin Wilson.[14] He was born in Brooklyn in 1908 and grew up there. During a large part of his childhood and adolescence he was the only Jewish boy in a non-Jewish suburb and came to think of himself as an outsider. Much of the time he was isolated and unhappy and preoccupied himself with books. As a youth he was shy, unsure of himself, and ill at ease with girls, but at twenty he married his cousin Bertha, the one girl with whom he had had a serious emotional involvement. His timidity apparently plagued him through most of his life, and he often experienced an acute panic before delivering papers. For the most part, however, his agony was not apparent to his audiences, who were more likely to be impressed (either favorably or unfavorably) by the bold sweep of his ideas.

As an undergraduate Maslow developed a strong interest in cultural patterns. The interest continued, and there were times when his work bordered on the anthropological realm, but it was psychology that he chose for a career. As a student he was greatly impressed by the ideas of John B. Watson and leaned toward the behavioristic view of psychology. His initial work was in the experimental area; while studying under Harry Harlow he wrote a doctoral dissertation on the sexual and dominance characteristics of monkeys. He earned all of his university degrees at the University of Wisconsin, where he received his doctorate in 1934. From 1935 to 1937 he worked as a research fellow at the Teachers College of Columbia University. He then served on the faculty at Brooklyn College until 1951, when he moved to Brandeis University. In 1969 he moved to Menlo Park, California, and there in 1970 he suffered a fatal heart attack.

While Maslow started his career as an experimental psychologist doing research with animals, he moved through the fields of social psychology, abnormal psychology, personality, and motivation theory

261

in the course of his career, and his outlook shifted to a position far removed from the narrow behaviorism of his youth. As a student he had known William Sheldon, Clark Hull, and Harry Harlow. During his years at Brooklyn College he had occasion to interact with psychologists of many different persuasions and to refashion his own views. He appears to have been influenced by Margaret Mead, Gardner Murphy, Rollo May, Carl Rogers, Kurt Goldstein, and Gordon Allport.

Maslow is often regarded as the leader of a "third force" in psychology, the alternative to both behaviorism and psychoanalysis. Despite the prominence accorded his ideas in the humanistic movement, however, Maslow refused to consider himself either antibehavioristic or anti-Freudian. He regarded himself as both a behaviorist and a psychoanalyst and referred to his own position as a holistic-dynamic point of view. He wanted to deal with the total person, and he wanted to incorporate and integrate the insights provided by all partial perspectives. He often seemed to manifest a curious combination of qualities. The earlier behaviorism, materialism, and atheism became tempered with a much more subjectivistic orientation. What emerged was the mystical atheist, a mixture of the tough-minded and tender-minded.

In his concern for the whole person, Maslow refused to preoccupy himself with minor details. He searched constantly for basic problems and tried to deal with them broadly, attempting to sketch the outlines of a total picture. He thought of himself as an innovator, a man more interested in breaking new ground than in completing structures, more interested in exploring new territories than in completing the work of mapping them. For this reason, his approach to theory was bold and inclusive but often appeared sloppy. He was inclined to issue his broad outlines at a point where most psychologists might have been inclined to continue gathering more data.

In attempting to deal innovatively with vast areas instead of following the more secure and common course, the patient pursuit of trivia, Maslow was capable of displaying great naiveté, for there were inevitable gaps in his understanding. There were serious flaws in his research methodology, and he often overlooked the relevant work of other major theorists. In his effort to achieve comprehensiveness, he

262

wove some rather simplistic assumptions about human nature and development into the fabric of his theoretical system. It is to his credit, however, that he was aware of many of his failings as a scholar and could entertain his own doubts about his methods and concepts. He was an honest man and did not pretend to be what he was not.

Maslow's ideas on motivation provide a foundation for most of his work in other areas. In his early work we encounter the idea of the need hierarchy.[15] He listed seven categories of basic needs:

1. physiological needs,
2. safety needs,
3. belongingness and love needs,
4. esteem needs,
5. need for self-actualization,
6. the desires to know and to understand, and
7. aesthetic needs.

These are all considered basic in the sense that they are species-wide, apparently unchanging, and genetic or instinctual in origin. Maslow differed from most other theorists in seeing the "higher" needs in this list (categories 5, 6, and 7) as being just as basic or innate as the "lower" needs at the top of the list. A Freudian might view them as disguised expressions of the lower needs, while the behaviorists or Gordon Allport might view them as derived from the lower needs through a process of learning. From Maslow's standpoint, the lower needs merely appear more basic, more an inherent part of our constitution, because they are prepotent over the higher needs. With respect to the first five categories in this list, Maslow argued for a hierarchy of prepotency that operates in such a way that the earlier needs in the list must be substantially met before the later ones can gain expression. Thus, one does not seek belongingness or love until the physiological and safety needs are met, and the belongingness and love needs in turn are prepotent over the esteem needs. Maslow did not explicitly apply this principle to the order of the fifth, sixth, and seventh categories on the list. The aesthetic needs and the desires to know and understand he viewed as overlapping with each other and with other needs.

This particular hierarchy is obviously an oversimplification. Taken very literally, it does not fit all the facts of human motivation. Still, the notion of an order to prepotency is a powerful and promising concept and may prove sounder in principle than the alternatives provided by other theorists. Maslow applied it in his later work to a motivational dichotomy. He distinguished two grand classes of motives: the lower needs are strivings to overcome deficiencies, while the higher needs, or metaneeds, are concerned with growth, or with the enhancement of being. In general, deficiency needs must be met before growth needs can emerge. He spoke also of D-values (those associated with deficiency needs) and B-values (those associated with growth or Being needs), and he distinguished two corresponding kinds of love: D-love and B-love.

According to Maslow, the B-values are one of the distinctive features of human nature, but they are not just products of culture. Like the deficiency needs, they are instinctoid in nature and form part of the "biological rootings of the spiritual life." They include such qualities as wholeness, perfection, completion, justice, aliveness, richness, simplicity, beauty, goodness, uniqueness, effortlessness, playfulness, truth, and self-sufficiency. These values do not constitute a well-defined hierarchy in the way that the lower basic needs do, claimed Maslow, because they are subject to great individual differences in emphasis. One person will be particularly sensitive to truth, another to justice, another to beauty, and so on. Furthermore, each of these values when fully defined is seen to imply all the others.

In general, according to Maslow, need deprivation leads to sickness and need gratification leads to health. He regarded neurosis as a deficiency disease that may result from the frustration of any of the lower needs—safety, belongingness, etc. In the healthy person these needs have been met and behavior is governed more by a striving for growth or self-actualization. Deprivation of the metaneeds or B-values is also possible, however, and this too yields a characteristic form of pathology, one characterized by valuelessness.

Maslow was concerned with psychopathology, of course, but he was far more interested in elucidating the characteristics of the very healthy individual, the person he termed the self-actualizer.[16] As a general thesis, he held that the self-actualizer is an individual who is metamotivated—an individual whose deficiency needs have been adequately met and whose life is governed largely by B-values. Maslow wanted to obtain a more detailed picture of the self-actualizer, however, by examining actual cases. He began early to keep a record of his ideas and observations in a "Good Human Being" notebook. He attempted initially to study self-actualization in a college population but ultimately concluded that college students in general were not sufficiently mature to yield good cases. He proceeded to compile a list of self-actualizers that included some of his friends and acquaintances and a large number of public figures, both contemporary and historical. Through examination of biographical data and through direct observation and interview, he gradually pieced together a global picture of the qualities of self-actualizers.

Maslow's procedure yields a uniquely full-bodied view of the optimal person as defined by Maslow. Unfortunately, it is a very circular method. One studies a case in detail to learn what a self-actualizer is, but one must have a preliminary criterion or definition in order to select the case in the first place. Sometimes after tentatively selecting a case, Maslow would decide that the person was not a self-actualizer after all and drop him from his study (psychopathology was one basis for exclusion). What the procedure ultimately yielded was a more detailed picture of the kinds of people admired by Abraham Maslow—a glance at his list of self-actualizers suggests that two prerequisites for his admiration were high intelligence and creativity. Maslow's method is thus subject to uncontrollable biases. Nevertheless, it does provide a well-rounded picture of people who are certainly functioning well in certain respects. Whatever his ill-defined initial selection criteria, they undoubtedly represent a value consensus of at least one segment of our society. I must confess that I, too, admire most of the people on his list.

What are the qualities of the self-actualizer that emerge from detailed examination? Maslow provides various descriptions of these, but the following is a fairly comprehensive list:

265

1. more efficient perception of reality and more comfortable relations with it;
2. acceptance of self, others, and nature;
3. spontaneity, simplicity, naturalness;
4. problem centering (investment in some problem, task, or mission outside oneself);
5. the quality of detachment and the need for privacy;
6. autonomy, independence of culture and environment;
7. continued freshness of appreciation;
8. the peak experience, or mystic experience;
9. *Gemeinschaftsgefühl;*
10. deep and profound interpersonal relations with a few people;
11. democratic character structure;
12. definite (but not necessarily conventional) moral standards;
13. philosophical, unhostile sense of humor;
14. creativeness (but not of the kind that depends heavily on a special talent); and
15. resistance to enculturation, the transcendence of any particular culture.[17]

While this brief list does not do justice to Maslow's more elaborate descriptions, it does afford an accurate overview of the picture he has drawn. It is a many-faceted portrait, and yet it can be aligned rather well with the pictures provided by such theorists as Allport and Rogers.

In addition to attempting to define the ideal person, Maslow sought to define the good social organization and the good society and, in fact, to define goodness in general. He was not the first to seek a scientifically based ethics, but his strategy is unique for it is tied to his work on self-actualizers.[18] He argued that the free choices of the very healthy, self-actualizing people provide the basis for a naturalistic value system. This means that good is to be defined as the values held by those people whom Maslow regards as good people. These values are, of course, the values that Maslow calls B-values, or Being-values.

The good organization is one that promotes self-satisfaction and growth in all its members. In the ideal case, perhaps, it would lead to self-actualization on the part of everyone. Maslow spoke of eupsychian management in the business world and contended that such management, which permits participation and facilitates growth on the part of

266

workers, is quite compatible with efficiency in business. Though Maslow was a socialist in his youth, he came to hold a highly optimistic view of our capitalistic society, just as he arrived at a highly optimistic view of basic human nature. The view manifested in his later writings is that we are progressively moving toward the good society—the synergic society, which functions in such a way as to support and meet the needs of its individual members.

FREDERICK S. PERLS AND GESTALT THERAPY

Much of the personal style of Frederick S. Perls as a thinker, as a therapist, and as a human being is reflected in the fact that in the last few years of his life he came to be known to thousands of people in this country simply as "Fritz." Born in 1893, he grew up in Germany and received training in both psychology and medicine. Early in his career, in 1926, he served as an assistant to Kurt Goldstein at the Institute for Brain-Injured Soldiers, and much of the holistic, organismic character of Perls's subsequent thinking can be traced to the influence of Goldstein. He was also attracted to psychoanalysis fairly early and underwent training analysis and supervision with several of the important pioneers in the movement. Some of his training was supervised by Karen Horney and Otto Fenichel. He underwent part of his own analysis under Wilhelm Reich, whose concern with character armor (the expression of character or of defenses in habitual muscular tension patterns) left a lasting impression on him. His analytic training was brought to a premature halt in 1933 with the ascension of Hitler to power in Germany. Foreseeing the danger in remaining in Germany, Perls fled to Holland in that year. He received a bit more training under Karl Landanner in Amsterdam. In 1934 he seized an opportunity provided by Ernest Jones and moved to Johannesburg, South Africa, where he established a practice and founded the South Africa Institute for Psychoanalysis. In 1946 he moved to the United States. By then he had developed all the essentials of his own theoretical position and methods of therapy, but it was largely in the last decade of his

267

life, when he was living in California and became associated with a growth center known as Esalen, that his ideas became widely recognized in this country. He died in 1970 at the age of seventy-six.

Fritz Perls was a man who plunged freely into life. He engaged in activities as diverse as flying airplanes and directing plays. He expressed his feelings and thoughts freely, without embarrassment or apology. He could be pompous and he could be ostentatious, and he readily admitted it. His personal style is clearly evident in his loose, rambling autobiography.[19] There he often lapsed into poetic form, evidently depending on his immediate mood at the time of writing. He freely divulged the most intimate details of his sex life as they came to mind and discussed many of the agonies of his past while maintaining a playful tone. Perhaps a Jungian would say that the work is dominated by extraverted feeling.

In his therapy Perls pressed for outer expression of the inner—of the deeper bits of feeling and impulse that people keep not only private but hidden from other parts of themselves. He usually worked with one individual at a time in a group setting, so that his method tended to require a willingness of the participant to reveal secret parts to a number of observers at once. He achieved fame by demonstrating his methods with volunteers before large audiences. Sometimes he appeared a bit brutal when the demonstration culminated in humiliation for the voluntary participant. He appeared to enjoy exercising power, to delight in manipulating his victim. His aim, however, was just the opposite: to help people take full responsibility for themselves, so that they could not be unduly manipulated by others. From his standpoint, he had no power over another person except the power that the other person gave him. This was something that a patient working with him ultimately had to realize. Partly because of Perls's own personal example, the system of theory and therapy that he introduced, which he called Gestalt therapy, tends to attract prospective therapists who are somewhat extraverted, often people who like to assume a strong social role in imitation of the master.

It is difficult to classify Gestalt therapy in terms of its relationship to other theories and movements. Historically it is an outgrowth of psychoanalysis, since Perls began as a Freudian analyst and moved progressively away from an orthodox position in both theory and therapy. Perhaps Perls was not suited by temperament to remain a pure psychoanalyst. He found the intellectual gymnastics of the strict Freudians tedious. In his one direct contact with Freud in 1936, he was greatly disappointed and annoyed. He had traveled a great distance to present a paper and to meet Freud, but he found that the great Viennese genius would tolerate only a very brief impersonal exchange with him. He was influenced more directly by Wilhelm Reich, who had begun to deviate from psychoanalytic orthodoxy when he served as Perls's analyst, and Perls adopted Reich's concept of psychic energy as excitement and his view of habitual movements and muscular armor as expressions of character.

In some respects, Perls is closer to Jung than to Freud, though he adopted none of Jung's terminology. Like Jung, he saw dreams as creative expressions of the self and rejected the Freudian view that one of the basic functions of dreams symbols is disguise. With Jung he also shared the view that our experience is characterized by a multiplicity of polarities, so that our conscious expression in one direction tends to be accompanied by a hidden tendency, often denied or projected, to do the opposite. With Adler he shared an emphasis on conscious experience and conscious self-direction, and like Adler, he concocted a populist form of theory, using plain language for ease of mass consumption and shunning any pretension of academic elegance. He shared with Rank an interest in the efforts of the patient to establish his individual identity separate from that of the therapist and other powerful individuals in his life, and he was clearly influenced by Rank's view of the constructive function of resistance on the part of the patient. Perls shared a rather flamboyant personal style with the great exponent of psychodrama, Jacob Moreno, and his use of certain dramatic techniques may be attributed to Moreno's influence.

There are strong influences in Gestalt therapy from sources more remote from the psychoanalytic movement. There is, of course, a stress on organismic wholeness that can be traced directly to Kurt Goldstein, and perhaps indirectly to Jan Smuts. A stress on experiential holism can also be traced to traditional Gestalt psychology, which inspired the label that Perls adopted for his own approach. From Ges-

269

talt psychology he adopted an emphasis on the figure/ground character of experience (the principle that whatever we perceive is composed of two or more mutually influencing parts) and the idea that all experience is characterized by a tendency toward the formation or completion of good figures, or gestalts. The traditional Gestalt psychologists were largely concerned with the perception of the external world, however, and Perls transported their concepts from that realm to the experience of the individual's own bodily sensations, feelings, emotions, and fantasies.

At times in his writings Perls allied himself with the existentialist movement and spoke of Gestalt therapy as one of the major existential approaches to therapy.[20] At other times he referred to existentialism as a form of "is-ism" and to Gestalt therapy as an alternative orientation.[21] In its basic orientation, Gestalt therapy may be viewed as a product of a phenomenological tradition that also embraces both traditional Gestalt psychology and existentialism. It stresses immediate experience and, like some other products of the tradition, de-emphasizes the interpretation of experience. Perls recognized in his emphasis on the unanalyzed *now* a kinship with Zen Buddhism, though of course he arrived at his own position by a Western route, rather than by borrowing from Eastern thought. As a therapist Perls assumed a powerful role somewhat similar to that of the Zen master, seeking to bring about an experience of illumination in the disciple without trying to impose his own insights—in a sense, the paradoxical role of nonauthoritarian manipulator.

Since its introduction by Perls, Gestalt therapy has become a collaborative venture to which many people have contributed and which continues to evolve after the death of its originator. Even the major theoretical work on the subject represents a joint effort on the part of Perls, Ralph Hefferline, and Paul Goodman.[22] According to Gestalt therapists, the basic subject matter of psychology is the organism/environment field. The events of greatest importance occur at the "ego boundary," the interface between organism and environment. This boundary itself is not fixed. What is experienced as organism and what is experienced as environment are subject to redefinition and change through processes of identification and alienation. The important events involve contact or interaction at the boundary. Conditions in both the organism and the environment are ever-changing, creating imbalances or needs, and there is a basic tendency for the field to move from imbalance to equilibrium. The self is said to have the function of effecting "creative adjustment" in the field. *Self* is variously defined as the system of contacts at the ego boundary, as "the power that forms the gestalt in the field," and as "the figure/ground process in contact situations." It is distinguished from three chief "partial systems" called *id, ego,* and *personality. Id* and *ego* are used in a sense akin to Freudian usage, although the ego is accorded such properties as self-awareness and a process of conscious identification. *Personality* is used in the sense of a system of attitudes and assumptions about one's own nature that serve as a basis for explaining one's actions to oneself and to others.

In his first major work, *Ego, Hunger and Aggression,* Perls presented a principle of organismic self-regulation.[23] According to this principle, the most pressing need at any time becomes figure and organizes behavior until it is satisfied. It then recedes and the need that is most important at that time takes over. Under natural circumstances, our chances of survival are enhanced by a continual shifting in the dominance of different needs. Unfortunately, in our society some needs become chronic and tend to interfere with the natural process. The concept of creative adjustment is closely related to the notion of organismic self-regulation, for it implies the spontaneous formation and dissolution of gestalts as conditions in the field change. This concept seems to stress the psychological aspect of organismic self-regulation.

Gestalt therapy rests on a Romantic view of human nature. Left to its own devices, the organism is perfectly self-regulating, and adjustment is characterized by creativity and spontaneity. Problems arise as a consequence of external manipulation. Certain needs are given undue emphasis and others are deemed unacceptable. As a result, the natural process is disrupted. We cannot attend adequately to some parts of the field, we misperceive others, and we fail to establish sufficient contact with the environment. Instead of a natural flow of gestalts, we experience confusion and indecision, we deliberate excessively, we cannot shift our attention as occasion demands, and our energy remains bound up in uncompleted tasks. These effects are viewed as symptomatic of neurosis. Perls, Hefferline, and Goodman spoke of retroflection, introjection, and projection as three of the major neurotic mechanisms that interfere with the natural flow and prevent proper contact.[24] In the case of retroflection, we suppress our responses to the environment and direct them toward ourselves instead, in effect reducing interchange between ourselves and the environment. In the case of introjection, we passively incorporate modes of acting and feeling provided by the environment without regard to how well they fit the inherent properties of the organism. Projection involves attributing properties of oneself to the environment, particularly to other people, and in the usage of Gestalt therapists this nearly always implies defensively disowning these properties at the same time. Each of these mechanisms will obviously interfere either with the way in which the dominant needs at any time are perceived or with the actions through which we attempt to cope with these needs.

We all make frequent use of these mechanisms, of course, and we all suffer from disturbances in the natural flow of awareness. To that extent we all are neurotic, and Perls stated in fact that the basic personality of our time is a neurotic personality, for we live in an insane society.[25] Perls, Hefferline, and Goodman noted that, in general, norms for health and abnormality are a matter of opinion once we move outside the strict domain of physical medicine, and tend to reflect the fashions of the society. They argued that even the basic psychoanalytic criterion, adjustment to "reality," amounts in practice to conformity to socially prescribed standards. By the usual rules of the game, the term *neurotic* would be used in such a way that it applied to only a certain deviant minority within the society in which the term is employed. From the standpoint of Gestalt therapists, however, we are all neurotic to the extent that there is interference with what they view as the natural process of experiencing and creative adjustment.

In further elaboration of the nature of neurosis, Perls described a series of layers through which we must proceed in order to recover genuine experience and expression. There is first the cliché layer, a layer of meaningless tokens of exchange. Then there is a layer composed of games and social roles—the "Eric Berne" layer. Next is a phobic layer of fears, of avoidances, of "should nots." After working through those first three layers, we reach the layer of the impasse, where we feel lost, stuck, helpless. According to Perls, we experience an impasse when we are deprived of environmental support and when authentic self-support has not yet been achieved. In the course of therapy, we experience this when we have dropped our accustomed defensive maneuvers but have not discovered how to proceed without them. Confronting the impasse, we move next to the death layer, or implosive layer, where we experience a kind of deadness or paralysis. If we fully experience this, there follows an explosion of genuine emotions of various kinds, a sudden return to authenticity.

Gestalt therapy employs a vast assortment of specific techniques, but in general they emphasize tuning in to one's immediate experience in the present moment. By virtue of all the devices we employ to avoid full awareness of assorted feelings and impulses, we tend to have many parts of ourselves that are sealed off. We contain many unintegrated fragments, and we contain polar splits, acknowledging one quality and denying qualities that run counter to it. Gestalt therapy aims to recover wholeness and to resolve our polarities by bringing everything into full awareness. The techniques are designed to evoke awareness and expression of all components and to bring opposing forces into contact so that they can be resolved. The procedures are mostly verbal, but techniques that rely on active motor expression are frequently invoked and help to undercut a common split between language and experience. Whatever the specific procedure, awareness in itself is the objective, and it is considered curative. It is both the core of the system of techniques and the goal of therapy.

From the standpoint of Gestalt therapy, the optimal condition is the natural condition that we have lost. It has a number of interrelated facets and can be described in several ways. It can be stated in terms of full awareness: to be fully aware is to be aware of every element that becomes salient in the organism/environment field. Experiencing an optimal state would mean being aware of every need that arises and aware of every feeling. It would involve being aware of any sense that one should or should not do something and aware of how these

273

"shoulds" and "should nots" affect the flow of awareness. It would involve being aware of the total flow of experience, including anything one does to block the flow of awareness or self-experiencing. It would involve awareness of one's polarities, one's opposing attitudes and impulses, awareness of any tendency to project these attitudes and impulses and hence a dissolving of projections. Such an awareness implies a clearer recognition of oneself as distinct from the rest of the total field but also as a part of it—an awareness of one's relationship to the rest of the field. The ideal condition is also stated in terms of the ability to live fully in the "here and now;" this is essentially another way of stating the idea of attending fully or being fully aware of the flow of immediate experience.

With an increase in overall self-awareness, there are many changes in the relationships among parts. There is less identification with fragments, with one end of a polarity to the exclusion of its opposite. As all parts are admitted to awareness and owned, there is greater "centering," a sense of one's being that is more in accord with the totality of experience. The character of the flow or process of experiencing also changes as the mechanisms that serve to block full attention to some parts of the field are eliminated. We experience less confusion and uncertainty, for gestalts are formed more freely and fully, and they quickly come into being and dissolve as needs arise and are met. Our actions and our experience are then characterized by greater spontaneity and creativity.

The optimal condition can also be stated in terms of an assumption of full responsibility for one's own feelings and actions. To accept this responsibility is to recognize that one is not an inevitable victim of either the actual or the imagined intentions of others. Of course, we are influenced by others and we become neurotic as a consequence of external forces, but the gestaltist view is that if we are aware, we can resist adverse influences from without, avoid giving away our own power, and assume personal responsibility. To some extent, particularly in infancy and childhood, we need external guidance, but maturing is viewed in terms of a progression from external support to self-support. At the same time, some common concepts of maturity are rejected, for maturity is often conceived in terms of a rather rigid pattern of conforming adjustment and a loss of the natural qualities of the child. To achieve true self-support, we must permit awareness and expression of the totality of our being, and this entails retaining the spontaneity, imagination, and playfulness of the child.

Gestalt therapy resembles Zen Buddhism in its emphasis on a nonanalytical full awareness of the present moment. It also resembles Eastern views in its stress on the falseness of the notions of personal identity, based on partial identifications, that we ordinarily carry around with us. Even with its emphasis on the total organism/environment field, however, there is an implicit emphasis on individuality. Individuality, independence (self-support), and creativity are elements more often found in Western traditions. Fidelity to one's own individual nature and a respect for the individuality of others are clearly expressed in the "Gestalt prayer," Perls's oft-quoted statement of his own ideal:

> I do my thing, and you do your thing.
> I am not in this world to live up to your expectations,
> And you are not in this world to live up to mine.
> You are you and I am I,
> And if by chance we find each other, it's beautiful.
> If not, it can't be helped.

HUMANISTIC PSYCHOLOGY AND THE HUMAN POTENTIAL MOVEMENT

The term *humanism* has a long history, and it has come to have a number of meanings. It was originally applied to a movement that began in the Middle Ages and attained widespread expression during the Renaissance. It emphasized a study of the Greek and Roman classics. Since the early humanists differed on many issues from the scholastic philosophers of the Church, the movement also represented an emphasis on the freedom of the individual to arrive at his own opinions through independent critical thought and an emphasis on the natural world rather than the spiritual world. The Renaissance as well as many subsequent developments that emphasize the free pursuit of

275

knowledge, the development of the intellect, and opposition to dogmatic authority—including the Enlightenment, the Reformation, science, and democratic government—may be viewed as ultimate outgrowths of early humanism.

The contemporary meanings of the word *humanism* include: (1) the study of the humanities; (2) any system of thought or ethics concerned with the interests and ideals of people; (3) the view that the welfare and happiness of mankind in the present life are of primary importance; and (4) a twentieth-century philosophy that rejects beliefs in the supernatural, considers the good of humanity to be the supreme value, and relies on the methods of reason, science, and democracy for the solution of human problems.

The fourth meaning, naturalistic humanism, is reflected in the views of most Unitarians and Universalists who consider themselves humanists. It also comes close to the essential position of the American Humanist Association, which was formed in the 1940s. The literature of that society expresses an opposition to dogmatic and authoritarian religion and an emphasis on moral values that grow out of human experience (rather than those prescribed by authority), on the liberating power of reason and the accumulating knowledge acquired by mankind, on the solution of present human problems, and on participatory democracy.

There are many psychologists of the past to whom the term *humanism,* is one or more senses, would certainly apply, but it was not until the 1950s that people began to speak of humanistic psychology with reference to a recognizable movement, and it was not until the 1960s that this label came into widespread usage. At that time, the notion of a "humanistic" psychology reflected a need felt by many psychologists and people in allied fields for a reversal of trends within psychology that they viewed as dehumanizing—notably a stress on detached observation, objectivity, and analysis that seemed to rob the individual of his full personhood either as an object of theory, as a research subject, or as a patient or counselee. This need was expressed in 1962 in the formation of the Association for Humanistic Psychology and in 1970 in the formation of a new Division of Humanistic Psychology within the American Psychological Association.

It is possible that *every* significant movement in science reflects developments in the larger society of which the science is a part. This is certainly true of humanistic psychology, for it blossomed at a time when young people in large numbers throughout the country were becoming very vocally critical of dehumanizing trends in American society as a whole. They were concerned about the burgeoning of technocratic controls and bureaucratization, about the arms race and the prospect of nuclear annihilation, about the maltreatment of the poor and ethnic minorities, and above all about the country's senseless involvement in a war in Southeast Asia. The controlling establishment in the United States seemed to them to be characterized by either ineptitude or cynical hypocrisy. Out of their quest for a society characterized by justice, love, and a respect for human life and human personality came the political activists, the hippie dropouts, the counterculture of the 1960s. In many ways, the movement of humanistic psychology shared the spirit and concern of the counterculture.

Humanistic psychology was a heterogeneous movement at its onset, and it remains a heterogeneous movement, but there appear to be some broad principles on which most humanistic psychologists agree. A brochure of the Association for Humanistic Psychology containing a statement prepared by Charlotte Buhler and James Bugenthal lists four major ingredients of the humanistic orientation:

1. A centering of attention on the experiencing *person,* and thus a focus on experience as the primary phenomenon in the study of man. Both theoretical explanations and overt behavior are considered secondary to experience itself and to its meaning to the person.
2. An emphasis on such distinctively human qualities as choice, creativity, valuation, and self-realization, as opposed to thinking about human beings in mechanistic and reductionistic terms.
3. An allegiance to meaningfulness in the selection of problems for study and of research procedures, and an opposition to a primary emphasis on objectivity at the expense of significance.
4. An ultimate concern with and valuing of the dignity and worth of man and an interest in the development of the potential inherent in every person. Central in this view is the person as he discovers his own being and relates to other persons and to social groups.

These points have many ramifications on which we could elaborate further. The first point suggests an emphasis on immediate experi-

277

ence or consciousness per se, and certainly a resistance to treating behavior without reference to experience. Humanistic psychologists usually object to viewing the human being merely as an animal organism or merely as an empty reactor or response-emitter. They tend to stress intentionality, values, meaning, and goal-direction, rather than interpreting behavior purely in terms of antecedent events. They stress autonomy, freedom, and the possibility of individual choice, in opposition to the instinctual determinism of Freud and the environmental determinism of behaviorists. They stress individual uniqueness. They emphasize understanding, rather than prediction and control, as the aim of science. They are interested in the achievement of synergistic relationships in groups, in communities, and in organizations.

There is sufficient coherence in this multifaceted outlook for it to claim the allegiance of a sizable number of psychologists. But should this outlook be called humanistic? Certainly it is in some senses of that word, but Skinner raised the question because he saw his own opposing position as a humanistic one.[26] He defined *humanism* as a concern for the future of mankind and saw this concern as quite consistent with the work of the behaviorist. He argued, too, that "humanistic" psychologists really misappropriate the word to the extent that they stress such "selfish" aims as the fulfillment, gratification, and spiritual growth of the individual, as opposed to the good of the culture or of mankind. From the standpoint of most humanistic psychologists, of course, Skinner loaded his argument with a false dichotomy of common good and individual fulfillment. Perhaps Skinner could envision an ideal society in which there would be no concern with the self-realization of individuals, but to a humanistic psychologist this is absurd. It is interesting to note that the American Humanist Association selected Skinner as "humanist of the year" in 1972, but this honor had previously been accorded to both Carl Rogers and Abraham Maslow. As for the matter of terminology, it can certainly be argued that Skinnerian behaviorism and objective science in general, as well as its product, the technocratic society, are all humanistic in a basic sense of that term, for they represent an effort on the part of mankind to control its destiny through the exercise of the intellect. Given the vagaries of the word they chose, perhaps it would have been better if the psychologists of 1962 had

278

settled on some other label—perhaps "personalistic psychology." By now, however, the use of the term *humanistic psychology* seems, for better or worse, to be well established.

The humanistic movement has proven to be a common meeting ground for people of many specific orientations. It embraces the views of Jungians, Adlerians, neo-Freudians, existentialists, and those who ally themselves with such contemporary theorists as Allport, Rogers, Maslow, and Perls. It also embraces the views of many who favor non-Western modes of thought, in particular Zen Buddhism, Vedanta philosophy, and Sufism. To some extent, the movement has also embraced an assortment of elements that have little directly to do with humanistic psychology but share with the movement a lack of conformity to, or lack of acceptance by, psychological orthodoxy. Thus, in the convention programs of the Association for Humanistic Psychology one may find sessions that relate to astrology, parapsychology, nudism, and Kirlian photography.

Closely associated with the development of humanistic psychology is the human potential movement. Humanistic psychologists tend to attach great importance to personal growth, and the human potential movement seeks to implement this aim in a practical way through the use of various procedures for helping the individual discover and realize his potentials. It is difficult to say which specific procedures are a part of this movement and which ones are not. A technique may be borrowed from almost any traditional kind of psychotherapy and then regarded in its new context as a technique not for treating pathology but for enhancing normal growth. Certain forms of therapy, such as Gestalt therapy and the procedures of psychosynthesis, lend themselves very readily to inclusion in the movement by virtue of their original rationales. Other procedures and approaches that have been regarded as part of the human potential movement would include neo-Reichian therapies (notably bioenergetics), primal therapy, rational-emotive therapy, techniques for enhancing sensory awareness, various techniques utilizing fantasy, Progoff's Intensive Journal, various forms of meditation, various yoga techniques, massage, creative dance, certain more stylized forms of movement or dance (such as T'ai chi ch'uan and Sufi dancing), psychodrama and related uses of dramatic procedures, and various uses of such artistic media as paints and clay.

The most distinctive ingredient of the human potential movement, however, is the encounter group. This term does not designate a well-defined procedure, since with respect to the events that occur in an encounter group it is not sharply distinguishable from therapy groups of the past. The encounter group is distinguished chiefly by the fact that it is viewed as a setting that facilitates personal growth and by the fact that people usually enter into it with some expectation that they will share their feelings and experiences more openly and honestly than people do in most social contexts. The group ideally comprises about ten to twelve people, but it may be smaller, and under some conditions many of the effects achieved in a small group may occur in a group of hundreds. In the sort of encounter group characterized by Rogers as a basic encounter group, the leader or "facilitator" imposes little structure on the group process and functions essentially as just another group participant.[27] In other encounter groups the leader may play a much more directive role and employ various standard techniques.

Given such an assortment of specific theories and practices within the domain of humanistic psychology, we may expect to find a variety of viewpoints on the nature of the optimal personality or the ideal goal of personal growth. Through the movement, there runs the theme characterized in terms of self-realization, self-actualization, or the actualization of all one's potentials. In elaborating on this theme, however, one may subscribe more specifically to the outlook of Jung, Maslow, Assagioli, Vedanta philosophy, or Buddhism. There are a number of more specific themes that also appear to be characteristic of the literature of the human potential movement. These themes seem to represent partial goals or subgoals related to the more general theme of full personal development:

1. full immediate awareness, sensory awareness, or awareness of feeling;
2. spontaneity of expression;
3. self-transcendence or "ego death";
4. joy or the peak experience;
5. autonomy, independence, or experience of individual will;

6. trust of others, relatedness, or intimacy; and
7. transparency.

Of these ingredients, transparency—the disclosure of one's thoughts and feelings to others—is perhaps the most novel. It is a quality that is obviously required in many human potential practices that involve groups. At least as a means to an end, many of the procedures encourage people to be less private, to share more of themselves with other people. Sidney Jourard, more than anyone else, underscored and attempted to document the value of transparency.[28] He argued that self-disclosure eliminates one source of illness, that it is conducive to further personal growth, and that it facilitates self-disclosure on the part of others. To the extent that this is all true, we can improve the whole society just by encouraging people to engage in more honest self-disclosure. Jourard did not go so far as to equate transparency with psychological health. From his standpoint, transparency is not itself the goal, but it will help us get there.

In consideration of the great variety of procedures that have been utilized and that are still being devised within the human potential movement, it might be illuminating to attempt a thorough systematic analysis of these procedures and of their actual and intended effects in order to gain a comprehensive picture of the growth goals sought in this movement. I have certainly not attempted to gather the data required for such analysis, nor has anyone else so far as I know, but I believe there are several obvious modes of variation in these procedures that are of psychological importance (i.e., they are important in that they have a bearing on what people are seeking and what they derive from the procedures). These basic dimensions of variation would include the following.

Technique focus versus *psychological content focus.* At one extreme, the basic encounter group de-emphasizes technique in the hope of achieving a full experience of persons. Other approaches emphasize standardization of procedure. At the extreme, this is tantamount to a quest for—or the claim that one has found—the one perfect ritual. Some people favor variety. William Schutz's open encounter amounts to a flexible eclecticism in the choice of techniques.[29]

Problem focus versus *growth focus*. One may emphasize either the overcoming of barriers or residues from the past or the experience or exercise of new possibilities. This may be more a matter of rationale than of procedure as such, but some procedures clearly entail one focus and not the other.

Developmental level. If we think of the life cycle as involving different stages with different subgoals, as in the theories of Jung and Erickson, then it is apparent that some procedures emphasize early life goals (such as trust in people or the experience of will), while others stress goals more appropriate for later stages of life (such as self-transcendence). Gestalt therapy tends to emphasize ego integration—from a Jungian standpoint, the goal of early adulthood. Some systems of procedures, such as the Intensive Journal and psychosynthesis, are intended in principle to embrace a wide range of developmental goals.

Experiental versus *conceptual emphasis*. An emphasis on the conceptual process, or on intellectual insight, is particularly evident in the use of transactional analysis in groups. Meditation and other nonverbal procedures are at the other extreme. Some procedures, such as Gestalt therapy and the Intensive Journal, make use of verbal procedures but are clearly designed to help the individual achieve greater immediate awareness and deal with his total experience, rather than promoting intellectual processing.

Interpersonal versus *intrapersonal focus*. A procedure may emphasize one's relationship to, or interaction with, other people, or it may focus strictly on the individual himself. The two are related, for a change in the one area inevitably affects the other, but any given procedure will tend to focus on either the interpersonal or the intrapersonal realm and assume that to be the preferable starting point. Transactional analysis is highly interpersonal in focus. Encounter groups are variable in focus, but they tend to emphasize feeling responses to other people. Fantasy techniques and the Intensive Journal stress the intrapersonal realm. Gestalt therapy has an intrapersonal focus in principle, but it may utilize the interpersonal realm to get at the intrapersonal. The specific procedures used by Perls and by those who follow his example tend to entail acting out the internal in a group setting, or

282

"extraverting" intrapersonal content and bringing it into the interpersonal realm.

The human potential movement is a meeting ground for people of various persuasions, and as people continue to try out different pathways they generate fresh ideas about appropriate life goals. For the most part, of course, as people try out different modes, they tend simply to select goals and procedures in keeping with their individual constitutions. Like the Catholic Church, the human potential movement contains niches and orders to fit people of various temperaments. Fantasy and journal techniques are most likely to appeal to introverts, while extraverts may prefer procedures that entail more active outward expression. Encounter groups demand a certain kind of extraversion—in particular, the interpersonal expression of feelings—yet an introvert who is in touch with his feelings and able to talk about them is likely to feel more at home in an encounter group than will an extravert who is accustomed to acting without reflection. A given procedure may attract people who need to experience power, people who need to express feeling in movement or in artistic creation, people who are seeking something spiritual, people who need to realize their feminine qualities, people who need to achieve greater autonomy, or people who need to vent anger. As people try out different procedures, of course, they often discover hidden facets—growth needs of which they have been quite unaware. As enlightened people continue to try out different pathways and to devise new pathways, totally new conceptions of the ideal goals of personal growth may evolve within the human potential movement.

TEN

THE OPTIMAL PERSONALITY: A REEXAMINATION OF THE DOMAIN

AVAILABLE RESEARCH STRATEGIES

We have now considered a great variety of views on the nature of the optimal personality. Several things seem immediately apparent from this survey. For one, there are a number of possible models of the ideal from which to choose in defining the optimal personality. These models have long histories, and it is possible to trace a number of themes from an early period in Western civilization to the present. At the same time, there is some recognizable variation from one culture to another in the definition of the ideal. Within the total array of ideal-person concepts are the modern Western ones that are cast in terms of mental health. We may tend to think of these as being the aseptic products of scientific discovery and thought and hence closest to some ultimate truth, but these ideas, too, can be viewed as modern expressions of ancient traditions, tempered a bit by the influence of modern societal conditions.

Perhaps some features or modes of human functioning are inherently desirable for everyone. A thorough analysis of extant models might reveal these as elements universally recognized as a part of the optimal personality. Thus, it seems likely that all traditions recognize the need for some kind of growth. They all assume that as we get

284

older we should abandon at least some of the ways of infancy. If we were to construct a picture of a universal ideal by piecing together elements common to all traditions, however, we should end up with a very meager sketch. To add sufficient flesh to obtain the semblance of a person, we should have to make a larger number of decisions about ingredients to adopt and ingredients to reject. We cannot escape the fact that the whole issue of the ideal personality is quite value-laden, and we cannot expect to find a solution that will meet with universal acceptance.

Obviously it is not possible by scientific research to arrive at *the* solution, to determine altogether what is optimal and what is not, but research can furnish a good deal of pertinent information. Human personality is an extremely complex puzzle, and we make many assumptions about it when we proceed to define something we call mental health, maturity, normality, or self-actualization. Through research, we can test some of these assumptions and find out more about the ways in which people actually do function. Research can serve to illuminate and clarify the choices we must make when we formulate an ideal concept.

There are three basic research strategies that seem to have something to contribute to our understanding of the optimal personality. One of these, noted in the context of Rogers' work, is the examination of the changes or effects yielded by psychotherapy. This strategy assumes that we have some condition or method of treatment wherein people will tend to move closer to an ideal condition; its most obvious flaw is the assumption that a particular method of treatment—client-centered therapy, in this case—is especially designed to permit natural, constructive growth. The assumption may be valid, but it could be applied with some justification to many other treatment methods. Perhaps it should be. It would be illuminating to apply this basic strategy to a variety of conditions, to examine in more detail the effects that result from undergoing three years of Freudian analysis, spending twelve years in an unstructured classroom, living for ten years in a Zen monastery, or taking 100 weekly doses of LSD. The effects would vary from one condition to another, but it would be interesting to see which ones were common to a number of different conditions.

285

A second strategy is the one employed by Maslow: we select a sample of people who all manifest some desired quality to a high degree and study the members of the sample in depth. This method has been employed very fruitfully in such realms as the authoritarian personality and creativity. Maslow applied it to the study of self-actualizers. The strategy eliminates the need to make any initial assumptions about the process that produces the criterion quality, but there is a kind of circularity inherent in this approach; what we ultimately find is implicit in our initial selection criterion. Any bias in our initial selection will affect the final results of deeper examination and may be magnified in them. But this strategy, too, has something valuable to offer, for it provides the most detailed picture of people who approximate some ideal model.

There is a third strategy, that of multivariate analysis, that can furnish still a different sort of information. In this strategy we assess a large number of personality variables in a large sample of subjects and employ factor analysis or something comparable to illuminate the relationships among the variables we have measured. Such a procedure may reveal patterns of functioning or basic dimensions of individual differences that we would not detect in applications of the other two strategies. Applied to the domain of variables embraced by concepts of the optimal personality, it can give us a much clearer idea of the overall nature of that domain and show us which ingredients naturally go together and which ones do not. This strategy has been applied extensively to the personality and ability realms, notably by R. B. Cattell and by J. P. Guilford. Some past studies have naturally included variables pertaining to various aspects of optimal functioning, but I believe that my own research, which I have reported in detail in an earlier book, represents the first major application of this strategy to the domain of ideal-person concepts.[1]

A MULTIVARIATE ANALYSIS OF THE IDEAL-PERSON DOMAIN

Before I attempted my own analysis, I had observed that the typical theorist who formulates a concept of the optimal personality tends to describe a constellation of traits that he sees as naturally cohering. The presence of one part of the constellation is assumed to call forth other parts. If all the desiderata do in fact tend to covary, we will find some people who possess them all to a high degree, some who lack them all, and many people who manifest them all to only a moderate degree. We would not expect to find some people who manifest some of the desired traits to a very high degree while showing a complete absence of others. To put it another way, with respect to their proximity to the optimal condition, people can be pretty accurately described in terms of one general dimension. The true self-actualizers are very high on it. Neurotics and psychotics are very low, and the rest of us are somewhere in the middle.

Unfortunately, in employing the first two strategies I noted above, it is all too easy to make this assumption and obtain results that tend to convince us that it is correct. In employing the second strategy—the in-depth study of highly selected cases—we can unwittingly choose a sample that totally misrepresents the most natural confluences of trait patterns. When I first encountered Maslow's research long ago, I noted that he had assembled a list of creative people who were fairly well-rounded. He had some creative geniuses on his list, but none with the social insensitivity and ruthlessness of a Richard Wagner or the proneness to psychosis of a Van Gogh. Obviously, if Maslow had assumed that self-actualization could occur selectively with respect to any one of several independent parts of the personality, he might have seen fit to study a few such lopsided people. It occurred to me that there might be many more lopsided people than well-rounded people in the world, and I decided that a multivariate study of a less select group might yield some pertinent information.

For my study I assembled a six-hour battery of tests. The battery contained some instruments borrowed from other people and a number of instruments devised specifically for this study, and it was designed to tap a wide assortment of variables that related in some way to common concepts of the optimal personality.[2] It included measures pertaining to phenomenal consistency, cognitive efficiency, perceptual organization, the experience of control, the scope of awareness, openness to experience, independence, the experience of time, reality contact, self-insight, logical consistency of the attitude-belief system, and various other aspects of attitudes, beliefs, and adjustment. The battery or parts of it were administered to several hundred university students. Some component instruments were separately analyzed. Ultimately I undertook a factor analysis of the total battery, using scores obtained for 291 subjects.

It was quite apparent from the correlations among the variables that there was no general dimension common to any large segment of the domain I was examining. My analysis culminated in nineteen obliquely rotated factors, which I interpreted as follows:

1. distress proneness,
2. object orientation versus personal orientation,
3. liberalism versus conservatism,
4. openness to experience,
5. acceptance,
6. pessimism versus optimism,
7. deliberateness versus spontaneity,
8. ideational fluency,
9. extraversion versus introversion,
10. general intelligence,
11. responsibility,
12. analytic versus global orientation,
13. organized simplicity versus uncontrolled complexity,
14. self-dissatisfaction versus self-satisfaction,
15. scope of early memory,
16. conceptual elaboration versus preference for constancy,
17. openness to unreality,
18. age stabilization, and
19. aesthetic versus practical interest.

Several of these factors appear to be concerned with facets of the personality that are prominent in current concepts of the optimal personality, but it is important to note that there is nothing that can be considered a general factor of personality integration, self-actualization, or positive mental health. Every global concept to which such a label has been attached encompasses several classes of variables that prove to be subject to independent variation. It should be noted, of course, that my factors form an oblique system. This means that there are some moderate correlations among the factors, but not a pattern of correlations that justifies the idea of a general factor of optimal functioning. Higher-order analysis definitely fails to yield any evidence of such a factor.

Thus, the finding that most conspicuously emerges when we examine either the correlations among the original variables, the composition of the factors that I extracted, or the correlations among the factors is that in the domain encompassed by optimal-personality concepts, there are a number of independent classes of personality variables. Reality contact, which is prominent in the Freudian view, appears in my study to be related to unconventionality of thought and to logical consistency of the attitude-belief system, but it bears little relationship to most other aspects of adjustment that I examined. Measures of intellectual functioning tend to be correlated with one another, but to manifest little relationship to anything else studied.

In addition to finding a number of independent subclasses of variables, I found that some qualities that are often combined in concepts of the optimal personality displayed correlation patterns that suggested mutual exclusiveness. Thus, self-insight and openness to experience apparently go together, but they both tend to be accompanied by a proneness to subjective distress, or anxiety, rather than a sense of emotional well-being. Furthermore, self-insight and openness to experience prove to be negatively correlated with various measures of experienced control (a sense of control over one's internal processes, a sense of confidence in one's ability to succeed at various tasks, a sense of one's ability to influence other people or environmental events, and the like).

THEORETICAL IMPLICATIONS OF THE ANALYSIS

My analysis indicates, then, that many of the qualities bound up in concepts of the optimal personality display little interdependence. Instead, they constitute a number of clusters that vary pretty independently of one another. Furthermore, some pairs of presumably desirable qualities tend to covary negatively, so that the more one has of the one, the less one is likely to have of the other. Within the realm we are

289

now considering, both my data and logical considerations point to a number of polarities in which a value choice seems required—polarities in which the contrasting modes seem both desirable but mutually incompatible. The most basic of these polarities would include:

1. a general openness to experience that permits richness or fullness of experience, versus the stable organization that provides freedom from distress;
2. an orientation toward harmony, toward relatedness, toward unity with other people and with the world, versus a sense of clear differentiation from others and striving for autonomy, self-adequacy, mastery, and individual achievement;
3. relating to oneself and others as persons versus the "objective" orientation that permits technological efficiency;
4. self-confidence, or a sense of control, versus a realistic appraisal of one's own limitations; and
5. an optimistic, confident attitude toward the world, versus a realistic appraisal of world conditions.

Some of these contrasts underscore differences among some of the traditions we have considered in this book. Much of the "mental hygiene" literature in this country has stressed order, stability, adjustment, and freedom from anxiety. In existentialism and contemporary humanism, however, we see a greater emphasis on openness and a recognition that the experience of anxiety and guilt may be a necessary price for accepting and exercising our freedom. The contrasting themes of individual fulfillment and union with others can be traced much further back to classical Greece and to the roots of the Judaeo-Christian tradition. The choice between person-orientation (or the I-thou relationship) and object-orientation (the I-it relationship) has been highlighted by modern humanists, but some earlier theorists have pointed to essentially the same issue. It corresponds to a characteristic difference between the humanities and the natural sciences, between Eastern culture and Western culture, and between women and men. This polarity is represented by my second factor, where my data reveal one of the most marked sex differences. On the whole, men display more emphasis on a detached, analytical, objective kind of orientation, while women show more inclination toward an orientation that involves feeling, intuition, and relatedness to other people.

It would be an oversimplification of the facts to say that we are dealing with totally incompatible qualities within these polarities and that we must decide in each case which aim is more important. Perhaps there are some desirable features of life that are inherently incompatible. To a greater extent, we are confronted with choices we must make simply because there is not enough time in one life to do everything. Choosing one course of action precludes another because we have committed a large portion of our lives in making the choice. For many years I have regretted that I could not pursue active careers in several other fields, such as music and literature, along with psychology, but every career demands a major personal investment, and the necessity of earning a living and the body's need for a certain amount of sleep impose additional constraints. The existentialists have recognized that it is not possible for an individual to realize all his potentials, and we must all be prepared to accept some developmental limitations.

It is possible that some contrasting attitudes and modes of expression that appear to most people to be incompatible are actually subject to resolution. Elements that have appeared to be mutually exclusive throughout the general population may prove subject to simultaneous expression in rare individuals who succeed in integrating them into a new pattern of adjustment. This is what Maslow claims to find in his self-actualizers with respect to many dichotomies.[3] The dichotomies that he mentions include those of reason and instinct, selfishness and unselfishness, kindness and ruthlessness, concreteness and abstractness, acceptance and rebellion, self and society, adjustment and maladjustment, detachment from others and identification with others, seriousness and humor, the Dionysian and the Apollonian, introversion and extraversion, intensity and casualness, seriousness and frivolity, conventionality and unconventionality, mysticism and realism, activeness and passivity, masculinity and femininity, lust and love, and Eros and agape. Maslow does not develop this point in detail, but it is a possibility that has been noted by many other writers. Perhaps it is developed most fully in Jungian theory, where the individuation process is seen to entail a transcendence of the opposition between thinking and feeling, sensation and intuition, and introversion and extraversion.

With respect to some polarities a total transcendence or resolution is possible. As we develop further, we reach a point at which the dichotomy vanishes altogether and there is no choice to be made at all. This happens on many levels with respect to the experience of self and mankind or group as we proceed to share our experience in encounter groups or probe the inner world through fantasy and meditation. We move from the social trivia on the surface to material that is more deeply personal, more hidden, seemingly more peculiar and socially unacceptable, until we reach a level where what seemed most wildly idiosyncratic proves to be universal. Then, boundaries suddenly vanish, we become aware of our utter inseparability from the group, from mankind, from all that is, and we experience simultaneously our wholeness as individual beings.

There is another form of resolution that consists in the recognition that it is not necessary to act the same way or to experience things in the same way all the time. Then the impulse, the need, the feeling that we have held in check at one moment for the sake of an immediate aim can be given expression in the moment that follows. The contrasting modes can all be given their due attention through alternating or sequential expression. It may not be possible simultaneously to solve an abstract reasoning problem, to repair a mechanical object, to respond with great emotional intensity to a work of art, and to engage in an intimate dialogue with another person, but it is nonetheless possible for one individual at different times to do all these things.

In the course of development we tend to shut off many possibilities. We choose one corridor and close the door leading to an alternative corridor, either because we expect to enhance one achievement through a single-minded pursuit or because we fear that a step across the other threshold would meet with disapproval. It is not just the unenlightened individual who denies some of his basic possibilities in this way. Many of the theorists and traditions we have considered stress the value of choosing one course and excluding an alternative that is recognized as possible but viewed as incompatible. For some alternatives, this is undoubtedly the wise thing to do. For a great many others, however, I should suggest that a flexibility that permits sequential expression of contrasting modes—and under some conditions, an integrative merging of them—is more consistent with our basic nature and permits something closer to a full realization of our developmental potentials.

I think the applicability of this point should be evident with respect to most of the polarities I have noted above. Most of them have in common a contrast between a mode that entails a kind of openness, fluidity, permeability, accessibility, or looseness and something more ordered or orderly that involves deliberate control, restriction of attention, and systematic thought and action. The open mode permits the emergence of new experiences, new actions, increased awareness, and greater intensity. The ordered mode favors stability and greater protection from painful and unexpected events. There is an obvious virtue in both modes. As I noted in *The Optimal Personality,* these two fundamental modes correspond to two opposing principles that have been recognized by many theorists in many contexts to be jointly involved in the creative process. Whether we are dealing with creative thinking, with biological evolution, with cultural progress, or with cognitive and personality development, it is possible to discern the interplay of two underlying processes—the destructive and the constructive, the mutative and the preservative, the diversifying and the unifying, the differentiating and the integrative. Jung more than anyone else applied this idea to personality development, and he saw the fully individuated person as one who has gone through a lengthy course of growth that involves both processes. I should like to suggest that at any one stage in development, we might appropriately describe the optimal condition as one in which constructive growth is possible because both processes are permitted to operate. If either process is excluded, something is lost. The life-style that capitalizes on the open mode and excludes the ordering mode is characterized by chaotic and ceaseless change, while the reverse life-style is one of stagnation.

I do not see the optimal, growth-conducive life-style simply in terms of an alternation between openness and ordered stability.

293

Openness itself implies flexibility with respect to many additional polarities that cannot themselves be characterized in terms of openness versus order. One such polarity, or set of polarities, concerns the multifaceted realm of masculinity versus femininity. We tend to segregate many of our possible modes of experience, expression, and functioning along sexual lines and to regard one mode as appropriate for men (hence, masculine) and regard a contrasting mode as appropriate for women (hence, feminine). Perhaps some of the resulting distinctions have a biological basis, while others are purely arbitrary conventions. The determinants of sex differences are complex and need not concern us at the moment. What should concern us is the pervasive attitude, which is gradually breaking down in our society, that it is important to go in one direction or the other. There seems to be little doubt that the people who appear to be most creative, most fully alive, most fully human are generally people who can realize and express in good measure both masculine and feminine qualities without worrying too much about the distinction. There is an overall tendency in Western culture as a whole to attach greater value to qualities that are usually viewed as masculine. To the extent that this is true, Western culture probably needs a bit of feminizing. Not only would this enhance our psychological well-being; it might greatly increase the chances for the continued survival of the human species into the next and subsequent centuries.

In my earlier book I suggested the need for flexibility with respect to many additional alternative modes of functioning. These would include:

1. the locus of attention,
2. the use of different sensory modes,
3. the Jungian functions: thinking versus feeling and sensation versus intuition,
4. introversion versus extraversion,
5. immediate knowing versus abstract conceptualization, or knowing about,
6. patterns of cognitive or intellectual functioning,
7. spontaneity versus deliberation,
8. living fully in the present versus preparing for the future,
9. optimism versus pessimism,

294

10. trust versus suspicion,
11. experiencing one's separate individuality versus experiencing union with others,
12. pride or self-esteem versus realistic self-awareness,
13. person versus object orientation,
14. social role: dominance, dependence, autonomy, etc., and
15. emotional response to others.

This is not an exhaustive list of possibilities, and the items overlap in various ways, but it is suggestive of the broad realm in which flexibility may be important. In general, flexibility permits the emergence of new insights and the discovery of new and valuable modes of experience, expression, and coping. Of course, it must involve more than access to an ever-changing succession of activities and sensations. There must be access to processes that provide some basis for organization and constancy. For creative growth to occur, we must be able to maintain certain commitments and preserve some of the insights and modes of functioning that we have discovered in the course of exploratory change.

Perhaps the need for this kind of balance and for the balance of contrasting modes in general has been recognized more clearly in the Orient than in the West. We can see it expressed in the opposing forces of the Hindu pantheon, in the doctrine of the yang and the yin, in the blending of Taoist and Confucian approaches to life, and in the years of rigid discipline the Zen monk accepts in order to achieve spontaneity and liberation. In the West, it is easier to find people who believe they can attain their highest goals either by rigidly adhering to old-fashioned law and order or by "turning on," "dropping out," and making schizophrenia a way of life.

BASIC MODES OF FULFILLMENT

What is the basic goal of human existence? What is the nature of the person who is fully himself, fully human, and fully mature? As we have seen, no one answer to such a question is generally accepted. Among the available answers, there are some basic themes that turn up in disparate cultures, and some themes find continuing expression over thousands of years. At the same time, however, we find certain differences in emphasis between cultures, and in any one culture we find contrasting themes that interweave. Furthermore, my data indicate that the various qualities embraced by definitions of the optimal condition do not fit neatly into one cohesive package.

I have one more suggestion for introducing a bit of order into this tangled state of affairs. I cannot pretend to have the final solution to the question of what is optimal, but perhaps it is possible to clarify further the choices that such a question entails. In Chapter 1, I suggested that five basic modes of human fulfillment or realization underlie most of our notions of the ideal human condition: efficiency, creativity, inner harmony, relatedness, and transcendence.

I arrived at this list after surveying many traditions and contemporary views and after weighing the evidence from my multivariate analysis. The five categories seem to me to provide as efficient a descriptive system as I can devise. They oversimplify to the extent that each category encompasses a number of separable things and to the extent that there are unavoidable overlaps between categories, but these categories preserve the most important distinctions. Most traditional models of the ideal may be viewed as expressions of single categories or of simple combinations of modes. Any given definition of the optimal personality represents a decision with respect to the mode or modes that should be stressed, with respect to particular elements within those categories that merit particular emphasis, and with respect to assumed relationships among categories.

I believe that available evidence shows these five modes to be relatively independent of one another. Thus it is possible to attain a high level of fulfillment, self-realization, or self-actualization within one of these modes without doing anything unusual with respect to the other four. Certain kinds of achievement, however, involve a combination of modes. Furthermore, there are probably certain prerequisite conditions that are common to two or more modes. A certain kind of openness, for example, may be a common precondition for fulfillment in the realms of creativity, inner harmony, and transcendence. Some of these points will be more obvious if we consider in a little more detail the constituents of each of the five modes.

296

Efficiency This mode embraces the primary ingredients of a number of models—ranging from the rational to the heroic—that have enjoyed popularity in the Western world, models that have in common an emphasis on efficient functioning in either the intellectual, social, or physical realm. The models tend either to stress or to assume certain kinds of functional competence. The competence may be essentially intellectual. It may entail effective use of all one's cognitive capacities, or there may be particular emphasis on the capacity for rational analysis or on contact with external reality. Effective use of the senses may be required. Freud stressed reality contact. The existentialists and theorists influenced by them (Perls, for example) emphasize awareness.

Effective psychophysical coordination is another possible emphasis. This would mean an absence of "psychosomatic" disorders and effective responsiveness to sensory impulses arising from the somesthetic receptors. Efficient use of the body in locomotion may be required, and a heroic model may call for the cultivation of certain physical skills.

While classical Greek culture emphasized the cultivation of capacities (both mental and physical) for their own sake, the efficiency models of recent centuries are more likely to call for work skills and for appropriate application of them. Fulfillment in this mode may be said in general to require such things as organization, an ability to plan and to carry through on plans, and a capacity for effective work. Thus, *energy, industry,* and *productiveness* (the effective use of energy) are terms that recur in some descriptions of efficiency ideals; the Protestant ethic provides one type of this ideal.

Another quality that is closely associated with efficiency ideals is a capacity for functioning without direction from without—what has been variously characterized as autonomy, independence, self-direction, or self-management. Unless the individual can function autonomously, he is failing to operate with total individual efficiency, for he is dependent on someone else to supply some of the thinking, planning, decision-making, energy, motivation, and so on.

Another aspect of performance that may be stressed is the meaning one invests in work. Many theorists have stressed the importance of a commitment to projects, or an investment in tasks, projects, or causes outside oneself. To an existentialist this would be a matter of accepting the responsibility for fulfilling certain possibilities in work. Maslow spoke of it in terms of problem centering; for Allport, it was an aspect of self-extension.

Creativity There is obviously some overlap between the constituents of fulfillment in the realm of efficiency and what is ordinarily called creativity, for we think of creativity in terms of some kind of production. It is distinguished by the fact that what one produces is in some sense original. It involves the discovery or creation of novel form or novel experience. Creative living, of course, may not involve an emphasis on industry or on production of quantity. It may be expressed more simply in terms of an original style of life. Both the actions and the experiences of the creative individual are free from stereotypy. Such a person experiences familiar things in fresh ways and finds value and beauty where it is not dictated by common standards. He develops a system of values and a morality that reflect his own nature. The image of the artist best personifies this mode, but creativity is possible within almost any occupation and any area of life.

There are a number of qualities emphasized in contemporary concepts of the optimal that may be viewed either as ingredients or as preconditions of creativity. Independence is important here, as it is for efficiency, but the important thing is not so much freedom from external direction as freedom from the values and the ways of perceiving and understanding provided by one's parents, one's group, and one's culture. If the creative person introjects these, he must also be capable of setting them aside and seeing a different kind of order or seeing without imposing an order on what is seen. The creative person would have an internal locus of evaluation (in Rogers' terms) and would be capable of transcending his particular culture (as in the case of Maslow's self-actualizers). Another obvious requirement is an openness to the novel, to the strange, to the socially unacceptable, to ideas and experiences that others are reluctant to entertain. Also related are those qualities that theorists speak of in terms of naturalness and spontaneity of expression.

Some models obviously combine the modes of efficiency and creativity. The ideal of the Renaissance certainly involved fulfillment along both lines. Any concept of the optimal person that stresses creative productiveness would combine them, requiring organization and industry along with creativity. One may attach various relative weights to the two modes, of course, and assign primary value either to sheer productiveness or to originality. Perhaps some aspects of efficiency, however, may be inherent in creative fulfillment. The total creative act involves not only the emergence of novel form but an organized processing of it that culminates in the creative product. The seemingly more spontaneous event, the emergence of the novel element, may itself depend on prior systematic preparation. We have noted that in the East a certain discipline is recognized as a precondition for spontaneity or naturalness, and this idea is not unknown in the West. Without some order and deliberate effort, freedom remains formless. And without energy and organized intention, new form cannot be carried into creative expression.

Inner harmony Something in the way of inner harmony seems to be a part of most popular notions of adjustment, normality, or happiness. The well adjusted person is free of disturbing emotions and apparently at peace with himself. He experiences a high level of self-esteem and self-confidence. He likes himself and feels capable of success. These are all qualities that point to inner harmony, but this harmony may rest on a shallow base. The person who appears best adjusted is often an individual who has simply accepted the views and the will of the surrounding society and failed to experience a very large part of himself. What passes for inner harmony is really the blissful unawareness of conformity. Of course, this sort of adjustment does entail inner harmony on a limited scale—a harmony of those parts, borrowed or otherwise, that lie within the scope of the individual's awareness. There may be other parts effectively excluded from awareness with which reconciliation would be difficult.

The basic precondition for a more inclusive inner harmony would be an openness to the total realm or the total flow of experience. This openness would entail more extensive self-awareness. It would entail what the existentialists call an acceptance of all one's possibilities, an acceptance of one's freedom. It would entail what Rogers describes as a recognition of oneself as process and as complexity. This broad experience of self requires both a capacity and a need for some amount of privacy and solitude. Permanent isolation would not do, of course, since there are parts of our being that can only be known through interaction with others, but in America the danger of escaping into society is much more prevalent than the danger of escaping from it.

Given an openness to the total flow of experience, I see the achievement of harmony with respect to the total person as involving two basic features. The first would be a coordination of all the ingredients that lie within the conscious phenomenal realm. Inevitably the individual will become aware of inconsistencies, of contrasts, of polarities, of opposites within his total nature, but it is possible to resolve conflicts between contrasting elements. A conflict exists only so long as we identify with one element and deny another—when we insist that we are neat and not sloppy, kind and not inconsiderate, masculine and not feminine. If we accept our multifaceted nature, we can tolerate the shifts within polarities. Some of the contrasts may prove to be necessary complements, and some may yield to a transformation that eliminates the contrast. In accepting all elements, we will be able to function with greater unity or coordination of purpose.

If we are open to all parts of our experience, nothing that can be consciously realized will be excluded from consciousness. We are capable of realizing only so much on a conscious level, however, and the second feature involved in the achievement of total harmony is harmony between what is consciously realized and what cannot be consciously realized. This, too, entails a kind of openness—an openness to forces underlying our action and experience that cannot themselves be directly perceived or understood. Perhaps we could describe this in terms of a trust or faith in the unknowable roots of one's own being. On this level, inner harmony shades into what I have called transcendence, and no sharp dividing line can be drawn between the two.

Relatedness Here the concern is with one's relationship to other people, and there are two principal forms of fulfillment on which we may focus. One is the sort of intimacy that is possible in a person-to-person relationship. This is central to the Freudian concept of genital character. It involves a full acceptance and valuing of the other person for the sake of that other person. The other form concerns our relationship to humanity, to people in general. Here a more pervasive altruism or a sense of union with other people—what Adler would call *Gemeinschaftsgefühl*—seems important.

There are many related concepts that point to aspects or requisites of relatedness that have received attention in recent years: empathy, social sensitivity, compassion, and others. A complete relationship with another person involves many components. True dialogue with another person involves not only a willingness to make one's self available, to be genuinely transparent, but also a willingness to receive what the other seeks to communicate. Too often our apparent acceptance of another person and of his messages is merely an acceptance of our own projections and constructions.

Models of the ideal that stress relatedness can be traced far back in the Judaeo-Christian tradition, but this mode has been given increasing emphasis in modern treatments of the optimal condition. Perhaps the need for fulfillment in the realm of relatedness has acquired fresh urgency in the modern world, for as James Baldwin says: "The moment we cease to hold each other, the moment we break faith with one another, the sea engulfs us and the light goes out."

Transcendence What I am calling transcendence has been described in many ways: in terms of our relationship to God, to the divine, to the whole of nature, and to the ultimate ground of being. It is sometimes difficult to distinguish this category from that of relatedness, since the relationship of the individual to God is sometimes described as a personal relationship and is assumed to share the features of an intimate relationship to another person. The concept of transcendence need not presuppose a personal concept of God, however, or any other theological doctrine for that matter. Obviously there are intermediate cases or cases that involve both relatedness and transcendence, but the additional category is clearly necessary.

There are essentially two ways in which we might make a distinction between relatedness and transcendence. One possibility is in terms of the nature of the others. Thus, we could speak of relatedness

301

with respect to our relationship to other individual people and transcendence with respect to our relationship, say, to the whole of nature, a realm that we would not experience as a single being and a realm of which we are a part. What about our relationship to the whole of humanity? Is this an intermediate case? And our relationship to living beings in general? Obviously there is a range of others from the very specific to the all-encompassing, and we can regard some of the larger wholes as including or not including ourselves.

I should prefer not to make the distinction along such lines, however, but in terms of the nature of the experience. I would propose to speak or relatedness to the extent that there is still an *I* and an *other*. I would speak of transcendence to the extent that the experience entails a loss of my experienced separateness as an individual distinct from the whole to which my attention is directed. The intimate person-to-person encounter is the basic expression of relatedness, while the mystical experience of unity with a larger whole is the basic expression of transcendence. There is reason to believe that we all need this kind of experience, for its value has been recognized in all known cultures, and in all cultures people have devised ways of achieving it. The individual who advances furthest in this mode has greater access to transcendent experience, realizes it in greater depth and intensity than others, and preserves in his usual state some of the awareness wrought by the transcendent state. In every society there appear to be a few such spiritually gifted people.

The transcendent experience has always been recognized as in some sense ineffable, and certainly it defies conceptualization in the moment of the experience. Any labeling or explanation must come afterward. Many of the experiences that Maslow would characterize as "peak" experiences involve transcendence, whether we describe them specifically in terms of religious ecstasy, mystical union with nature, aesthetic experience, or love. We more often think of self-transcendence with respect to our relationship to some all-encompassing totality, which we may call nature, being, or God, but the stimulus for the experience is often something more concrete and specific, such as a work of art or another person. Transcendence is not entirely a matter of something that occurs in special states or in brief moments of enlightenment. There is a kind of awareness that one may attain in the special moment or state that carries over into ordinary experience and alters the basic manner in which we view ourselves and the rest of reality, and within a given tradition this persisting awareness may be more important than the special moment that initiates it.

The special moment of ecstasy or mystical union is not essential for a persisting sense of self-transcendence, and some forms of transcendence may depend very little on such moments. In the course of a group endeavor, the individual may merge with the group and function as an inextricable part of it, losing all sense of separateness but without experiencing a discernible "peak." Similarly an individual who labors long and hard for a cause may experience a merging with some larger purpose in the course of his solitary work. An individual like Karl Marx, who disavows all ties to traditional religion and displays little obvious inclination toward the spiritual or mystical realm, may manifest a high degree of transcendence in this form.

CHOICE, BALANCE, AND THE OPTIMAL CONDITION

The five modes I have described are subject to many possible combinations in specific treatments of the optimal condition. Some contemporary theorists who have dealt extensively with this issue, including Erikson, Allport, and Maslow, list qualities that involve most of the five modes. The individualistic traditions of the West tend to stress either efficiency or creativity or a combination of the two. The mode that is most characteristic of Eastern traditions is transcendence. Inner harmony and relatedness have been stressed to some degree in both the East and the West, and in both parts of the world they have probably been stressed more in recent times than in the past.

It may be worth noting that both transcendence and relatedness can provide a balance for the more individualistic modes. Just as we have traditions that stress the full realization of one's being as a separate individual, we have traditions that regard our experience of individual separateness as the fundamental problem in the human condi-

303

tion. In the East, this is seen as an illusion and as the source of suffering, and the primary solution is held to be a kind of transcendent awareness of the whole and a dissolution of the duality of *I* and *other*. In the West, there are theorists who recognize a similar problem. In the Judaeo-Christian tradition, the original sin is recurrently construed as the advent of experienced individuality. In the work of religious writers the solution is generally held to lie in our relationship to God. Depending on the conception of God, this will mean either transcendence (a recognition that one is only an expression of the more fundamental reality) or relatedness (though one has no choice but to be a separate willing being, one can subordinate one's will to God's or seek a close relationship with him). In the work of some religious thinkers, it is difficult to say whether the emphasis is essentially on transcendence or relatedness. We find the same alternatives in the work of psychological theorists who do not cast the matter in theological terms. Thus, Fromm also saw separateness as a fundamental problem, and his solution was basically one of relatedness to other people. Other psychological theorists, such as Rank and Progoff, seem to stress something more in the way of transcendence. Jung's solution is perhaps an intermediate one, for he did not believe in giving up the ego but stressed the need to accommodate to a broader and deeper reality (the self), which actually includes the ego but which we cannot directly know in its totality.

What then is the ideal human condition? Obviously each of the five modes represents a possible line along which people can develop, and if it is important for the individual to realize all his human potentialities, we could argue that he ought to attain fulfillment in some sense with respect to each of the five modes. Perhaps there is some natural sequence of fulfillment. Both in Jung and in Eastern traditions we encounter the notion that individualistic goals are appropriate for the earlier stages of life and that the achievement of inner harmony and transcendence is a task for the latter years. Erikson's theory embodies something comparable, but his developmental progression is more complicated. But is there one course that we can properly prescribe for everyone? We can find some admirable people who excel in just one mode and who follow a developmental course that defies the general rule. Perhaps we should try to understand them better before setting forth to show them where they have failed and offering dogmatic prescriptions. If someone asks us to what condition he should attain, perhaps we should ask, "What are you seeking?"

NOTES

ONE / BASIC PERSPECTIVES ON THE OPTIMAL PERSONALITY

1. Abraham H. Maslow, *Toward a Psychology of Being* (Princeton: Van Nostrand, 1968).

2. Peter F. Drucker, *The End of Economic Man: A Study of the New Totalitarianism* (New York: John Day, 1939).

3. Edward C. Tolman, *Behavior and Psychological Man: Essays in Motivation and Learning* (Berkeley: University of California Press, 1951).

4. Philip Rieff, *Freud: The Mind of the Moralist* (New York: Viking, 1959).

TWO / TRADITIONS IN WESTERN THOUGHT

1. Carl Gustav Jung, *Psychological Types,* trans. H. Godwin Baynes (New York: Harcourt, Brace, 1926).

2. Gilbert G. Chesterton, *What's Wrong with the World* (New York: Dodd, Mead, 1920), p. 48.

3. Paul Tillich, *A History of Christian Thought, from Its Judaic and Hellenistic Origins to Existentialism* (New York: Simon and Schuster, 1967), p. 236.

4. Max Weber, *The Protestant Ethic and the Spirit of Capitalism* (New York: Scribner, 1958).

5. This couplet was written by Alexander Pope and intended as an epitaph for Isaac Newton.

THREE / WESTERN THOUGHT IN THE MODERN ERA

1. Darwin's theory was set forth in more elaborate form with massive supporting evidence in the following year in his monumental work *The Origin of Species.*

307

Notes

2. See Julian Huxley, *Knowledge, Morality and Destiny* (New York: New American Library, 1960).

3. Jan Christian Smuts, *Holism and Evolution* (New York: Macmillan, 1926).

4. Karl Marx, "Economic and Philosophical Manuscripts," trans. T. B. Bottome, in Erich Fromm, *Marx's Concept of Man* (New York: Frederick Ungar, 1961).

5. Rollo May, *The Meaning of Anxiety* (New York: Ronald Press, 1950).

6. Abram Kardiner, *The Psychological Frontiers of Society* (New York: Columbia University Press, 1945).

7. Romain Rolland, *Michelangelo* (New York: Albert & Charles Boni, 1915), p. 161.

8. May, *Meaning of Anxiety*, p. 218.

9. George Orwell, *1984*. (New York: New American Library, 1949).

10. Alvin Toffler, *Future Shock* (New York: Random House, 1970).

11. Theodore Roszak, *The Making of a Counter-Culture: Reflections on the Technocratic Society and Its Youthful Opposition* (Garden City: Anchor Books, 1969).

12. Charles A. Reich, *The Greening of America: How the Youth Revolution Is Trying to Make America Livable* (New York: Random House, 1970).

13. The significant events included not only the expansion of the war but the assassination of such charismatic leaders as Robert Kennedy and Martin Luther King and the slaying of four students by National Guardsmen in the course of a demonstration at Kent State University.

14. The ideas covered in the remainder of this section are expressions of Buber's personal philosophy, but that philosophy reflects the Hasidic influence.

15. Martin Buber, *I and Thou* (Edinburgh: T. & T. Clark, 1937).

16. The ideas summarized here are derived from Paul Tillich, *The Courage to Be* (New Haven: Yale University Press, 1952).

17. The ideas we are considering here are most systematically expounded in Pierre Teilhard de Chardin, *The Phenomenon of Man* (New York: Harper & Brothers, 1959). Some of their implications are further developed in Pierre Teilhard de Chardin, *The Future of Man* (New York: Harper & Row, 1964).

18. Teilhard de Chardin, *Future of Man*, pp. 122–23.

19. Thomas S. Szasz, *The Myth of Mental Illness* (New York: Harper & Row, Hoeber Medical Division, 1961).

20. Thomas Szasz, *Ceremonial Chemistry: The Ritual Persecution of Drugs, Addicts, and Pushers* (Garden City: Anchor Books, 1974).

21. R. D. Laing and A. Esterson, *Sanity, Madness, and the Family: Families of Schizophrenics* (Harmondsworth, Middlesex: Tavistock, 1964).

22. *R. D. Laing, The Politics of Experience* (New York: Pantheon, 1967).

308

FOUR / TRADITIONS IN EASTERN THOUGHT

1. Albert Schweitzer, *Indian Thought and Its Development* (Boston: Beacon Press, 1936).

2. D. T. Suzuki, "Lectures on Zen Buddhism," in D. T. Suzuki, Erich Fromm, and Richard De Martino, *Zen Buddhism and Psychoanalysis* (New York: Grove, 1960), p. 5.

3. Alan W. Watts, *Psychotherapy East and West* (New York: New American Library, 1970).

4. Ibid.

5. Sri Aurobindo, *The Life Divine* (Pondicherry, India: Sri Aurobindo Ashram, 1970).

6. Ibid., p. 911.

7. Ibid., pp. 995–96.

8. Ibid., pp. 971–72.

9. Schweitzer, *Indian Thought.*

10. Lama Anagarika Govinda, *Foundations of Tibetan Mysticism, According to the Esoteric Teachings of the Great Mantra Om Mani Padme Hum* (New York: E. P. Dutton, 1960).

11. Ibid.

12. Chögyam Trungpa, *Born in Tibet* (New York: Harcourt, Brace & World, 1966).

13. Of Suzuki's numerous works, the one that can best be recommended to the general reader as an exposition of the fundamentals of Zen is Daisetz Teitaro Suzuki, *Introduction to Zen Buddhism* (New York: Causeway Books, 1974). Watts deals with Zen thought in a number of books; his most systematic treatment is Alan W. Watts, *The Way of Zen* (New York: New American Library, 1957).

14. Watts, *The Way of Zen.*

15. Ibid., p. 118.

16. Suzuki, *Introduction to Zen Buddhism.*

17. Alan W. Watts, *The Book, on the Taboo Against Knowing Who You Are* (New York: Collier Books, 1966).

18. Ibid., p. ix.

19. Watts, *Psychotherapy East and West.*

20. Ibid., p. 143.

21. Ibid., p. 149.

22. Ibid., p. 134.

FIVE / SIGMUND FREUD AND PSYCHOANALYSIS

1. Actually it seems virtually impossible to identify a specific point at which any fundamental idea in psychology appeared for the first time. As Jung argued, every significant idea has its historical antecedents.

2. Henri F. Ellenberger, *The Discovery of the Unconscious: The History and Evolution of Dynamic Psychiatry* (New York: Basic Books, 1970).

3. Sigmund Freud, *The Interpretation of Dreams,* trans. and ed. James Strachey (New York: Avon Books, 1965).

4. Ellenberger, *Discovery of the Unconscious.*

5. Sigmund Freud, *Zur Auffassung der Aphasien: Eine Kritische Studie* (Leipzig: Deuticke, 1891).

6. Ernest Jones, *The Life and Work of Sigmund Freud* (New York: Basic Books, 1961).

7. See Sigmund Freud, *The Standard Edition of the Complete Psychological Works of Sigmund Freud,* vol. 1, ed. James Strachey (New York: Macmillan, 1964).

8. These works are included in Sigmund Freud, *The Basic Writings of Sigmund Freud,* trans. and ed. A. A. Brill (New York: Modern Library, 1938).

9. It can be easily contended that Freud did not provide a very adequate theory of moral or ethical development. He paid little attention to the major contributions to the individual's value system that ordinarily come in preadolescence and adolescence. In these later stages, ethical development is less a matter of an uncritical introjective process and presumably would be conceptualized in Freudian theory in terms of ego development.

10. Included in Freud, *Basic Writings.*

11. Still another way of stating the conflict is in terms of the biological and the social. The question has often been raised as to whether Freud overemphasized either biological or social-environmental determinants. At the core of the Freudian position is the idea that the individual is at the mercy of both sets of forces and tends to be pulled in opposite directions by them.

12. Sigmund Freud, *The Future of an Illusion* (New York: Liveright, 1928).

13. Sigmund Freud, *Leonardo da Vinci and a Memory of His Childhood,* ed. James Strachey and trans. Alan Tyson (New York: Norton, 1964).

14. Ernst Kris, *Psychoanalytic Explorations in Art* (New York: International Universities Press, 1952).

SIX / CARL JUNG AND ANALYTICAL PSYCHOLOGY

1. Henri F. Ellenberger, *The Discovery of the Unconscious: The History and Evolution of Dynamic Psychiatry* (New York: Basic Books, 1970).

2. Several of his papers dealing with Eastern thought are contained in *The Collected Works of C. G. Jung,* vol. 11, *Psychology and Religion: West and East,* ed. Herbert Read et al., trans. R. F. C. Hull (Princeton: Princeton University Press, 1969).

3. C. G. Jung, "Psychological Commentary on *The Tibetan Book of the Great Liberation,*" in *Collected Works,* vol. 11.

4. Ibid.

5. Three valuable sources provide differing perspectives on the relationship: Ernest Jones, *The Life and Work of Sigmund Freud* (New York: Basic Books, 1961); Jung's autobiography, *Memories, Dreams, Reflections,* ed. Aniela Jaffé (New York: Vintage Books, 1963); and *The Freud/Jung Letters: The Correspondence Between Sigmund Freud and C. G. Jung,* ed. William McGuire (Princeton: Princeton University Press, 1974).

6. Ellenberger, *Discovery of the Unconscious.*

7. C. G. Jung, *Psychological Types,* trans. H. Godwin Baynes (New York: Harcourt, Brace, 1926).

8. Ira Progoff, *The Death and Rebirth of Psychology* (New York: McGraw-Hill, 1956).

9. See R. W. Coan, "Dimensions of Psychological Theory," *American Psychologist* 23 (1968): 715–22; R. W. Coan, "Toward a Psychological Interpretation of Psychology," *Journal of the History of the Behavioral Sciences* 9 (1973): 313–27.

10. C. G. Jung, "Synchronicity: An Acausal Connecting Principle," in *Collected Works,* vol. 8.

11. Ira Progoff, *Jung, Synchronicity, and Human Destiny: Noncausal Dimensions of Human Experience* (New York: Julian Press, 1973), p. 113.

12. J. R. R. Tolkien, *The Lord of the Rings,* 3 vols. (New York: Ballantine, 1965).

13. Jung, "Psychological Commentary on *The Tibetan Book of the Great Liberation,*" p. 484.

14. Alan W. Watts, *Psychotherapy East and West* (New York: New American Library, 1970).

SEVEN / OTHER THEORIES RELATED TO PSYCHOANALYSIS

1. Alfred Adler, *Study of Organ Inferiority and Its Psychical Compensation: A Contribution to Clinical Medicine,* trans. Smith E. Jeliffe (New York: Nervous and Mental Diseases Publishing Co., 1917).

2. Alfred Adler, *The Neurotic Constitution: Outline of a Comparative Individualistic Psychology and Psychotherapy* (New York: Moffat, Yard, 1917).

3. Otto Rank, *The Trauma of Birth* (New York: Harcourt, Brace, 1929).

4. Otto Rank, *Will Therapy and Truth and Reality,* trans. Jessie Taft (New York: Knopf, 1945). This translation was first published in 1936 in two separate volumes.

5. Otto Rank, *Beyond Psychology* (Camden: Haddon Craftsmen, 1941).

6. Ira Progoff, *The Death and Rebirth of Psychology: An Integrative Evaluation of Freud, Adler, Jung, and Rank and the Impact of Their Insights on Modern Man* (New York: McGraw-Hill, 1956), p. 262.

7. Erich Fromm, *Beyond the Chains of Illusion: My Encounter with Marx and Freud* (New York: Pocket Books, 1963).

8. Erich Fromm, *The Sane Society* (Greenwich, Conn.: Fawcett, 1955); Erich Fromm, *The Revolution of Hope* (New York: Harper & Row, 1968).

9. Fromm, *Revolution of Hope*, p. 1.

10. Erich Fromm, *Escape from Freedom* (New York: Farrar & Rinehart, 1941).

11. Fromm, *Sane Society*, pp. 180–81.

12. Ibid., pp. 241–42.

13. Fromm, *Beyond the Chains of Illusion*, p. 193.

14. D. T. Suzuki, Erich Fromm, and Richard De Martino, *Zen Buddhism and Psychoanalysis* (New York: Grove, 1960).

15. Erik H. Erikson, *Young Man Luther, A Study in Psychoanalysis and History* (New York: Norton, 1958); Erik H. Erikson, *Gandhi's truth: On the Origins of Militant Nonviolence* (New York: Norton, 1969).

16. Robert Coles, *Erik H. Erikson: The Growth of His Work* (Boston: Little, Brown, 1970).

17. Erik H. Erikson, *Childhood and Society* (New York: Norton, 1963).

18. In addition to *Childhood and Society*, see Erik H. Erikson, "Identity and the Life Cycle," in *Psychological Issues*, ed. George S. Klein (New York: International Universities Press, 1959), 1:1–171; Erik H. Erikson, *Identity, Youth and Crisis* (New York: Norton, 1968).

19. Erikson, *Identity, Youth and Crisis*, p. 50.

20. Erikson, *Childhood and Society*, p. 268.

21. Roberto Assagioli, *Psychosynthesis: A Manual of Principles and Techniques* (New York: Viking, 1965).

22. Roberto Assagioli, *The Act of Will* (New York: Viking, 1973).

23. Assagioli, *Psychosynthesis*, p. 7.

24. Ibid., p. 22.

25. Ibid., p. 250.

26. Eric Berne, *Transactional Analysis in Psychotherapy* (New York: Ballantine, 1961); Eric Berne, *Games People Play: The Psychology of Human Relationships* (New York: Grove, 1964).

27. Berne, *Transactional Analysis*, p. 11.

28. Eric Berne, *What Do You Say After You Say Hello?* (New York: Grove, 1970).

29. Thomas A. Harris, *I'm OK—You're OK: A Practical Guide to Transactional Analysis* (New York: Harper & Row, 1967).

30. Berne, *Games People Play.*

EIGHT / EXISTENTIAL PHILOSOPHY AND PSYCHOLOGY

1. Rollo May, Ernest Angel, and Henri F. Ellenberger, eds., *Existence: A New Dimension in Psychiatry and Psychology* (New York: Basic Books, 1958).

2. Martin Heidegger, *Being and Time,* trans. John Macquarrie and Edward Robinson (New York: Harper & Row, 1962).

3. Søren Kierkegaard, *The Concept of Dread,* trans. W. Lowrie (Princeton: Princeton University Press, 1944).

4. The following works deal with these stages: (1) Søren Kierkegaard, *Philosophical Fragments,* ed. H. V. Hong, trans. David Swenson (Princeton: Princeton University Press, 1936); (2) Søren Kierkegaard, *Concluding Unscientific Postscript to the Philosophical Fragments,* trans. D. F. Swenson and W. Lowrie (Princeton: Princeton University Press, 1941); (3) Søren Kierkegaard, *Either/Or,* trans. W. Lowrie (Princeton: Princeton University Press, 1944).

5. Friedrich Nietzsche, *Thus Spake Zarathustra: A Book for Everyone and No One,* trans. R. J. Hollingdale (Baltimore: Penguin Books, 1961); Friedrich Nietzsche, *Beyond Good and Evil,* trans. Helen Zimmern (Chicago: Henry Regnery, 1949).

6. The ideas covered in this section are those expounded by Heidegger in *Being and Time.*

7. See Karl Jaspers *The Perennial Scope of Philosophy,* trans. Ralph Mannheim (New York: Philosophical Library, 1949); Karl Jaspers, *Reason and Existenz,* trans. William Earle (New York: Noonday Press, 1955).

8. The reader must be prepared for the fact that the basic categories or distinctions vary from one existentialist philosopher to another and that overlapping terminology is sometimes misleading. Thus, *Dasein* (existence) is not used in quite the same way by Jaspers and by Heidegger. Sartre also speaks of being-in-itself (*être-en-soi*), but with a meaning much different from that of Jaspers.

9. The main source for this section is Gabriel Marcel, *The Mystery of Being* (Chicago: Regnery, 1950).

10. Jean-Paul Sartre, *Being and Nothingness: An Essay on Phenomenological Ontology,* trans. Hazel E. Barnes (New York: Philosophical Library, 1956).

11. See the sections written by May in *Existence* and those in Rollo May, ed., *Existential Psychology* (New York: Random House, 1961).

12. R. D. Laing, *The Politics of Experience* (New York: Ballantine, 1967), p. 53.

13. Rollo May, "Contributions of Existential Psychotherapy," in May et al., eds., *Existence,* pp. 37–91.

14. The main sources of material for this section are the papers of Binswanger included in May et al., eds., *Existence,* and Ludwig Binswanger, *Being-in-the-World: Selected Papers of Ludwig Binswanger,* trans. Jacob Needleman (New York: Basic Books, 1963), which includes a valuable introduction to Binswanger's work written by Jacob Needleman.

15. See Medard Boss, *Psychoanalysis and Daseinsanalysis,* trans. Ludwig B. Lefebre (New York: Basic Books, 1963).

16. Ibid., p. 32.

17. Ibid., p. 34.

18. The account is contained in the first part of Victor Frankl, *Man's Search for Meaning: An Introduction to Logotherapy* (New York: Washington Square Press, 1963). The material for this section is derived essentially from that book and from Victor Frankl, *The Doctor and the Soul: From Psychotherapy to Logotherapy* (New York: Vintage, 1965), and Victor Frankl, *Psychotherapy and Existentialism: Selected Papers on Logotherapy* (New York: Simon & Schuster, 1967).

19. R. D. Laing, *The Divided Self: An Existential Study in Sanity and Madness* (Baltimore: Penguin Books, 1965).

20. R. D. Laing, *Self and Others* (Baltimore: Penguin Books, 1969).

21. R. D. Laing, *Knots* (New York: Vintage Books, 1970).

22. See, for example, R. D. Laing and A. Esterson, *Sanity, Madness, and the Family: Families of Schizophrenics* (Baltimore: Penguin Books, 1970).

23. R. D. Laing, *The Politics of Experience* (New York: Ballantine Books, 1967), p. 27.

24. Ibid., pp. 144–45.

25. William Shakespeare, *Hamlet,* Act I, Scene 3.

26. This prayer was composed by Reinhold Niebuhr in 1933. Since then, it has been adopted by various groups and has been widely quoted with several variations in wording.

27. The origin of this quotation is uncertain. It has most often been attributed to Stephen Grellet, a Quaker who lived from 1773 to 1855.

NINE / OTHER CONTEMPORARY PERSPECTIVES

1. I would argue, however, that behaviorists cannot achieve a comprehensive understanding of the learning process so long as they treat the learner as an empty organism. Under some conditions they can achieve very efficient prediction, and they often generate procedures that have great practical utility. The behavioristic dominance of the learning area is reflected in the tendency in this country to define learning in terms of a change in response. If instead we define learning in terms of a change in expectancy or in terms of a change in properties of the phenomenal field, then the response change

becomes only an indirect indicator of learning, and the need for an analysis that includes more than the stimulus, response, and reinforcement becomes apparent.

2. B. F. Skinner, *Walden Two* (New York: Macmillan, 1948).

3. See B. F. Skinner, *Beyond Freedom and Dignity* (New York: Knopf, 1971).

4. I would not argue that language has nothing to do with self-awareness, but the relationship is a complex and subtle one. We should distinguish between self-description in terms of general categories or attributes and a more immediate awareness of self-referable events or phenomena. The former is obviously language-dependent and may fit Skinner's rule. In the case of the latter, I would recognize only a very limited dependence on language. Perhaps in the early ordeal of learning to use the words *I* and *me,* we acquire an initial disposition to differentiate between self-referable events and events ascribable to the rest of the universe, but such differentiation can take place throughout life without much verbal structuring.

5. Gordon W. Allport, *Personality: A Psychological Interpretation* (New York: Holt, 1937).

6. Ibid.

7. Gordon W. Allport, *Pattern and Growth in Personality* (New York: Holt, Rinehart, and Winston, 1961).

8. See Richard I. Evans, *Gordon Allport: The Man and His Ideas* (New York: Dutton, 1970).

9. Gordon W. Allport, *Becoming: Basic Considerations for a Psychology of Personality* (New Haven: Yale University Press, 1955).

10. This is a summary of the description presented in Allport, *Pattern and Growth in Personality.*

11. See Carl R. Rogers, *Counseling and Psychotherapy: Newer Concepts in Practice* (Boston: Houghton Mifflin, 1942); and Carl R. Rogers, *Client-Centered Therapy: Its Current Practice, Implications, and Theory* (Boston: Houghton Mifflin, 1951).

12. Rogers' theoretical system is presented in greatest detail in *Client-Centered Therapy* and in Carl R. Rogers, "A Theory of Therapy, Personality, and Interpersonal Relationships, as Developed in the Client-Centered Framework," in S. Koch, ed., *Psychology: A Study of a Science, vol. 3* (New York: McGraw-Hill, 1959), pp. 184–256.

13. Several pertinent papers will be found in Carl R. Rogers, *On Becoming a Person: A Therapist's View of Psychotherapy* (Boston: Houghton Mifflin, 1961).

14. Richard J. Lowry, *A. H. Maslow: An Intellectual Portrait* (Monterey, Calif.: Brooks/Cole, 1973); Colin Wilson, *New Pathways in Psychology: Maslow and the Post-Freudian Revolution* (New York: New American Library, 1974).

15. The need hierarchy and Maslow's later ideas on motivation are covered in Abraham H. Maslow, *Motivation and Personality* (New York: Harper & Row, 1970).

16. The term *self-actualization* has come to be used by a number of theorists. Maslow borrowed the term from Kurt Goldstein, who was never particularly pleased with the way in which Maslow employed it.

17. This list is based essentially on the description provided in the 1970 edition of Maslow, *Motivation and Personality.*

18. In particular, see Abraham H. Maslow, *Toward a Psychology of Being* (Princeton: Van Nostrand, 1968).

19. Frederick S. Perls, *In and Out the Garbage Pail* (Lafayette, Calif.: Real People Press, 1969).

20. Frederick S. Perls, *Gestalt Therapy Verbatim* (New York: Bantam, 1969).

21. Frederick S. Perls, "Four lectures," in *Gestalt Therapy Now,* ed. Joen Fagan and Irma Lee Shepherd (New York: Harper & Row, 1971), pp. 14–38.

22. Frederick S. Perls, Ralph F. Hefferline, and Paul Goodman, *Gestalt Therapy: Excitement and Growth in the Human Personality* (New York: Dell, 1951).

23. Frederick S. Perls, *Ego, Hunger and Aggression* (London: Allen & Unwin, 1947).

24. Perls et al., *Gestalt Therapy.*

25. Perls, *Gestalt Therapy Verbatim.*

26. B. F. Skinner, "Humanism and Behaviorism," *The Humanist* 32 (July/August 1972): 18–20.

27. Carl R. Rogers, *Carl Rogers on Encounter Groups* (New York: Harper & Row, 1970).

28. See Sidney M. Jourard, *Disclosing Man to Himself* (Princeton: Van Nostrand, 1968); Sidney M. Jourard, *The Transparent Self* (New York: Van Nostrand Reinhold, 1971); Sidney M. Jourard, *Self-Disclosure: An Experimental Analysis of the Transparent Self* (New York: Wiley-Interscience, 1971).

29. William C. Schutz, *Here Comes Everybody: Bodymind and Encounter Culture* (New York: Harper & Row, 1971).

TEN / THE OPTIMAL PERSONALITY: A RE-EXAMINATION OF THE DOMAIN

1. Richard W. Coan, *The Optimal Personality: An Empirical and Theoretical Analysis* (New York: Columbia University Press, 1974).

2. I had data for my subjects on 147 variables altogether, but these were not all included in any single analysis that I undertook.

3. Abraham H. Maslow, *Motivation and Personality* (New York: Harper & Row, 1970).

INDEX

317

Index

318

Index

Index

Socrates, 20, 23
Spencer, Herbert, 42
Spinoza, Benedict, 37
Spiritual Man, 6, 8
Spranger, Eduard, 251
Stability, 1, 290, 293
Stern, William, 251
Stoicism, 23
Subject-object dichotomy, 207-8, 215
Sunyata, 100-1
Superman, 13, 16, 214
Suzuki, D. T., 82, 107, 176, 309n2, 309n13
Swedenborg, Emanuel, 134
Szasz, Thomas, 68, 71, 308n19, 308n20

Tao, 105-6
Taoism, 104-6, 295
Technology, developments in, 51, 53-55
Teilhard de Chardin, Pierre, 57, 63-66, 89, 196, 308n17
Terullian, 25
Thomas à Kempis, 28
Thomas Aquinas, Saint, 27-30
Thoreau, Henry David, 46
Tillich, Paul, 33, 57, 60-63, 206, 307(Ch. 2)n3, 308n16
Toffler, Alvin, 51, 54, 308n10
Tolkien, J. R. R., 148, 311n12
Tolman, Edward C., 7, 244, 307(Ch. 1)n3
Transactional analysis, 196-205

Transcendence, mode of, 17, 296, 301-3; in Greek thought, 24; in Eastern thought, 303
Transparency, 281
Trungpa, Chögyam, 102, 309n12
Tulkus, 102

Vaihinger, Hans, 158
Van Gogh, Vincent, 287
Vedanta philosophy, 85
Viet Nam war, 52-53
Virgin Mary, 27
Vivekananda, 88-89

Wagner, Richard, 287
Watson, John B., 243-44, 248, 261
Watts, Alan W., 85-86, 107, 110-11, 152-53, 309n3, 309n13, 309n17, 311n14
Weber, Max, 35, 307(Ch. 2)n4
Wilhelm, Richard, 134
Wilson, Colin, 261, 315n14
Wundt, Wilhelm, 43
Wu-wei, 106-7

Yang and yin, 104
Yoga, 86-87

Za-zen, 109
Zen Buddhism, *see* Buddhism, Zen
Zimmer, Heinrich, 134
Zwingli, Huldreich, 32-34